Newham London

D0766528

Sept 4		
0 3 APR 2012		
0 8 OCT 2012		

24 hour automated telephone renewal line
0115 929 3388
Or online at www.newham.gov.uk

This book must be returned (or its issue renewed)
on or before the date stamped above

Douglas Thompson is the author of more than 20 books. A biographer, broadcaster and international journalist, he is a regular contributor to major newspapers and magazines worldwide. His books, published in a dozen languages, include the television-based anthology *Hollywood People* and bestselling biographies of Madonna, Clint Eastwood, Michelle Pfeiffer, Dudley Moore, John Travolta, Nicolas Cage and Leonardo DiCaprio. He has been involved in the writing of many Hollywood stars' memoirs.

He collaborated with the billion-dollar dancer Michael Flatley on his top-ten story *Lord of the Dance*. With Christine Keeler, he wrote her revealing memoir *The Truth at Last*, an instant bestseller, and he worked as a consultant on the tie-in television documentary on the Profumo Affair. Working with eminent psychotherapist Pauline Sutcliffe, he told the poignant story of her brother Stuart, who named and helped found the Beatles with John Lennon, in *The Beatles' Shadow*.

His book *The Hustlers*, about gangsters and gambling in 1960s London, is being developed as a major motion picture and was the subject of a Channel 4 documentary. *Mafia Princess*, on which he worked with Marisa Merico, is also being developed for film. He recently contributed to a documentary celebrating Clint Eastwood's career that was included in a special DVD box set of Eastwood movies.

Douglas Thompson divides his time between a medieval English village and California, where he was based as a Fleet Street foreign correspondent and columnist for more than 20 years.

SHADOWLAND

HOW THE MAFIA BET BRITAIN IN A GLOBAL GAMBLE

DOUGLAS THOMPSON

MAINSTREAM
PUBLISHING

EDINBURGH AND LONDON

First published in Great Britain in 2011 by
MAINSTREAM PUBLISHING COMPANY
(EDINBURGH) LTD
7 Albany Street
Edinburgh EH1 3UG

ISBN 9781845967796

A catalogue record for this book is available
from the British Library

Printed and bound by
CPI Group (UK) Ltd, Croydon, CR0 4YY

1 3 5 7 9 10 8 6 4 2

'American Roulette', Robbie Robertson, 1987

For Alexandra

'When it [the shadow] appears as an archetype . . . it is quite within the bounds of possibility for a man to recognise the relative evil of his nature, but it is a rare and shattering experience for him to gaze into the face of absolute evil.'

Carl Gustav Jung

'The victor belongs to the spoils.'

F. Scott Fitzgerald

Acknowledgements

'It's Only a Paper Moon', *The Great Magoo*, 1933

Official answers, explanations and, more often, lies disguised as diluted information, administered to us because it was decreed anything stronger would be too difficult to swallow, have followed, surrounded and ambushed most events in the following narrative for as long as I can recall. It has been a pleasure to find one person in particular, but others, too, who have generously brought clarity to my thinking and understanding of what was indeed the shadowland of the twentieth century. Roger Huntman has been illuminating, shining a spotlight into the dark corners of the past, and he has been brave to do so. It's taken him his long lifetime to confront what his unconditional love of and loyalty to his father involved him in. In countless conversations with me, he never shirked a question or gave an evasive answer. He never speculated. David Cornwell, who had not seen Roger Huntman in more than 40 years, appeared on my radar by happenstance; he brought with him decades of experience in gaming and a first-rate mind with which to analyse it. Roger Huntman led the troops, of whom there were many, who provided guidance and information as well as their energy and time.

The splendidly single-minded Bobby McKew, who has an encyclopedic and primary knowledge of many aspects of the events described here, kept me on a straight road, away from improbable avenues even when they offered fantastic views; this astonishing story did not need extraordinary embellishments. He also helped with introductions to friends in America and throughout Europe who brought me to a new comprehension of a banking system that doesn't have high-street branches.

Charles Richardson helped with a hindsight he alone

possesses, as did the dignified and sadly missed John Burke and the always honest and forthright CMK, with her sharp and distinct memory of events and her political insight. The late Mark Birley was instructive, as was the lively and entertaining Mark Sykes. Most instructive was the generous help of Dino Ricardo 'Ricky' Cellini, who provided me with much pertinent and never-before-disclosed information; he has remarkable inside knowledge through lifetime relationships with many major players in *Shadowland*, including 'Uncle' Meyer Lansky and 'Uncle' Santo Trafficante Jr, for whom he acted as an honoured pall-bearer. Muriel Davidson told me many stories of the Bahamas and the Mafia that she had witnessed at first hand with her husband, Bill, when they investigated the specialised entertainment going on there in the 1960s for the *Saturday Evening Post*. Sadly, some of that information, which might still attract our learned friends, must wait for another opportunity to be disclosed, as must some intriguing tales from the worlds of boxing and gambling and Hollywood.

I will always be indebted to the newspapers and magazines that indulged the reporting that gave me first-hand interviews and encounters with many of the eclectic cast – stars and cameo performers – in *Shadowland*, from Judith Campbell Exner, mistress to JFK and Mafia don Sam Giancana, to Frank Sinatra, Dean Martin, Peter Lawford, Sammy Davis Jr and Angie Dickinson; from Thomas 'Coroner to the Stars' Noguchi MD to lovable George Raft, gentleman Cary Grant, monster Mickey Cohen, incorrigible President Richard Nixon, Robert Vesco and Bernie Cornfeld; from Jackie Kennedy Onassis, Aristotle Onassis and Reg Kray to Joe Louis, Muhammad Ali, Henry Cooper, Joe Bugner, Jake LaMotta and beyond, to the many throughout America (especially in Phoenix, Arizona, and in Hollywood, Las Vegas and Miami), the Bahamas, Cuba and Europe who would not thank me for name checks.

The marvellous Bill Campbell of Mainstream Publishing arrived with the company cavalry at the perfect time.

But, again, I must thank Roger Huntman, who has learned the hard way to be very wise indeed.

CONTENTS

Preface

Summer in the City

'Catch Us If You Can', The Dave Clark Five, 1965

Let's call them Laurel and Hardy, for anybody who knows their real names is either dead or terrified of telling and being so.

Anyway, it's most appropriate, for the two New Yorkers arriving at Heathrow off the noon Pan Am flight from JFK resembled the film funnymen. One was tall, with his good living bursting over his tan crocodile belt. The other was much shorter and slim, with a friendly, impish grin that disguised his somewhat alarming attitude to life.

On command, he was happy to end anybody's. Which was no laughing matter   simply business.

When they appeared in the arrivals hall, they looked like tourists on a short trip: open-necked white shirts, camel-hair jackets, grey slacks and overdrive affability. Their two small, identical jet-set suitcases, Hartmann 707s, advertised money and a week or so out of town. It was a useful image that summer of 1965 because it provided the security of anonymity. For Laurel and Hardy, their safety depended on just that: a lack of identity. It depended on being who they weren't.

They'd been told the English guy would meet them, had made all the arrangements. They knew him from New York, from Miami. He was OK, one of them. Jimmy had told them to say hello.

Jimmy Blue Eyes had fixed everything, including their ride across to Idlewild – to the airport they'd renamed after that interfering bastard Kennedy, God roast his soul – after joking with them: 'You know why they call it "Swinging" London?'

Laurel looked blankly at Hardy.

'Because anything goes,' chuckled Jimmy.

Laurel and Hardy, wanting to get going, wondering whether

11

to take the bridge or the tunnel to their flight, looked at him. Jimmy ordered the kid by the door to get their car and driver. 'London, ya know? Anything goes . . . Make sure it's not your wallet.' Jimmy lost his laugh as he walked them over to the car, whispering to them, 'I'll know when it's done.'

For Laurel and Hardy, the novelty was not that they were going to commit murder but that they'd be doing it in London. And everything was looked after, including the extra discretionary expenses and their exit from events.

They had a few days before they had to perform. Maybe there'd be time to see the Queen. She wasn't far off from their hotel in Piccadilly Circus. They'd been told it was the heart of tourist London, so it'd be crazy not to see the sights, take a walk along Carnaby Street, keep an eye out for the Beatles – something to tell the girls about.

At Heathrow, they saw the Limey. He had a young guy with him whom he introduced as his son. He didn't ask for their names in return, just offered a quick shake of the hands. He'd been more relaxed in Miami.

'Jimmy says hello,' Hardy told the Limey, who acknowledged the message with a nod of his head.

They all got into a Bentley that was a deep-blue colour, almost a navy, and must have been hell to keep a shine on. The kid in the front said nothing, his father not much more. Laurel and Hardy looked at the back of a couple of heads, the view they'd had all the way over the Atlantic.

'It's all going to go away, be good,' said Laurel.

'Yeah,' mumbled the Limey.

The New Yorkers, lacking the emotional vocabulary, didn't push any more conversation. Whaddayagonnasay? The Limey had been a friend of the guy they were going to kill for a very long time.

PROLOGUE

TOLEDO BLUES

'You Ain't Heard Nothing Yet', Al Jolson, 1919

Jack Dempsey was as rough as his trade when he became boxing's heavyweight champion of the world, but the edges were quickly chipped away by his fame and polished by those scrapping over it.

When he fought Jess Willard for the title on 4 July 1919, a galaxy of smooth operators – the grifters and the hustlers, the ten-dollar girls and the ladies who charged rather more for similar services with better hygiene and conversation – ran away to this particular Independence Day circus to witness the champ become the champ a lot of money wanted him to be.

A good deal of it was his manager's. Tilting against sports-page opinion (including that of Wyatt Earp's sometime sidekick Bat Masterson in the *New York Morning Telegraph*) and bootleg wisdom, Jack 'Doc' Kearns, who snapped out instructions like Masterson had bullets in Dodge City, had wagered $10,000 at 10–1 that his fighter would see off his Goliath opponent in the first round.

Dempsey, despite standing an inch over 6 ft tall and weighing in at around 190 lb, did have the David role. Jess Willard would have got Fay Wray's heart thumping. He towered at nearly 6 ft 7 in., weighed (after a strict training diet) 250 lb, could reach out 83 in., and when he wanted to he could hit you hard all over – left, right, again and again.

Ten big ones on Dempsey at 10–1 riding on the event in Toledo, Ohio, looked like an idiot bet. Doc Kearns had distinctive big ears and dressed like a clown, in taupe pants, a red and white striped shirt and white shoes, but he'd never been known as one. Still, it seemed a crazily loyal gamble on his man.

The crowd liked the look of Dempsey, 24, handsome yet not a matinee idol. He had a toned physique and an outdoorsman's bronzed skin. Even his haircut, the sides shaved to the head, shouted youth and energy; it was meant to make him look tougher but instead promoted a boyish, clean and highly marketable look. You'd buy aftershave from this guy.

Willard, though, was a big champion, a huge man who in Havana in 1915 had gone 26 rounds with Jack Johnson and still had the power for a zinger knockout punch to take the world title from the first black heavyweight champion. Dempsey's father picked Willard, 37, over his son. For his part, Willard asked for 'legal immunity from murder', fearing he might kill Dempsey. Wall Street brokers made it 15–5 Willard, while in Toledo, where the weather was getting as hot as the betting, it was 5–4 Willard.

In all this, it was only slightly obscured that the amiable Willard didn't like to hurt anyone. For money, he could. But he just didn't like to bash out punishment, something that had been deeply compounded when he'd broken the neck of opponent 'Bull' Young with an uppercut. In contrast, Dempsey was a boxer who'd punched his way to the title fight, taking out a mixed assortment of fighters, some hard, some soft, including 'Gunboat' Smith and 'Fireman' Jim Flynn. The most talented was Fred Fulton, known as 'the Rochester Plasterer' and a 1918 title contender, but he'd lasted only 18 seconds in the ring with Dempsey before calling it an evening.

The wise money was on Willard. The speculative dollars were speed-boating booze – near-beer was as strong as you could get legally in Ohio – over Lake Erie from Canada as the Temperance Movement applauded the upcoming nationwide ban on alcohol heralded by the Volstead Act. In Toledo that Fourth of July, if any fight fans were crying about that they were doing so, at a premium, into real beer and whiskey that would stay down.

Yet the real seller in and around the 80,000-seat stadium (the greatest ever built, shouted the headlines) was water. Iced, it went for 15 cents a glass in the 114-degree temperatures. It wasn't just the heat, it was the oppressive violence of it, broiling brains and biting into bodies that were already prime attractions for the swarms of mosquitoes.

Even the stadium, built for $100,000 by engineer Jim McLaughlin from San Francisco, suffered in the sun. The 24 miles of seats were made of fresh pine, which swelled and oozed sap. The cushion concession was voted a winner; it went for a remarkable $2,500, in the belief that the crowd would be unwilling to soil their clothes on the seeping pine planks. But word spread even faster than the sap and rather than pay 50 cents a cushion the fight fans, the players, the card sharps and tricksters, the dice mechanics, the scam artists, the chisellers and clip artists, the girls, one real actress (the flustered Ethel Barrymore), the former champs, the near-champs, the never-weres, the punch-drunk and the plain drunk brought their personal cavalcade of vices – and cushions.

They didn't sit on them for long. Dempsey and Willard played cat and cat at first – it was never clear who was stalking whom – but it suddenly became jaw-droppingly clear that Dempsey was hitting Willard, hitting him again and again in a combination of punches: right hook, left hook, classic hook, short right and a hook of cruel carnage that shattered Willard's cheekbone in 13 places. The crowd were up and down, moving, almost synchronised, to the brutal solo ballet surefootedly being danced in the ring. When Willard was knocked down for the second time, the left hook sent half a dozen teeth soaring from his mouth. The frenzy was given revolutionary zeal by one woman pushing to ringside and demanding not Willard's guillotined head but: 'Give me one of the big guy's teeth! I want his teeth!'

Dempsey, as he was allowed to, stood over his floored opponent and hit him as soon as both Willard's knees had left the white canvas, which he'd stained a vivid claret. Those ringside said Willard looked like a fountain of blood as he went down a total of seven times in the first round. With the crowd howling, the round ended in confusion. Kearns, dreaming of his $100,000 first-round triumph, hustled his champion out of the ring. But the fight was not over. The first round had ended before Willard had been counted out. Kearns had lost his $10,000 stake money, for a confused Dempsey was brought back into the ring for round two.

The battering went painfully on until Willard threw in the white towel, soaked in his blood, as was Dempsey's body, before the fourth round got started. Willard, who with insane instinct had got up again and again, floundering around the ring to take harsher and harsher punishment, looked like a building had fallen on him – several times. He'd suffered a broken jaw, broken ribs, a mouthful of busted teeth and deep fractures to his facial bones: a startling amount of damage in boxing. His face was a gargoyle of swelling, his right eye trapped shut. His professional world had been as battered and beaten up as his face and body, and he grasped at the only available security his mangled mind could manage to find. Through the damage and the cheers and cheers for Dempsey, he was heard muttering as he was led from the scene of his terrible destruction, 'I have one hundred thousand dollars and a farm in Kansas, I have one hundred thousand dollars and a farm in Kansas, I have one . . .'

When Jack Dempsey woke up the next morning as heavyweight champion of the world, the controversy was already rolling. The suspicion and then the word was Dempsey had cheated, he'd used loaded gloves. How else could he have inflicted so much damage on Willard without hurting himself, fracturing his own knuckles? There wasn't a mark on Dempsey; all that had got to him was Willard's blood, and lots of it. Claims that plaster of Paris had been added by Kearns to the gauze tape wrapped around his big hands, which were then soaked in the corner bucket – insurance for Kearns' big bet – that Dempsey had worn knuckledusters or weighted his glove with a railroad spike or possibly a heavy iron bolt swiftly became barroom and gym talk, one-for-the-road conspiracy theories. Yet an hour after the fight, Willard had said, 'I was fairly beaten and thoroughly beaten.'

That didn't make it any easier on the punters who'd lost big, including some who'd made their bets from barbershops a couple of hundred miles away from the fight across the state's Route 80 in the coming steel city of Steubenville. They'd believed their believers at Rex's Cigar Store when they'd said that Willard would triumph in a fair fight. That was one blow Willard did soften some time later, when he was gifted an excuse by big losers claiming that the Mob had fixed the fight. When the bruising had gone and the battered bits had healed and the teeth been replaced with dentures, he found one word to explain why he'd lost the fight, lost his lucrative title: 'Gangsterism.'

That was easier to accept for those who didn't like being wrong or even the thought, the hint, that Dempsey's victory was self-tarnished. Heroes were welcome, needed, and big Jack Dempsey fitted the part, and his fur coats and new Brooks Brothers suits, to perfection. By then, it was the 1920s and many of the evils of America were being blamed on what had become a popular trade. Some of the more powerful exponents called it a vocation. As with most things, it's all about who's defining the definition.

The cognoscenti said Dempsey's manager Jack Kearns, who had a penchant for pungent colognes, was a 'ballyhoo artist'. The fanciful enjoyed his stories of being managed as a young boxer by Wyatt Earp and surviving Alaska with the novelist Jack London. One tale of Kearns' youth was confirmed: before he got anywhere near Dempsey's glory, he'd served three years in Leavenworth State Penitentiary, Kansas, for selling fake shares in an oil well that wasn't where Kearns said it was, indeed wasn't anywhere at all. Inside legendary Leavenworth, you make connections.

But it was because of his instinctive skill in his management of the champ that many went the way of Willard and didn't answer the bell after Dempsey confronted them. With his fierce capacity in the ring, Dempsey held the world heavyweight title from that Fourth of July in Toledo until 1926, when he lost it on points to Irish-American Gene Tunney in Philadelphia. Al Capone supposedly offered to fix the rematch a year later, but if he did it didn't help Dempsey. It didn't hurt him, either; he remained one of the most popular personalities of the age, the first $5-million sports star.

He moved about America like a prince at court, acknowledging acclaim, and all he had to do anywhere was to turn up to make a dollar. He appeared in a Hollywood one-reeler, sadly not as dashing or entertaining as its title, *Daredevil Jack*, and was paid for public appearances and exhibition boxing.

The French philosopher Nicolas Chamfort, thinking a century or more before Dempsey got his 15 minutes, maintained that chance was another word for Providence, but you wonder what strange divine intervention was involved when, as champ, Dempsey sailed the North Atlantic in 1925. Much to Jack Kearns' suspicious anger, Dempsey had been tempted into marriage by the ambitious starlet Estelle Taylor, who, after appearing in the silent version of his *The Ten Commandments*, told anyone who would listen, 'I'm under personal contract to Cecil B. DeMille.' She sailed with her husband, her dog Castor and Jack Kearns, and the contest was over who was the most nippy on the voyage. There were complications, many revolving around beloved Castor's seasickness, and time and the champ's commitments became a concern. Dempsey was adamant he wouldn't miss his enthusiastically anticipated exhibition bill on the 1925 Fourth of July holiday, this one even further from home, in Brighton, England. For it, he delayed his trip back to America. The schedule was for a run of warm-up contests before Dempsey, the grand attraction, went twelve rounds with four different British boxers to raise funds for the Royal Sussex Hospital.

On the day, he gently punched a baker's dozen of rounds, including an encounter with the infamous 'Phaintin'' Phil Scott, who had an absurd reputation in the ring. Phil Scott, the British champion, didn't like being hit. He'd turned avoiding being hurt into an art form. At the hint of a blow anywhere below his eyeline, he'd claim foul, a low blow. He was clever at it and won nine fights straight by collapsing, fainting to the canvas and proclaiming he'd been fouled. He talked about opening a pub when they called time on his boxing, but it was regularly pointed out to him that it wasn't a good choice: every time the cash register rang, he'd have doubled up and stretched out on the bar. His charades had helped him to a profitable 12-year career.

Although Phaintin' Phil was a terrific show (they'd bet on when he was going to do his act), the magnet for everyone's attention was Dempsey, one of the most famous men in the world, a sportsman who had beguiled most everyone, *the* founding figure of sport as big business, the heavyweight champion of the world. He was as good as it gets. Benny Huntman watched Dempsey in awe. He'd read about the champ in the papers, seen him on newsreels. Dempsey was a legend of Roaring Twenties America, a sharp dresser with a thick wallet who'd married a Hollywood movie star, and here was Benny Huntman, just 19 years old, not only in the same stadium but on the same bill that particular American Independence Day. Over time, that happenstance would come to matter very much, and it would give those who thought of it goose-pimples.

Three years earlier, as an amateur lightweight for the Limehouse and Poplar club in London's East End, quick and wiry Benny had achieved an open competition final; since then, he'd had twenty-one contests as a professional. The last one was to be at this Royal Sussex Hospital benefit. It was to change his life, and the lives and fortunes, for good and bad, of many others. That day, everyone wanted a sprinkle of the Dempsey stardust: he was living the American Dream just as they were inventing it. Benny Huntman wanted to shower in it.

PART 1

DEAD MAN'S HAND

'You Never Can Tell', Chuck Berry, 1964

1

OPPORTUNITY KNOCKS

'Nobody Knows the Trouble I've Seen',
Marian Anderson, 1925

When he spoke, Benny Huntman sounded like trouble. He
was not much more than a toddler when one of his brothers
gave him a cup of boiling-hot water to drink. It scalded his
throat and from then on his speech had a sort of griddled
sound to it, attractive but edgy, a little like his personality.

It was that loud, distinctive voice that echoed when he
returned from the Brighton exhibition and announced to his
family: 'Dempsey's the king of the world. You wanna see how
they look at him. He's like a god.'

No one had that role in the Huntman family. And no one
paid much attention to Benny; he was talking out of his and
their league. His parents had six children: Benny and his
brothers, Sammy, Harry, Ruby and Sonny, and their sister,
little Millie, whom everyone adored and cared for. For the
rest, it was open season.

Benny, the youngest, had to battle from moment one. His
siblings, having arrived before him, had established what
hierarchy there was room for. He was born on 13 June 1906,
at the family's rented home, 31 Radlix Road, Leyton, London,
to Hyman Huntman, a bootmaker, and his wife, Annie,
formerly Annie Levy, who signed his birth certificate with an
'X'. It was a long birth and the boy, named Benjamin, emerged
screaming.

Maybe he knew what he was getting into. He was the son of
Jewish immigrants in a city of casual racism and extravagant
violence. The local ghouls still spoke in gin-inflamed paranoia
of Jack the Ripper, who'd been stalking and killing around
Whitechapel not that long before. Home – dingy, damp and
air-conditioned by doors that didn't quite squeeze shut –
didn't look quite so bad in candlelight; there was no electricity,

no running water. Life revolved around a big iron stove that took the bite off the cold of the place and cooked their meagre meals.

They shared their clothes but never, never ever, their shoes. Hyman Huntman, as a bootmaker, took pride in his skills and in keeping his family walking as tall as they could around the rubbish-strewn cobbled streets. Hyman made extra money making sweets and jellies and selling them from a stall in Green Street Market. As Benny grew up, silent movies began showing and his father would sell to the queues outside the cinemas, a little something to go with the latest Lillian Gish celluloid offering. Street life was a world of jumping in and speeding out; the prizewinners had quick wits and legs. In this half-a-sixpence turbulence, there were rascals, and sometimes downright hoodlums, trying to make off with the little cash being made. Benny, wiry and athletic and growing in height and attitude, would go out with his father, there being protection in numbers.

He listened to the other stallholders complaining about bully boys but didn't say much. The Huntman boys grew up fast. If Benny ever felt fear, he disguised it and confronted it in pursuit of what he wanted. He despised the concept of fear in itself but recognised it as an effective, manipulative business device in dealing with others. In his world, you punched your philosophy, and for profit.

Benny was in his early teens when he became one of the protectors of the stallholders around Green Street. He worked it up slowly, helping one and then another with street toughs trying to muscle in on their profits. It was a good business plan; he was tougher than the extortionist tearaways.

The market men allowed Benny a few pennies, sometimes shillings, and it added up. He liked the arithmetic and expanded his protection patrol around the East End. He saw an opportunity, as did Jack Cohen, who in 1919 started selling groceries from a stall at Wall Street Market in Hackney, putting down the foundations of his Tesco empire. Benny (whom Jack Cohen would later tell, 'There wouldn't have been Tesco without you') was equally an entrepreneur. He had some style and liked to play the part of a man of substance. He invested in a handmade suit, sharp and in his favourite rich navy blue, and planned to wear it for the first

24

time at a dance the next Saturday night.

But on the night the suit had vanished. He found it at the dance hall, hanging off his brother, who'd never been forgiven for that cup of scalding water. Benny didn't say anything. He marched across the dance floor to his brother, pulled him forward by his shirt (not the suit) and planted his fist several times in his face.

As his brother lay on the floor, surrounded by friends and other locals, Benny stripped him naked. The punches had made his point; his brother's humiliation came from somewhere deep inside Benny. There was a rage in him, but he usually managed to restrain it. That was a quality that protected him from unnecessary trouble; he almost always calculated the odds before acting – unless he was absolutely intoxicated by anger.

Also, Benny had his own charisma. Dark-haired and attractive, with a wiry athleticism, he dressed too well for the money from the stallholders and, later, his professional boxing. He spent freely, and by the Christmas of 1925 he was running a Mercedes, a Ponton model.

At Brighton, along with the other young fighters on the exhibition bill, he spoke to Dempsey. There was a kindness about Jack, the sort that comes from being good at what you do. He'd signed off from Brighton with a big grin, telling the young boxers, 'Fellas, see you in New York.' It was a throwaway line, but Benny dreamed about America, about New York and Times Square. He followed Dempsey's career – the staggering $15,000 a week for exhibitions, his regular sailings across the Atlantic on the giant liners of the day – and became even more intrigued by the tales and prospects of the US. Every time he picked up a newspaper, it seemed to mention America, offer details of the lavish living of Dempsey, of a greener land.

Benny was a practical young man. He knew his limitations. He was a good but not a brilliant boxer, more of a street fighter. He wasn't going to be a champ, a title and money winner. His family had their own lives to keep going. It couldn't be any tougher in America; they kept calling it the land of opportunity. All that London's East End, with its ongoing influx of Jewish immigrants, had to offer was a different sort of fight – one to escape increasingly difficult and deprived circumstances.

Such thoughts drove Benny Huntman to the port of Southampton on the south coast, where, on 18 April 1926, he took a slow boat to infamy. The *Berengaria*, a star of Cunard's luxury fleet and often packed to its 5,500-passenger capacity, was about to sail for New York. With his street-market smarts, Benny sold his Mercedes on the dockside. The £35 sale bought him steerage passage. Whatever the accommodation, it would have made the trip no different. He paced the decks most of the voyage, unable to sleep, his heart pumping with the excitement, the adventure, the trip into the unknown.

On docking, he changed his remaining sterling for dollars. He had only a handful of greenbacks and a small suitcase to start life in America, but Benny was a fighter. Circumstances didn't intimidate him: as with everything, you just had to hold your nerve. A container-load of chutzpah was all to the good, but it was nerve that mattered, and never losing it.

Benny arrived in central New York in the middle of Prohibition. In the era of anything goes, the US had the clock set at high noon (the time some illicit punters got up and others went to bed). It meant that for those who sought profit in selling watered-down, high-priced, high-proof alcohol – ban something, everyone wants it no matter what it tastes like – the heat was always on.

For a young, quick-on-his-feet man, this was an outlaw opportunity. Benny wasn't out of place in the city; lots of people had accents, and he had a Mediterranean look that they were stamping into America daily out at Ellis Island. He got a room in a boarding house off-off-Broadway, down a back street and over the road from a coffee place with endless refills and raspberry-jam doughnuts. He found a job as a waiter at The Compton, near Broadway; it called itself a restaurant. Benny looked the part: well shaved, clean, dark hair neatly cut and swept back – an engaging young man. He worked hard and got on well with everyone, especially behind the private entrance to The Compton; the place did serve food, but it made its profit from providing high-quality, imported alcohol at the back of the two-storey building.

It wasn't a unique spot. By the time Benny got to New York, there were tens of thousands of speakeasies in the city. With a nod and a password, you could get a drink in any building on 52nd Street between 5th and 6th avenues. Benny didn't drink, but he understood the immense value in those who did. By the late 1920s, getting around the liquor laws had become an art form. Prohibition was truly an experiment in temptation. America continued to drink. Imbibers concealed their tipples in prams, hot-water bottles, garden hoses and coconut shells. One enterprising individual who liked life sunny side up went to work on an egg: he was stopped with half a dozen eggshells that had been drained and filled with booze.

The Compton was rarely hassled. The beat cop got another score or two of dollars a week on top of his regular graft to be somewhere else when the liquor lorries delivered. The speakeasies (speak easy, quietly, when you order) were lucrative for those serving the booze and for the federal agents, the cops and the New York District Attorney's office. Benny was taught where the alarms were at The Compton, and when the bell button was pressed it cut out power to the sliding doors to the caches of booze that were cradled behind fake panelling. If there was a 'show' raid, the majority of the stock would remain safe.

Benny enjoyed this cavalier life. Despite the long hours, the hands raced round the clock, for it was all so new to him. Every hour brought something different. He'd been there for six weeks when one evening the illegal booze got to work on one of his customers. The big man was at a table with his wife and two other couples. Benny was their waiter. The diner became loud and his language colourful; Benny asked him to keep it down, not to swear in front of the ladies. He got a nasty glare in return: 'I'm not taking orders from a fucking Limey.' The guy sprang to his feet and punched Benny. The retaliation was swift but professionally done. Benny, his face hard and furious, grabbed the man's arm, shoved it up his back and marched him out to the alley. The punishment was relentless, and Benny beat the stars and stripes out of his customer.

With his adversary spread out by a broken, steaming manhole in the cobbles, Benny pulled himself up straight, stretched his shoulders and glanced back at The Compton. Standing there casually framed in the doorway, with a warm smile on his lips, was a smartly dressed young man. He took a half-smoked Caporal from the corner of his mouth: 'Didn't give you no trouble, did he?'

Benny wasn't flustered, but he spoke like the young Londoner he was: 'He was drunk. He was an idiot, a real slag.'

The man dragged in a cloud of smoke, looking puzzled, and then said, 'Oh, you mean *asshole*.'

'Yeah – arsehole! His aim wasn't too good, either, even if he caught me. I thought I was gonna calm him down and then he chinned me.'

'He won't be doing it again.'

'I can't leave him here . . .'

'Yeah, you can. He'll take off. An ass like him won't show up again. If he does, we'll sort the little sucker.'

Benny was impressed. This friendly character seemed to know all about handling the tough-guy stuff. They were about the same age, but there was something about this man whose kind smile never left his lips. There was a confidence, an air of devilment; he gave off the impression of being a man who knew so much more than he ever said. There was something going on in his eyes. Benny was a good judge.

This was the dangerous manipulator most consistently known as Frankie Carbo. He'd been born in the blistering hot August of 1904 in a thin-walled tenement on the Chinatown end of the Lower East Side of Manhattan. He was christened Paolo Giovanni Carbo by his parents, who'd arrived in New York the century before from the south shore of Sicily, from Agrigento, known for ancient remains, poverty and the Mafia. Carbo inherited many interests from the old country, but one that never attracted him was poverty. From a young age, Paulie, who became Frankie, was an intimidating little beast. He was officially a juvenile delinquent at the age of 11, establishing a criminal record and being sent to a state reformatory. There, Frankie found friends, not innocence.

When he first met Benny Huntman, he was 23 years old, endlessly connected and fighting a murder charge. The DA's office said he'd shot dead a yellow cab driver who wouldn't pay his protection money. Carbo protested and his lawyers argued it was self-defence. The man with the smile didn't seem to care.

He hung around with Benny, whom he called 'the Limey', and before too long Benny wasn't just waiting tables any more. There were people to visit, things to organise. Carbo told everybody that Benny was a good organiser, neat and tidy in look and habits, a man to watch your back and the details. A reliable man.

The Limey suddenly found himself a welcome guest of some of the most unwelcome people in America: the Mob. He talked about boxing, about being on the same bill as Dempsey, and that made him even more popular, for this new crowd all followed the fights.

One of them was Frankie Carbo's associate Frankie Yale, who had been born Francesco Ioele in Reggio Calabria, the home of the brutal, earthy 'Ndrangheta Mafia. He was now Americanising their methods in Brooklyn. Everything he touched was intended to look like a legitimate business, and usually did, but was always a front for the rackets, for protection, gambling joints and the supply of booze and girls. It was a flickering, Charlie Chan world and Yale's outfit was known as the Five Points Gang. He put his profits into the Harvard Inn in Coney Island, Brooklyn. It was there that a waiter called Al Capone had had his face badly scarred. He'd upset the sister of a very drunk mobster, who, in a lopsided attempt to cut Capone's throat, had slashed his face instead. It didn't make Capone a freak show, for many of his bruised, bashed, shot and knife- and razor-cut fraternity had features like something the neighbourhood dog had been playing with.

By the time Benny was in New York, 'Scarface' Capone had moved on in the underworld, to Chicago. Yet around Frankie Yale there were still killers, like the feared hit man Albert Anastasia and Willie 'Two Knife' Altierri, who (you get the idea) didn't use a gun but got his job done.

Yale himself was so useful a stone killer that Capone invited him west to Chicago for some political murders he didn't want botched. But the mobsters' friendship was upset by their constant companion: greed. Yale imported Canadian liquor and supplied it to Capone, charging for the bootlegged whiskey and the protection of it on the run to Chicago. Any successful hijacks off the convoys was just bad luck; you couldn't legislate for that. But there were too many booze heists. Capone suspected something was wrong and sent in a spy, who reported back that Yale himself was indeed stealing the booze and reselling it, often back to Capone – a high-proof double dip.

A fatal one, too, in time. First, just after the Fourth of July in 1927, the not-too-clever spy, Jimmy D'Amato, was shot down as he crossed a street in Brooklyn. Capone, given his long association with Yale, tried to talk rather than shoot away the problem. He invited Yale out to the big fight, Dempsey's return match against Gene Tunney at Soldier Field on 22 September. The rematch was an astonishing, dramatic event, a $2-million gate, and after a 'long count' Tunney won on points in the tenth round. Capone and Yale's encounter was almost as frenetic.

And, as with Dempsey, their relationship was never champion again. Getting on for a year later, Yale got a call at his Sunrise Club telling him that his wife was unwell. He drove off in a panic, piloting his new armour-plated Lincoln coupé towards home. He was intercepted by a Buick carrying four assassins. They machine-gunned the coffee-coloured car, but the armour stopped the bullets. The car dealer, however, had cheated Yale and scrimped on the bulletproof windows, which were shattered by the gunfire. Yale's car careened into a brownstone building. One of the killers leaped out with a .45 and finalised the contract by sending a chamber of bullets into the rival gangster's head.

The boys gave the Brooklyn Beau Brummel – at his death he was wearing a gift from Capone, a belt buckle engraved with his initials in 75 diamond chips – a wonderful funeral, the best ever. It was a gangland event. All the guys were there, including friends Frankie Carbo and Benny Huntman. Thousands watched the procession as a couple of dozen cars carried the floral tributes and around a hundred Cadillacs purred along with the mobster mourners. Dozens and dozens of roses were scattered into the air by the sleek crowd gathered around the grave before the opulent, $25,000 silver casket that the always overdressed Frankie Yale was wearing was buried. The only moment of discord was when three women began arguing over which one was Frankie Yale's real wife. As it transpired, it was easier to work out who'd killed him than who had been married to him – or who would fill the New York power vacuum he left.

For the next three years, there was a machine-gun debate in which at least sixty mobsters with ambition died. The discussion was straightforward: the Sicilian Way against the

American Way. The new, young guard was led by Charles Luciano, born Salvatore Lucania in Palermo, who emerged as a charismatic, clever, wily and lethal leader of a multi-ethnic criminal conglomerate. He'd had an impressive adviser. As a nine-year-old, he'd started a protection gang working in and around the Lower East Side. He offered little Jewish boys the choice of paying up or being beaten up. Most handed over nickels and dimes. Maier Suchowljansky, who'd not long arrived with his family from Grodno in Poland, where he'd been born in 1902, wasn't taking any such nonsense. His reply to being told to pay ten cents a week was a rapid 'fuck off'.

Luciano attacked, for his brutal nature said he had to. His opponent fought back just as hard, for he didn't know any different. The fighting finished, it was the beginning of a dark friendship between 'Lucky' Luciano and the boy whom he came to know as Meyer Lansky. Lansky also became friendly with another young tearaway, the Brooklyn-born Benjamin Siegel, the son of Russian Jewish immigrants, who began his gangster career, like so many, by trading protection for dollars. They formed the Bugs and Meyer Mob, dealing in muscle and murder and mayhem for the Prohibition-busting gangs of bootleggers operating throughout New York and New Jersey.

Benjamin Siegel – 'Bugsy', but never to his face – was a psycho pistolero, a cowboy of a mobster who wanted to be in at the kill, if not pulling the trigger himself. Yet, as did Luciano, he listened to the counsel of Meyer Lansky, who, although as much a killer as his associates, saw that only as a business necessity, for he had a corporate brain. Lansky, they said, could see round corners.

He could also cut them. He and Luciano and Siegel worked with the addicted gambler and genius Arnold Rothstein, a New York mastermind who conceivably peed iced water. He was known as having a great criminal mind (after his death, during the post-mortem, it was found that Rothstein's brain weighed 1,400 g). Cold and calculating, he'd envisaged a nationwide crime organisation. It was an idea he talked about with his students, who also included Francesco Castiglia (older than Lansky by some ten years), who, as Frank Costello, was the greatest corrupter of politicians and policemen and judges, those known as the 'foreign dignitaries', powerful men outside the organised-crime fraternity. Costello had worked as a bootlegger alongside Joseph Kennedy and said the patriarch of the Camelot clan and Rothstein were the only men he ever admired.

Rothstein, teetotal, a non-smoker, saw his life and future as a spreadsheet. 'The Brain', as he was known, appeared in Scott Fitzgerald's *The Great Gatsby* in 1925 as Meyer Wolfsheim, who wore human teeth as cufflinks. Wolfsheim/Rothstein supposedly fixed baseball's 1919 World Series, but the fact from the fiction is that Rothstein probably only profited greatly from it. He followed only hot horses, those that always, always won. He might not have fixed it himself, but he probably knew which way to bet.

He was an able tutor and his class was eager, hungry for knowledge and opportunity. He taught them about forming organised groups, affiliations for no other reason than business, about 'looking after' politicians at local and national level, that the dollar was non-denominational and its nationality was profit. Money and the making of it was, he said, an international business. 'Have gun, will travel' was the crucial job description, and an utter allegiance to profit was a requirement, too.

When Rothstein, at 46, was shot in Room 369 at the Park Central Hotel in November 1928, a single bullet went through his custom-tailored Harry Beck silk shirt, blasting a hole where the initials A.R. had been hand-stitched. It was a nasty gut-shooting and Rothstein died the next day. The murder, which was never truly investigated by the New York authorities, was dismissed as the result of a falling-out over gambling debts. Rothstein, the great fixer, had angrily protested to his associates that gambling sessions in which he'd lost had been fixed. He died in that belief. His students were never brought into enquiries about their mentor's passing.

In gangland politics, it was a landmark moment, like the stock market crash in October the following year would be for the straight world. Rothstein's students had learned well. What happened outside their world was of no importance. They had their own agenda. When the battle for gangland dominance ended with a couple of final assassinations in New York in 1931, it was already abundantly clear that the boss was 'Lucky' Luciano, which for him and Lansky was neat diplomacy. Luciano kept the Italian factions content, while his quieter – and privately equal – partner brought in the Jewish mobs, who, unknown to the Italians, outnumbered them.

That year saw the establishment of the new American Mafia, the National Crime Syndicate, and gambling, prostitution, graft, corruption, numbers, loan-sharking, hijacking, criminal receiving, counterfeiting, pornography, smuggling, white-slave and narcotics trafficking, along with all other nefarious and profitable activities on the wrong side of the street, were about to prosper.

The savagery, the unconscionable number of deaths brought about by Luciano and Lansky to make it into pole position, sent a high Richter rumble across gangland America. The old had been shaken out by men who had grown up faster than anyone could remember, a bunch as young as they were single-minded and ruthless.

The New Deal gangsters also established an enforcement arm: Murder, Inc. It recruited rub-out men from the Bugs and Meyer Mob and comprised a bunch of made men, including Siegel himself, Louis 'Lepke' Buchalter and Albert Anastasia, 'the Lord High Executioner'. Still, no task for Murder, Inc. was taken forward without the personal approval of Meyer Lansky. He signed off on every deal, as it were. Other triggermen included Martin Goldstein and the colourful if nervy Abraham 'Kid Twist' Reles, who killed from a sweet shop known as Midnight Rose's. The killers got a salary and two to five thousand dollars per successful hit.

Enjoying that sort of cash was Gaetano 'Tommy' Lucchese, also known as 'Three-Finger Brown'. The one legitimate job the Sicilian took had cost him his right index finger, lost in a mangle machine. He decided such employment was too dangerous for him. A cop who later booked him nicknamed him 'Three-Finger Brown' after the Chicago Cubs pitcher. It was appropriate, for Tommy Lucchese loved sports, especially boxing. He talked about it all the time in 1931 with a Mafia soldier who worked alongside him in Murder, Inc. – Frankie Carbo.

Carbo was still the smiling man. He had reason to be. He'd pleaded his murder of the taxi driver down to a manslaughter charge and, a couple of months after Frankie Yale's fond farewell, had been sent 30 miles north, 'up the river', to Sing Sing Correctional on the Hudson. He'd served only 20 months. Now he was tight with Bugsy Siegel (they'd double up on hits) and getting on great with Tommy Lucchese.

And the Limey was still around. Carbo had introduced him to Ben Siegel and the others. They were all young guys, willing to learn. They talked boxing more and more. Capone and Dutch Schultz and Luciano, most of the more precocious mobsters, had owned or part-owned fighters. They didn't just identify with the violence of the ring; they understood it. There was the bonus of the gambling and glamour, of the prestige. There was also the fun. The rival gangsters quietly competed to see who could fix what fight and win the most in bets. Some fights were straight but that was rare, and it was suggested that only the ring was square. It was an intriguing time and business.

Frankie Carbo had eased Benny Huntman into a comfortable corner, into the management game, in the preceding years. Benny was held in high regard; he walked on the gold dust of loyalty and dependability. He didn't steal, which in the underworld is the mark of an honest man, one you can do business with. He had balls and he had sagacity, a rich combination. There were those around who were keeping an eye out for and on him. Sometime, he'd be brought in properly.

The Carbo crowd still liked to tease Benny Huntman about his accent and his Englishness, saying that, being from London, he knew all about bad weather, fog and rain and that stuff. He'd like Canada, they chuckled. That was where he'd gone on his first mission for Carbo. He'd been put in charge of a fighter called Ernie Jarvis, which was like home from home. Jarvis was from Millwall in London and a useful flyweight.

He had a shot at the title against Albert 'Frenchy' Belanger, who had a solid reputation, especially in his home town of Toronto, where the fight, for the National Boxing Association's world flyweight championship, was held half a dozen days before Christmas in 1927. Frenchy was already known as 'The Champ' and the home crowd expected an easy time of it. Benny, however, had trained and sweated Jarvis to a perfect weight and fitness, and the Englishman made a marathon of the fight, which Frenchy took only on a decision. Back in New York, they reckoned Benny had the makings of a manager. They kept him working with fighters. He had a future.

Carbo maintained his other prime interest at the time: murder. He remained on parole from Sing Sing when in 1931 he slipped off to Atlantic City, to the Boardwalk, to disrupt the empire of Philip Michael 'Mickey' Duff, who controlled beer supplies throughout New Jersey and Philadelphia. Duff's set-up had upset the controllers with failed payments and betrayals, and, on the basis that bad smells start at the top – in Sicilian, '*U pesci fet d'a testa*' – he had to be eliminated. Which he was, by two bullets in the head at the Ambassador Hotel.

The wily Carbo evaded arrest for a little while, time for alibis and the like to be established, and when he finally allowed himself to be found, in a plush Manhattan hotel, the headlines loved him. Here was a hired assassin charged with killing a multimillionaire bootlegger and with him was a teenage moll, a redheaded showgirl named Vivian Malifatti who called herself Vivian Lee: the ingredients for tabloid nirvana. Money went into the hands that could free Carbo and he was soon released, as was Vivian, who, louche legend has it, changed her name and hair colour and became a star of talking pictures.

At the top of the empire, Meyer Lansky and Lucky Luciano were more concerned with the accountancy department than the murderous minutiae of nine-to-five gangsterism. These men, especially Lansky, were highly controlled in a business in which the huge daily profits emanated from people abandoning their inhibitions. They were looking ahead, looking further afield. They were interested in wherever the dollar could profit, for there were zero parameters in their world. Their particular creative cast of mind did not allow for geographical or legal barriers. Success would be delivered by focus and forward planning, with the right people in the right places.

By the time they'd taken control, it was politic to manoeuvre Bugsy Siegel out of New York to keep the noise down. The flamboyant killer was sent to California to police and enlarge the Mob's interests on the West Coast. Hollywood and Bugsy Siegel were made for each other: they both wanted to put on a show.

Others were moved down to Miami to work the hotels and control or set up new 'carpet joints' (illegal but lavish casino-nightclubs with high stakes and good lobster, shrimp and girls – it had a carpet, therefore it was upmarket) and keep watch on 'the islands' – the Caribbean, especially Cuba, which was only a swimming pool or two away. And there was England and the Continent to think about, too. Benny would take their ideas over there and work some money magic with Carbo's fighters. He could get started with that strange kid, Alfonso Teofilo Brown. He was a character, quite a character.

'Panama Al' Brown was tall for a bantamweight. His reach helped him to a bit of history in June 1929, when he became the first Hispanic world title holder ever, taking out Antoine Merlo in Paris, a city whose culture and people the new champ adored. He enjoyed diverse pursuits in Paris, joining Josephine Baker's La Revue Nègre as a tap dancer and becoming a favoured lover of the man of letters and all talents (including 'boxing manager') Jean Cocteau. For Panama Al, boxing was the chore that financed his avant-garde lifestyle.

When Benny Huntman returned to London, the much-liked Panama Al was his fighter. Benny promoted his boxer like a star and 'the Man from Panama' was a sensation, the first non-white boxing world champ that Britain had seen since Jack Johnson had fought before a small crowd in Plymouth in 1908.

Benny had established his home in central London: there was never a problem with money for Benny; it always materialised. He took to training his fighter in Hyde Park. Doing his road work, Panama Al, with his soft cap set rakishly at an angle, would jog along with Benny, in a three-piece suit, and a couple of minders to keep the fans from crowding around them.

Benny Huntman knew it was never good to have anybody too close. People like that usually had to disappear. A mystery, indeed a man of mystery, only remained so if answers were never given. And mystery had its own power, like darkness.

2

RAZOR EDGE

'Life Begins at Oxford Circus', Jack Hylton and His
Orchestra, 1934

The England Benny Huntman returned to had changed as much as him. The images the boys in New York had laughed about – the gaslit streets with their parades of hansom cabs and Holmes and Moriarty as wispy figures in the fog – had by 1931 vanished with his illusions.

He'd arrived with an American invasion. That same year, the Ford Motor Company began operations at a huge new factory in Dagenham in the east of London. Ford's plan was to make their cars in Dagenham for the British market but also to expand sales throughout Europe, from a headquarters in London to Paris, Rome and on and on until the world was driving Ford. It was a smart marketing idea, if not a unique one, for the Mob had it too.

The city itself was striving to be part of the modern age, with improved communications and transport systems. It was the better broadcasting of news that broke into Benny Huntman's days. He was supremely aware of the suffering his parents and siblings and thousands of others had endured to escape tyranny and poverty in Europe. Most of the men he'd mixed with in New York had been members of refugee families. Now the threat of Fascism was overwhelming. He'd witnessed Jew-baiting on the market stalls. Now Jewish refugees were increasingly adding to London's already swelling population of around eight million, and groups of them were constantly fighting against Fascism.

Meanwhile, Benny and much of the capital prospered, despite the struggle of the Depression elsewhere in Britain and abroad. News from New York would tell Benny a similar story. Carbo and the other callers always wanted to know about the fights, the boxers, the upcoming events, the profits. With Carbo's help, his American connections made, Benny as a boxing manager had a special springboard. By representing Panama Al, he had brought in the money via Paris, but Benny wanted to be a player on his home turf. The welterweight Harry Mason was a little ring-worn, but Benny saw him as an opportunity. He convinced Harry to make a comeback eight years after he'd lost his title to Jack Hood (who regularly featured on New York and New Jersey bills in the 1920s) at the Holland Park Link in London. There was a little back and forth, but in November 1933 a deal was done outside a cinema in Whitechapel, not far from Mason's home.

The boxer signed for a five-shilling fee, cash, for a title challenge against the rated Birmingham boxer Len 'Tiger' Smith. Seven months later, on 11 June 1934, at the Embassy Rink, Birmingham, Harry Mason was the British welterweight champ once again.

And Benny Huntman had boosted his management career with the making of a champion. It was an era of strong-willed men, those establishing themselves in an increasingly changing environment; tradition was in dispute with the new but being dragged along anyway. The wireless dominated daily entertainment; in the East End there were fifty cinemas, all showing two programmes (two movies, one cartoon, one newsreel) every week, and the Whitechapel 'spielers', the illegal gambling joints. And there was boxing in arenas such as Premierland, in Back Church Lane off Commercial Road, and Wonderland in the Mile End Road. All the time, Hitler's shadow loomed over Europe as Britain celebrated George V's silver jubilee. There was also a terrible fear, almost a hysteria, brought on by the rise of Oswald Mosley and his British Union of Fascists (BUF), the Blackshirts.

When the BUF announced a mass march through the predominantly Jewish borough of Stepney, there was general alarm in the east of London. Politicians, as ever, dithered. It would be undemocratic to ban the march. Opposition groups thought it would be an outrage if it went ahead without protest. Benny Huntman knew plenty of tough guys who would join the anti-Fascist brigade. Mosley knew how to make things howl: on that Sunday, 4 October 1936, his followers were to parade in full uniform, a hybrid Nazi/Italian Fascist jackboot affair, to meetings in Shoreditch, Limehouse and Bow, before rallying in Bethnal Green.

Benny and his dozen or so lads gathered with the anti-Fascist groups in the maze of tight little lanes and alleyways around Leman Street and then moved on to Cable Street, where they were joined by groups of Irish, socialist and Communist demonstrators from Gardiners Corner (Aldgate). They looked about for Fascists to fight. What confronted them were thousands and thousands of police, including the Metropolitan Police's entire mounted division. The horse police had been instructed to keep the streets open for the legal BUF march; the crowds would not clear and a baton charge followed. Benny and two of his friends grabbed police batons and used them to fight their way through the police and closer to the Blackshirt marchers.

At Gardiners Corner, a driver had stopped his tram and, with the huge numbers of protesters, it blocked the way into the centre of Stepney. To the south was St George's Street, but it led to Catholic Wapping. The Blackshirts wanted to goose-step into Jewish Stepney, and Cable Street was the only route open. They met with growing counter-demonstrations. Paving stones were torn up, smashed and used as ammunition. Fireworks and marbles were thrown under the police horses' hooves as the crowds took up the Spanish Republicans' chant: 'They shall not pass.'

Benny watched the Blackshirts with increasing dismay. They hurled abuse at anyone with a Jewish appearance and spat openly on them. And these animals were being protected by the police? It was for him an example of the absurdities that arose when power was not properly controlled or contained. He saw an Orthodox Jew in a silk suit fighting alongside an Irish docker with a grappling iron. After three hours, the Battle of Cable Street was over. Mosley was ordered to abandon his rally and, instead of marching east into Stepney, the hordes of Blackshirts were sent westwards and back along the Embankment, like another river through London, to Westminster and their headquarters.

Benny always told the story of the Battle of Cable Street (which he had to provide to Meyer Lansky in detail) as one of people getting and sticking together to fight for their rights – the victory of commitment. Lansky had used his connections in New York to disrupt gatherings of the German American Bund and meetings and rallies of the Brownshirts and Friends of the New Germany. Hitler and all aspects and forms of Fascism became the common enemy of underworld and establishment Jews in New York. Some extraordinary political allegiances were formed. Everything, as Lansky preached, is an opportunity.

When Benny told Lansky of the Cable Street conflict, he described to him how the celebrations had gone on until the early hours and how the people giving thanks all had glory on their faces. And they hadn't achieved their victory by doing anything subtle: they'd hurled bricks, brimming chamber pots and any heavy missile to hand at the police and the Fascists. The Mosley mob, the police, the British Government had been intimidated by the violence and the numbers against them. They'd been frightened off. His nerve had never wavered.

Outwardly, however serious his preoccupations, Benny could be loud and sociable. It was good business to like a good time, within limits. The energetic Al Burnett always cheered him up. The club-owner/man-about-London favoured the sunny side of the street; for him, life was a party that went on 24 hours a day. Al Burnett's world was defined by music, champagne and women who wore red lipstick and silk; there, every girl was in a show or in moving pictures, or was only a couch or two away from being so. He was socially and otherwise superbly connected. Al Burnett was his own cabaret.

He was very Americanised, for, like Benny, he'd spent much time there, mostly in Miami. He'd go on stage at his cabarets, look at his watch, and announce in strange-sounding transatlantic tones, 'It's four minutes past seven diamonds.' He hosted many Americans in London, both household names and ones you wouldn't want in the house. He was an enthusiastic gambler and Benny's flatmate. He'd say they were two Jewish boys from the East End who'd made it to the West End. They moved into expansive rooms in Store Street, above the newly established restaurant Olivelli's. The young owners, Rita and Enrico Olivelli, who began their business in 1934, were part of a Sicilian family from the south shore, like Frankie Carbo's parents.

The Olivellis were into fine food. It was the Sabini family in London who were into the other traditional Sicilian activities. They haunted Clerkenwell, the city's Little Italy, and fought fierce battles with other gangs for dominance of the rackets they favoured: loan-sharking and protection. The Sabini brothers also provided the muscle, using barbershop open razors, for bookies operating illegally at the racetracks at Brighton and across the south of England. They provided a chilling addition to the lexicon. When racetrack razor gangs were in action, if an opponent 'took the scenic route' they had their throat cut from ear to ear. The phrase had variations, including one that gave new meaning to 'taking the train to Brighton'.

In a mirror image of the American alliances, the illegal Jewish operators formed a partnership with the Italian tough guys. The leader of the Sabini clan was Darby Sabini, who was christened Ollovia but called himself Charles or Fred, the names of his brothers, as well as Darby. He scattered employment around the racetracks for runners such as a young Scots-Italian lad called Albert Dimes. Darby Sabini, who had a black heart, also ran about three hundred 'soldiers' including a string of gunmen who had fled debts or vendettas and usually both in Sicily to join him. His was a wicked, evil bunch.

Benny Huntman had no time for Sabini and his mob, whom he called 'pretenders'. There was boxing history between him and Darby, a one-time professional who had Desperate Dan fists. He had impressed crowds in London and Paris when he and Benny were both into exhibition boxing.

The animosity between the two men erupted late one evening in 1937 in Olivelli's. Benny and Al Burnett were playing cards when Darby Sabini walked in the door of the restaurant, where a few customers were still eating. Benny quickly looked up at Sabini and just as fast looked away. Why trouble his blood pressure even if he despised the man? Yet Sabini, with the confidence of power and reputation, demanded to join the card game. Benny and Burnett ignored him. Sabini started shouting, threatening. The emotional explosion took a moment. And then Sabini was on his back. Benny had punched him out. All the controlled control went.

41

Benny grabbed a dining chair and viciously smashed it into jagged pieces across Sabini's body. He bashed him half a dozen times, hurt him, and then gave the floored gangster a couple of kicks. Al Burnett was trying to hold Benny back as the anger gathered on his friend's face.

Benny stood over Sabini, and it was in an icy, measured voice that he slowly told the writhing hoodlum, 'If you ever, ever . . . ever come back in here, I'll kill you.' Sabini limped away. Benny Huntman had fearlessly beaten up possibly the most powerful gangster in Britain. He never heard another word from Sabini or his men. They'd got an outfit-style message and they'd translated it correctly.

That evening, Benny did what he always did so well: he took the diplomatic route. There were two couples freeze-framed over their dinners in the aftermath of the violence. Benny apologised to them 'for the interruption', saying he would pay for their evening. They weren't going to argue. Benny smiled, told the Olivellis to give him the couples' bills. He went back to the card game, Al Burnett eyeing him curiously through his permanent cloud of cigarette smoke. Benny was holding a flush of diamonds, ace high. He won the hand. He was a man on a roll.

While visiting his family in the East End, he went to see a Jimmy Cagney movie at the Biograph Cinema on the Commercial Road; he liked the gangster movies, which transported him back to New York, and would imitate Cagney's tough-punk shrug. At the till selling tickets was a young, dark-haired girl who he would quickly find out was called Mae. 'After Mae West?' he cheekily tried.

Benny liked the film, *Angels With Dirty Faces*, but he liked Mae Pope even more and asked her out. They quickly became a couple, but it was an uneasy romance. Mae lived in a broken-down building in Custom House and from the age of nine – she was born on the memorable 11 November 1911 – helped to care for her younger two brothers and two sisters. It was a zoo. Benny's heritage was despised by Mae's father, who worked in East India Docks. In turn, the Huntman family regarded Mae as a faithless intruder, but they hid their disdain from her and Benny.

Mae's father was a bully, an ignorant man and angry about being so. His violent temper flared even more when he was drunk, and he beat Mae and her mother, Emily. Benny – the boxing manager and businessman who was custom-fitted all over, handmade suit, shirt and shoes – bought a café near the docks for Mae's mother to run, providing money for the family. Mae's father always drank his wages. That kindness didn't help; it inflamed the situation.

One Tuesday evening, Benny went to pick Mae up and was told she wasn't well and couldn't see him. Benny demanded to see her and Emily let him in. When he saw Mae, it was obvious she'd had a beating, and his face narrowed to a blade of fury. He made a phone call, a very quiet man arrived and together they raced round to the entrance to East India Docks and waited for her father.

When he appeared, Benny didn't say a word, punched him in the face, grabbed hold of him and pushed his face in some horse's mess. It was all over very quickly. Benny told Mae's father that if he ever hurt Mae or her mother again, he'd cripple him. Mae's father muttered obscenities from his bleeding mouth. He walked out of their house a few days later and was never seen or heard of again, even at the docks. Thereafter, his name was never mentioned by any member of either Mae's or Benny's family.

Benny and Mae separated after that. She was frightened and confused by the violence between her boyfriend and her father. They reluctantly agreed it was best not to see each other, but neither of them was happy about it.

Mae had taught herself to read and write, although challenged daily with the household drudgery, washing, sewing and preparing meals. Her skills had helped her to get the job at the local Biograph. She loved the musicals they screened. Her strong voice and personality had won her a talent competition at the London Palladium; she was presented with her prize by the actress Anna Neagle, the leading lady of British cinema, whom Mae had adored in *Good Night, Vienna* with another favourite, Jack Buchanan. She'd have loved to have stepped into that film world, but such dreaming conflicted with her circumstances.

Her escape was to go dancing with a friend, and the regular spot was the London Coliseum in the West End. The two girls couldn't afford the tram fare and would walk to and from the East End into Soho and the dance hall. One Saturday night, fate did a quickstep and across the dance floor was Benny Huntman.

Benny and Mae were married in 1941 at a London registry office. Their families were not present. Jack Solomons, who held the big diamond wedding ring and the fat, 12s 6d, 12-inch cigar, was Benny's best man.

Solomons, half a dozen years older than Benny, was another East End Jewish boy, from Frying Pan Alley off Middlesex Street, which was better known around the world as Petticoat Lane. Solomons was, in every way, larger than life. His bonhomie was as loud as his ties. He was a ten-year-old when his sister married boxer Joe Brooks and his lifetime fascination with the fight game began. He worked in the family fish shop in Ridley Road and tried other jobs, a little gambling here and there, but the East End boxing lifestyle was a powerful magnet.

With a business syndicate, he converted an old church in Mare Street, Hackney, into a sports arena and dance hall, the Devonshire. It was tough in and out of the ring, and Solomons was the syndicate's survivor into the better times when his matchmaking began to show profits.

As he began to promote more and more fights, he linked up with Benny Huntman, of whom he fondly told everybody: 'I like Benny. He's a simple guy at heart. The trouble is, it ain't simple to get at his heart. He's a keen bargainer and an astute businessman. He is a non-stop worker, except when he goes out to play. And when Benny goes out to play, you'll be safer stopping at home with your arm around the waist of a stick of dynamite. Whatever anybody tells him, Benny still does as he likes.'

Theirs was a beautiful friendship. They had the luck of chance and Benny made some for them, too. The chance arrived on a bicycle from Cambridgeshire on 10 March 1935, in the fighting shape of a young lad called Eric Boon who lied about his age but not his ability as a boxer. 'Boy' Boon became a running attraction at the Devonshire Club, a fresh-faced success who filled many stadium seats, if not the more expensive ones at ringside. A lightweight, he would fight twice a week and after every fight be asking Benny when the next contest was. The challenge was finding opponents for Boon to go up against.

He'd fight anyone, no matter what. In one victory, he'd banged up his right hand quite badly on Conn Flynn's chin. He was due to fight Llew Thomas in Bury St Edmunds, Suffolk, three evenings later. Boon insisted the fight would go ahead. You can't fight with a hand like that, he was told, but he chirped back, 'Why not? My left hand's still good. I can knock Thomas out with that.'

Which he did, in the third round. Thomas fell over into Boon's corner and the referee began the count: 'One, two . . .' The referee had got to six when Benny Huntman leaned through the ropes at his fighter's corner and repeated the count: 'One, two, three . . .' When the referee said 'Out!', the confused Thomas was hearing Benny in his ear saying, 'Seven . . .'

The exceptional Eric 'Boy' Boon went to the Harringay Arena in north London and took the British lightweight championship from Dave Crowley on 15 December 1938. He retained it in the same arena only a few weeks later, on 23 February 1939, in an extraordinary and punishing fight with Arthur Danahar that was stopped in the 14th round. Boon had been hurt early on, his right hand was gone again, his left eye closed by the third round, and to words of concern from Benny he told him, 'I'll catch him in a minute,' which he did, in a continuing flurry of blows.

It was the first time a British boxing championship had been televised. The following month, Jack Solomons, Benny Huntman and Boy Boon flew for a series of meetings in an expectant New York, where Solomons arranged future fights.

It was early in the Second World War, on 9 December 1939, when Boy Boon held on to his title against Dave Crowley. The young boxer who'd turned up on his bike at the Devonshire Club had kick-started Jack Solomons' boxing legend, but it was Benny Huntman who would turn him into an international entrepreneur.

In September 1940, the first Italian bomb to fall on London flattened the Devonshire Club, but throughout the conflict the friends, in a reserved occupation and excused active duty, found venues in which to stage exhibition events and charity boxing contests, including Seymour Hall and the Queensberry Club in London, King George's Hall in Blackburn, Lancashire, and Watford Town Hall. They raised substantial sums for the war effort. To their pride and delight, Benny and Mae's son Roger was born in 1943, not too long before his father received a letter of thanks for his fund-raising signed from Clementine Churchill, on behalf of herself and Winston Churchill.

Benny was also getting letters from Frankie Carbo. The smiling Carbo was now a licensed boxing manager and looking after the interests of fighters including Henry L. Pylkowski, who fought for him as Babe Risko. Carbo wasn't regularly in touch, however, as he was so often dealing with the authorities, usually the New York cops and sometimes the federals who worked for J. Edgar Hoover, who didn't believe that organised crime, the Mafia, existed in America. Hoover, as so often, was in a pantomime universe, for oh yes, they did.

Carbo was known as 'Mr Gray' when he was fixing fights or killings. The more theatrical called him 'the Gray', like a Marvel Comics super-villain, and there were other names that were sometimes admiringly but always fearfully offered: Dago Frank, Mr Fury, Mr Fix, Frankie Tucker, the Man Down South, the Ambassador. Some cops told the newspapermen that Mr Gray was 'the nicest killer you could ever meet'; odds-on Carbo was paying them. He'd escaped a double murder charge from a Dutch Schultz bootlegging feud when, happily for the accused, the body of a participant who'd offered information was found buried in quicklime. Carbo was indicted in 1940 for the demise in Hollywood of Harry 'Big Greenie' Greenberg, an original player in the fellowship that had created the national syndicate of Luciano-Lansky. 'Big Greenie' had developed a foul disposition, had stepped out of order and had to be dealt with, which he was, in the first syndicate hit in California.

Bugsy Siegel was by then partying with movie tough guy George Raft and was 'friends' – in the Hollywood-degree-of-sincerity sense – with Cary Grant, Clark Gable and Gary Cooper. He was also very fond of British actress Wendy Barrie and, it seemed, all the starlets living on and off La Cienega south of Sunset Boulevard. However, he used to take time away from his celebrity associates to mix with those whose modus operandi he understood rather better. Frankie Carbo and Lepke Buchalter, the CEO of Murder, Inc., were flown to the coast as the triggermen, but Bugsy, shrugging off his matinee idol guise, went along to make an evening of it the night before Thanksgiving 1939.

A young researcher at Paramount Studios, Peggy Schwartz, heard five gunshots as she walked outside Greenberg's safe house, a hideout off Santa Monica Boulevard in West Hollywood. Moments after the shots, she saw Carbo, a cigar clenched in his teeth, running from the house. Another witness, a prominent lawyer, identified Carbo and Siegel as the hit men. Bang, bang, bang, bang, bang to rights, the legally minded would have believed.

But the wheels of California justice took some remarkable spins in the months before the case reached Spring Street and the Los Angeles courts. Carbo had slipped away to Pennsylvania, 'outlaw country', then down to Florida and over to Cuba, where a typist-clerk army sergeant turned administration usurper, Fulgencio Batista y Zaldívar, was now a colonel and settling nicely into corruption and casino profits half a dozen years after taking control of the island. For the moment, his wardrobe of uniforms was better organised than the nation.

Eugene Williams, who was running the District Attorney's case in Los Angeles, quizzed an internecine-curved Hollywood blonde whom Carbo had been seeing before he vanished. The Lolita-like leading lady who performed naturally uplifting acts with sweaters couldn't help in that particular matter. Siegel was also unavailable. But the investigators weren't too bothered. They'd arrested Abe 'Kid Twist' Reles, who in return for mercy was talking – and singing more than anyone so elevated in the syndicate had ever done before.

The authorities had had no concept of the rope-trick killings Reles had been involved in, but after one candid conversation they'd 'solved' forty-nine murders in the borough of Brooklyn. The rest of New York and America followed and it was astonishing arithmetic, almost 1,000 killings for 'business reasons' by members of Murder, Inc., to protect the interests and freedom of the syndicate's board of directors.

Reles was known as Kid Twist because of his expertise in strangulation. He had strong, pliable fingers. One of life's enthusiasts, he was adept at getting the last breath out of his victims. Targets were trussed up like turkeys with the head pushed down on the chest and the legs folded into it, the hands in between. The rope was around the neck and under the feet. With every little movement, the rope tightened around the throat until, after a long time, when the killers were many miles away, it was all over. If speed in killing and disposal was required, then ice picks were employed to do the job instead.

Kid Twist ran up a whodunnit of an indictment. He seemed to enjoy talking and was proud of his lethal achievements, of the icings and especially the sadistic stranglings. After his killings, he'd go out early the next morning to get a newspaper to find out who he'd murdered. He was only ever given targets, not names. Yeah, he said, he took an interest in his work.

As did the authorities. They had Reles under close 24-hour protection in a room on the sixth floor of the Half Moon Hotel in Coney Island. He had a team of six guards with him constantly. He was cordoned off so well the DA's office said the precautions 'would've made the Queen's crown jewels safe in Jesse James's parlour'. That view was optimistic. Especially for Kid Twist. He was flipped out of the window; he smacked into the roof of an extension to the hotel and died on impact.

They said that he jumped. That he tried to escape with roped sheets and slipped. That the maid pushed him. They never mentioned a butler. The body landed 27 ft from the Half Moon, and that's remarkable jumping. There was an elaborate cover-up and investigations that offset each other. Few knew that Frank 'Mr Fixit' Costello had distributed $100,000 among the New York Police Department for Kid Twist to take a high dive and become a legend: 'The Canary That Sang But Couldn't Fly'.

With his demise, Frank Carbo and Bugsy Siegel appeared in public once again. Siegel walked away, his shoulders leading, from the murder charges, as Kid Twist wasn't around to link him to Big Greenie's shooting. And without Reles's testimony, Frank Carbo got the benefit of a hung jury. The Los Angeles DA muttered that the jury should be hung.

It was decided then that Carbo would concentrate on the fight game, using his keen knowledge of boxing and his expert awareness of human nature and the deviousness and greed around the sport. Still, he was expected to be available when his triggerman talents were required. Carbo smiled, as always, when he was told this. He liked to get along with people unless they didn't do what he said – and he had associates who carried lead pipes to deal with such misdemeanours.

He had no need for any of that with Benny Huntman. They had their neat transatlantic set-up all worked out. When they got Hitler and company out the way, Benny would get the big-name American fighters for title contests in Britain and throughout Europe. The bigger the attraction, the bigger the money. And, of course, the bigger the venue, the better for all. It was the Meyer Lansky mantra. He wanted to rule the world. Or, rather, the global underworld.

That was the simple business plan of the little man with high expectations. Lansky was blessed, or maybe it should be cursed, with self-direction, which relies on never having anyone change your mind or, arguably, touch your heart. He'd artfully created a network, like a government would with its spies, and they were everywhere. He and his associates had made many millions of dollars during Prohibition, and from its demise on 5 December 1933 the National Crime Syndicate had bloodily emerged. Throughout the turbulent times, the chilling and calculated readjustment of gangland control, Lansky had pursued profit. He wasn't going to stop now. Control of gaming was the way forward.

However, once again he was up against the law. Betting on games of chance was illegal in every state but Nevada. Yet there were always places and ways to place a bet, for Lansky and his partners (for there always were partners, fall guys if required) to make their money. Across and down through the states, most towns had gambling houses of one sort or another, usually in a backroom of a bar or the barbershop. Many were low rent, with sawdust, peanut shells and all manner of UFOs – unidentifiable filthy objects – on the floor. Often the craps games were played on the floor, too. These heathen places were traps for the naive, providing temptation for hopelessly addicted gamblers and always a good night's takings for the owners, who had help to deal with any complaints.

In the steel-mill town of Steubenville, Ohio, there were a couple of such places. There was also a better establishment, closer to a carpet joint, called Rex's Cigar Store; it was overseen by an associate called George Sadlo, who, after running casinos, guns and revolution with Pancho Villa down in Mexico, found life there easier, even if the climate was much more vicious with his bones.

The syndicate had rolled out scores of similar roadhouses, offering every possible way to lose money – poker, faro, craps, baccarat – and they were all operated by trusted, connected men like the capable Sadlo. Lansky laid some down in Saratoga Springs, a couple of hundred miles north of Manhattan, where his mentor Arnold Rothstein had pioneered the opportunity: every August, the Vanderbilt-led society, the rich and usually bountiful, gathered for the horse races. His interest developed into the lakeside Piping Rock, which he co-owned, if not too comfortably, with Frank Costello and Joe Adonis, the boss of the New Jersey gambling franchise.

The Saratoga Springs operation was the model of the upper-echelon carpet joints, where luxury and floor shows performed by headline entertainers were subtly cordoned off from the real action, the money-making gambling. It was a casino in all but name, and a provider of early deposits for confidential Swiss bank accounts on Rue Merle-d'Aubigné in Geneva.

If you were a betting man, you'd always wager on the house winning in the end, yet honesty was the true hallmark of the Lansky gambling policy. The big money was legitimate and ideally it should be taken from its owners quietly, shrewdly, in grand circumstance and the most sophisticated of ways.

In all of Lansky and company's gambling emporiums, the back rooms and the palaces, often taking over the premises of speakeasies, there were managers and dealers who had an extraordinary ability in gaming. These men had remarkable expertise, and if a man with a gun carried their luggage it was only insurance, for guile was their hold card. There is no substitute for knowing what you are doing. The key was to bring in the high rollers and keep them in house with gourmet girls, food and drink. The percentages were indeed with the establishment and so, therefore, would be the profit: the bigger the cash turnover, the bigger the cut of their percentage of the gross. All quite legitimate – if gambling had been legal.

Of course, if the house was genuinely losing big, or some other necessity called for it, then good fortune could be reversed. There was honesty and honesty. Wasn't there? There were 'mechanics' who could change dice mid-play, deal a winning or losing hand of cards and, good or bad, it couldn't be called anything but luck. The mechanics were that good.

You couldn't do that too often, though. Nothing killed the gambling goose quicker than bad word. The business model was to increase the number and the opulence of the gaming establishments to lure big money, wherever it might be in the world, to the games, which – the clever twist – were not fixed.

Meyer Lansky saw the future in being an honest crook. Up, of course, to a point – often the point of no return for someone.

3

Big Potatoes

'You Are My Sunshine', The Pine Ridge Boys, 1939

Always ambitious, Jules Kaufman was a chancer out of Chicago who made a great deal of money gambling on commodities and earned his nickname with one particular coup. 'Potatoes' Kaufman many times boasted that he'd bet on anything, but that didn't include his life. When he was presented with a disagreeable takeover conundrum involving his brain, a revolver and a partnership, he went into business with the syndicate.

What attracted the boys to Potatoes was the sunshine state of Florida, where, after his protective political connections in Chicago had shut down and Al Capone had said he'd kill him, he'd built up an extensive gambling business. In Chicago, Potatoes and would-be master mobster Bugs Moran had run the Sheridan Wave Tournament Club, which was so pretentiously high-tone it risked laryngitis. All the gimmicks to tempt the privileged to lose their money were glitteringly present: flunkey waiters, doormen in fine uniforms and velvet hats, and concierges for all little extra desires; admission was by exclusive invitation and, as standard, the girls, food and drink were free and imported. It worked.

The take each night at the deep-pile carpet joint was thousands and thousands of dollars, of which Moran took a quarter share for protection and the police got 10 per cent. The silent partner, the prostitution entrepreneur Jack Zuta, also received 10 per cent on his investment. Jake Lingle, the cash delivery man for the cops, was a long-standing friend of the chief of police. He tried to cut himself into the game big time, wanting half of every evening's money. He was an arrogant man and felt protected, as you might, by being the police chief's best friend. Lingle was walking through an underpass in the city centre when a gunman put a revolver to his head and a bullet through it. It caused a fuss and a lot of headlines, and Capone blamed Kaufman-Moran-Zuta, which wasn't remarkable thinking, for all the very unwanted attention. He wanted scapegoats. Dead ones.

He got Jack Zuta. The premier pimp had wisely left town and was hiding, as 'James Goodman', at the Lake View Hotel resort near Delafield, Wisconsin. It was a busy, fun place in the summer sun and Zuta was having a good time. He was in the hotel lobby playing a piano machine that tinkled your favourites for five cents a time. 'Flying High' by the Big Bernie Orchestra had him tapping his toes when he turned to the shout, 'Hi, Jack!' He found himself, confusingly, smiling at seven heavily armed men.

The up-front guy carried a machine gun and the others an assortment of shotguns and rifles, which were increasingly favoured for accuracy at medium and long range. A spray of bullets took Zuta down instantly. As he dropped, he was dragged to a chair and his body perched on it. His body was sprayed with 28 more bullets.

Potatoes Kaufman got the message. He didn't want to die. The only way to stay alive was to find and pay for an operator with better connections. He went to New York and to Vincent Alo, a confident, steady, made Mafia man to whom Capone and his crowd were nobodies, guys with no class. Potatoes paid Vincent Alo and stayed alive. Time made the question of life and death a little less heavy for him and he moved on from Manhattan. Yet, even with the syphilis-raddled Capone in prison for cheating on his taxes, Potatoes took no chances. He got well out of town.

He headed for the sunshine, for the Florida coast, where the climate and the Atlantic air and the waves that did cavalry charges over the sand tempted with a better lifestyle, one that was starting to attract more people and dollars. If there is a rule of intelligent gangsterism, it's 'always follow the money'. Sunshine and great crab cakes are a bonus.

Hallandale, 18 miles north along the potholed coastal road from Miami, was a lonely place in fruit-farm land, but Potatoes profited from that. What went as officialdom was instantly available for corruption. He teamed up with the bookmaker Claude Litteral, who'd lost an arm in the war and was factually known as 'the One-Armed Bandit'. They worked a bookie service out of a barely converted hot and horrid fruit-packing warehouse, which, when the gaming paraphernalia was added, they named The Plantation. It wasn't high-class Chicago or New York; rooms at the local hotel were one dollar a night and the fee included the eclectic assortment of resident bed bugs.

When the outwardly genial Vincent Alo arrived in 1938, the enterprise involved all forms of gambling, from craps to lottery games, which had a huge following. But it was a sawdust-in-the-sticks enterprise. The respectable new American money wanted clean and safe, silk-stocking emporiums in which to be entertained, eat, dance and gamble. As such, the potential of The Plantation spoke the language of profit, especially if it was taken upmarket.

Alo, the polite man they respectfully called 'Jimmy Blue Eyes', had spent three years in the Sing Sing finishing school, like Frankie Carbo. He was out, but his friend Charlie Luciano was in jail long term, for decades they said, on fanciful but effective charges of controlling prostitution. Now Alo was working with Meyer Lansky, whom he'd met with Luciano in their Lower East Side lives. Originally, the role for Jimmy Blue Eyes was to look after Lansky, *and* keep an eye on his activities for Luciano, but Lansky and Alo had established a friendship and trust that guarded their own and Luciano's interests. The two men were close in temperament and height. Both stood 5 ft 3 in. tall. Both were contained, didn't take chances and rarely made a move unless they knew what the result would be. You wouldn't want to cross them and competitive types might want to avoid chess games with them.

Potatoes couldn't have acted better when Jimmy Blue Eyes told him they were all going to be partners, which was a life-saver. He said he was delighted and, in time, he truly was. Together, they wrapped up Dade County and Broward County and down to Miami Beach and Miami itself, where hotels were appearing, like the sharper vaudeville acts, all over the place – dozens and dozens of them in every shape and size.

Lansky and his brother Jake ran the Colonial Inn on the edge of Miami and they'd sit on the balcony there and look out towards the islands, to Cuba. They did more than talk about the offshore potential; they planned for it. Meyer

Lansky could already envisage a financial bonanza over the water and soon over the Atlantic in Europe. Everything could be bought up front.

In Florida, if there were problems with local people or authority, they were paid off – donations to this charity, support always for the churches and schools, stuffed blue airmail envelopes in this pigeonhole – and if a nuisance couldn't be bought, then Jimmy Blue Eyes wasn't so genial. He was one of the first to make offers sensible folk couldn't refuse. Nevertheless, said the chorus, a nice guy.

Why else would he pay for Broward County to elect Sheriff Walter Clark who ran on the gambling issues as 'a goddamn liberal', promising not to 'stick my nose into private business'? Clark fitted the role of a southern sheriff perfectly, with his big belly, hands, hat and mouth. His officers provided security and traffic control at the casinos. They escorted armoured trucks supplied by his younger brother Robert to transfer each evening's takings to safe keeping. A club was opened in Fort Lauderdale, a bookie operation in Hollywood, Florida, and many others throughout Hallandale and Broward County, a huge attraction for the many who walked on and over the borderline of legality in America. With the money arrived scores of banks and investment companies, a Wall Street with humidity.

The surprisingly nimble on his feet Robert 'Big Barney' Baker, more than 300 lb of bad news, a mob enforcer who'd left New York and a couple of dead bodies behind to seek employment in Florida, found a spot open at the Colonial Inn. Frank Costello and Benny Siegel took a look around The Colonial, as did Abner 'Longie' Zwillman, who'd taken over the New Jersey rackets after Dutch Schultz was wiped out. Georgie Ranft from New York's West Side, who in Hollywood was the actor George Raft, appeared in a fashionable bespoke suit, like his smoothest movie gangsters, and the boys were visibly impressed by the tailoring. Zwillman, a lover of Hollywood and Jean Harlow (a liaison she advertised by driving along Sunset Boulevard in the red – it set off her platinum hair – Cadillac he'd had gift-wrapped for her), was a player who harboured corporate ambitions, like Lansky.

He was not made aware of the next move by Lansky, Frank Costello and Jimmy Blue Eyes. They were keen to wash the cash profits out of Florida for longer-term investment. They established the Emby Distributing Company, which enforced a franchise on Wurlitzer jukeboxes as well as cigarette machines in and around New York. They controlled what was available on jukeboxes with an exclusive US East Coast licence. The deal helped make a big star of Frank Sinatra, but they took their percentage: one of Frank Costello's divisions pressed bootleg copies of Sinatra's recordings. Hey, give a little, take a little.

The Emby money, though legitimate, couldn't compete with the profits available in gambling. The games were everywhere in South Florida – often in dives off unpaved roads and played with dollar bills not chips – and to the north and east: the outlaw fiefdom of Hot Springs, Arkansas, doubled as a rehab spot for stressed hit men, and winning would always take the chill off Omaha, Nebraska. Serious mobsters Moe Dalitz and Morris Kleinman, who ran liquor out of Cleveland, Ohio, for Lansky during Prohibition, operated carpet joints for and with him in Kentucky. Still, the sunshine state could trump most of America. Rival entrepreneurs opened their own establishments in the Miami area, but the connected city cops who enjoyed their weekly high retainers raided them out of business. The basic foundations established by Potatoes Kaufman were soon skyscrapers. Horse racing parks, dog tracks, bingo halls all joined in the wealth-deprivation of punters attracted to the venues by the weather and the excitement that went with losing their money.

Keeping track of the carpet-joint profits was a never-missed and hands-on nightly ritual for Lansky or his brother Jake or George Sadlo. When the last table had closed for play, all the cash was taken to the cashiers' cage. One of the brothers or George Sadlo would personally count it. With customary prudence, Lansky and Jimmy Blue Eyes had cushioned themselves with a coterie of clever and dependable experts, George Sadlo, Joe 'Doc' Stacher and Dan 'Dusty' Peters being the leaders. Sadlo, who was given the respect of a veteran – 'Pancho Villa, for Chrissake!' – had survived by being a careful man. His indulgence was talent-spotting, looking out for operators who could be groomed for syndicate stardom.

His instincts in Steubenville – where his Rex's Cigar Store

was the leader in a town of several such establishments, fronts for indulging in liquor, bookmaking, numbers, eight-ball pool and dice (including an intriguing Greek version, barboot) – had proved solid. He'd discovered Giardino Cellini, whose father, Marcello, ran the Lindbergh Restaurant, which he cheekily opened three days after Charles Lindbergh's solo transatlantic flight in May 1927; after a bother over selling illegal booze, it later became the Roma Restaurant. Sadlo favoured Dino Cellini over an Italian barber's son, the confident, broken-nosed part-time boxer Dino Paul Crocetti, a teenage bootlegger, roulette stickman and blackjack dealer for Sadlo.

Crocetti was a contender, but Cellini was the man to bring in, a man to train, Sadlo enthused to Lansky. His sister Julia was clever but quiet, as a girl should be. His brothers Bobby and Eddie were good, the other brother Goffredo, 'Goff', a nice boy – but Dino Cellini was magic. He could make straight dice talk the right language. He knew the pure maths of the percentages and he'd learned the mechanics of crooked dice: the 'six-ace flats', the 'shapes', the 'tops and bottoms', also known as 'tees', the most dangerous to deploy. They carried the same number of spots on each side, so that only three numbers were ever in play. These high-risk 'bust-out' dice had to be switched away for straight dice in a moment; the dexterity with which he made the switch was part of what some said was Dino Cellini's supernatural skill. He could police any craps game, manipulate moves so a hustle was never detected. He'd also worked on his own, gone on the road with his dice, operating throughout the Midwest, getting a tough education travelling with funfairs. He'd stopped off sometimes, in Louisville, St Louis, Cleveland, Columbus and, for a spell, Chicago. He was known as a gypsy and one of the best dice men ever. He was cool, he was collected, he was a gambling genius, with all the physical and mental skills he needed in spades – and diamonds, hearts and clubs, too.

He had depth of character and charm; Lansky and Jimmy Blue Eyes agreed that Dino Cellini was a contender but that he had to stop looking as though he dressed in the dark. Cellini wasn't that much out of his teens when he was sent off to New York to get a better tailor and improve himself and the financial interests of his mentors.

Meyer Lansky also went out of town to make more money. In 1937, with Doc Stacher, he took an hour-long Aerovias Q flight to Havana. Earlier, with the enthusiastic support of Charlie Luciano, he'd put an arrangement in place to persuade Fulgencio Batista y Zaldívar of their good and generous intentions. Batista, whom they'd seen as coming controller of Cuba, had facilitated their Prohibition rum-running. America, with fevered official machinations in Washington, had long yearned and tried to take over Cuba, a land of invasions and blockades and boycotts. The Mob was going to buy it. Cash.

This move was another level in the creation of a labyrinthine criminal empire. It involved Doc Stacher helping Lansky take to Havana six special-sized suitcases packed with dollars, which, on counting, the astonished Cuban leader realised added up to $6 million. It was neatly packaged at $1 million a case. There was a great grin on his greedy baby face.

Lansky and Batista shook hands over the suitcases: the syndicate had a casino monopoly throughout the island, centred on the memorable Hotel Nacional and the Oriental Park Racetrack; Batista could look forward to annual gifts of around $5 million. All cash bribes and gambling profits were to be personally deposited by Doc Stacher in Batista's own code-only-accessed Swiss account.

The syndicate had soared over the rainbow and found never-ending pots of gold. No two men could have had such a perfect understanding as Lansky and Batista that sunny day in Havana.

Damned if all that wasn't spoiled by violence and corruption – by other people. In the sugar-cane nation, it seemed, life wasn't sweet enough. When General Gerardo Machado was overthrown, he flew into exile with the only friends he had and all five of them were wearing their pyjamas. The liberal leader was dressed in a tunic suit and carried five revolvers and seven bags of gold. Batista had control of the military after Machado flew, but the president's followers, the Machadistas, insisted on their rights, although they'd never enjoyed any when he was in power. Still, they were the catalyst for an almighty inconvenience for the gangsters.

There was medieval mayhem on the island. Agitators were paid to provoke trouble on the streets, bodies were found beneath coconut palms, there was torture and kidnapping.

There were horrifying images of people mauled by attack dogs, their genitals eaten, others barbecued, their bodies blackened, still others hanged from street lights and left to rot.

It was no advertisement for the delights of sex, fun and sun. The Cuban tourism industry was already suffering in fickle economic times. And the attractions of gambling on the island had vanished: the racetrack was a mess, with races fixed, horses doped and punters duped; the casinos were being ripped off by mediocre mechanics, who would quickly have been dead on the mainland, and who were splitting their winnings with bent dealers.

In 1938, Batista finally and brutally cleared out the agitators. He announced all gambling was now in the control of the military, but his efforts to clean it up failed. The high rollers were still not arriving. He turned to Meyer Lansky, the man with the heavy suitcases, for help.

The Jewish Lansky was amused at the thought of this as a Christmas present – Santa Claus indeed. He went down to Havana in early December 1938 and stayed for a dozen weeks, overseeing the restructuring not just of gambling but of power itself in Cuba. No matter what it said on his epaulettes, Colonel/General Batista was in partnership with Lansky and the Mafia, and nothing profitable or political could happen unless an agreement was reached between them. Batista knew how easy it was for a couple of million dollars to drop into his confidential Geneva account, and consequently the good soldier was agreeable to all plans.

Lansky liked Havana. It wasn't the live sex shows or the rumba and rum, but something about the place cheered him. With men of his nature, an anything-goes society will bring colour to the cheeks, put a skip in the step. There was also that strange and special pleasure of being in a familiar city in familiar circumstances. He felt comfortable. Most of the senior guys from Florida came over and the fresh-faced Dino Cellini and the younger crowd came down from Manhattan to look after the tables and keep things straight and profitable. This was legitimate gambling and had all the benefits of good odds for those in charge.

The following year, Lansky spent four consecutive months in Cuba. By then, the war was taking its toll on Europe.

America couldn't stay out for ever. He knew the war would mean delay. He saw it as a postponement, not an abandonment of his intent. Lansky pondered that there was always change somewhere, and his long-range opportunity-seeking brain searched for where next to stretch his growing empire.

He didn't look far from Cuba, only across the Straits of Florida to the broken necklace of islands that comprise the Bahamas (themselves only a boat ride from Miami), where the political fix was strong and connections throughout the police department exceptionally solid. Which, it turned out, was a good thing, for there were some intriguing characters there who didn't quite fit the islands surrounded by transparent waters and white beaches.

One of the square pegs was the Duke of Windsor, the former King Edward VIII, who had abdicated the throne to be with 'the woman I love', the American Wallis Simpson. The Bahamas were a tranquil escape, a delightful discovery, but the Duke and Duchess of Windsor found them 'third-rate colonial'.

The British government had been anxious about the duke's being naively sympathetic to the Nazi cause and had decided that far away was the best place for him. When Hitler had occupied France, he'd sent envoys to the duke, who'd taken refuge in Portugal, vainly trying to persuade him to say publicly that he would retake the British throne following a German victory. The situation was untenable. With Churchill's high-treason threats echoing in his ears, the duke reluctantly took up the appointment of Governor of the Bahamas.

A precious man, always conscious of his status, he became acquainted with Sir Harry Oakes, an ebullient and colourful companion. Sir Harry had another enviable quality: he was the richest baronet in the British Empire. He had discovered the largest gold deposits in Canada, but when his taxes had reached $3 million a year, he had decamped and became a pioneer developer of the British dependency. Sir Harry was also an early member of the offshore trusts that enjoy homes in the sun. If anything, he was the token governor before the official one was deposited, under sufferance, on the Bahamas by the Royal Navy. They had many contacts in common, and they both liked their whisky drunk out of small crystal glasses, as well as gossip and money.

The duke and the mining magnate became embroiled in a get-richer scheme to ship gold bullion to, they convinced themselves, the Middle East. American investigators determined that the treasure, looted from occupied countries, was being trans-shipped by the Nazis to Mexico. The shipment was aborted.

However, US Treasury agent John Davis, who'd become a resident alien in the Bahamas in 1940, was conducting surveillance on the duke and Sir Harry when he noticed other visitors. He was aware of the type; these were criminals. Davis had published newspapers throughout Ohio and could recognise the species, and he was cognisant of Morris Kleinman and Moe Dalitz from the bootlegging days. The men whose faces he did not know, George Sadlo and Dusty Peters, visited Sir Harry's estate in Nassau.

What was this? The diligent John Davis knew that the duke and the Swedish billionaire business genius Axel Wenner-Gren were under investigation by the US Internal Revenue Service (IRS). Wenner-Gren, who owned 80 per cent of Hog Island (later renamed Paradise Island) just offshore in Nassau harbour, had Nazi links. They'd breached wartime currency-control regulations. The implications were devastating. A charge of treason against the former king could not be ruled out. And now gangsters?

Meyer Lansky liked to make big-money deliveries himself and, again with Doc Stacher as insurance, he arrived on the islands by yacht from Miami, docking at Nassau's natural sheltered harbour. His contact was Harold Christie, one of the 'Bay Street Boys' group that controlled all the nefarious Bahamian financial affairs in the isles with no income tax. The link between the two men was the lawyer Stafford Sands. Christie was known to the syndicate from Prohibition, when he had been a fixer helping to bring bootleg booze into mainland America from the islands. Now he was close to both Sir Harry and the duke, the men who, between them, had the money and power to control the islands.

The visitors John Davis had spotted were the usual careful Lansky emissaries, and now the little man himself arrived to do business. He saw himself as a salesman with something to sell. The $1 million he had brought for Sir Harry Oakes was 'an encouragement' for his help in green-lighting casino

61

licences from the Bahamian authorities for the syndicate.
Lansky had an uncanny understanding of greed. He was not
a greedy man himself, but he divined it in others; it was a
weakness. The rich, and those who have, always want more,
and they want a deal. They regard a life led at cut price, a
bargain always available, as their entitlement. This being the
case, it was all most civilised and Sir Harry agreed to an
arrangement that was out of his experience.

Lansky returned to Florida and, with America in the war
after Pearl Harbor, he commuted between there and New
York. In the city, Frankie Carbo, who'd been freed of police
restrictions since March 1942, had slowly spread his influence
through boxing. In December that year, the fight world's
crowd-pleasing star prospect Sugar Ray Robinson was
instructed to carry his opponent Al Nettlow through the
rounds and make an event of the contest. But when he took a
punch, Robinson reacted instinctively with an angry left hook
and knocked Nettlow out in the third. Only Nettlow got hurt.
They were all learning the ropes.

Carbo persevered. He even had an office set up at one of
the dining tables at Jack Dempsey's Restaurant on 8th Avenue
and 50th Street, across from where the fight-fixing money
was made, Madison Square Garden. It was useful revenue, for,
with the war stopping Americans flying for fun, the action in
Cuba was dormant.

And that made the development of the financial potential
of the Bahamas somewhat more urgent than it might have
been. Lansky wasn't obviously impatient, but other syndicate
members wanted to get on. Sir Harry Oakes was asked to put
more effort into arranging the rubber-stamping of all the
necessary paperwork. He blustered. It was the wrong reaction.

In turn, Harold Christie, the real-estate businessman, was
invited to use his influence on Sir Harry but the legendary
gold miner wouldn't be told what to think, couldn't, he said,
be bothered. He was 69 years old and a self-made success. He
was completely unlettered in the language of the underworld,
unversed in the society that he'd recklessly joined. Lansky
and the syndicate agreed Sir Harry would have to be taken
out of the equation: business was business, profit the
paramount objective. They were also about to do some
prominent people a kindness.

Sir Harry Oakes' body was found in the master bedroom of his Cable Beach house. The discovery was made by Harold Christie, who said he had slept in the bedroom two doors away but claimed he had heard nothing disturbing during the night. Christie said he'd not left the house, that he'd slept well, and he must have done if Sir Harry breathed his last just down that red-carpeted corridor on Wednesday, 7 July 1943. Sir Harry had not had an easy death. He'd been struck with an object that smashed triangular indentations into his skull – four holes in the left temple. A tiny pillbox and some papers were undisturbed on the bedside table.

Petrol had been splashed over his corpse, around the room and down the stairs, and set alight. A torrid tropical downpour, slanting through the open windows, seemed to have doused the fire and prevented it from spreading and incinerating the whole estate. Oakes's half-charred body lay on the smouldering mattress, his blistered skin covered in white dust. His corpse was also decorated with white feathers, his genitals all but burned off. From somewhere came the suggestion of a voodoo revenge killing. The lively baronet, some floral-hatted ladies suggested over yet another pink gin, had been having an affair with a native Bahamian.

The society murder, the suggestions of white mischief and black magic, pushed the war off the front pages – and sent the Duke of Windsor into a tizzy. He had no wish to have bureaucrats and London policemen prying into his and the island's affairs.

On 3 June 1937, he'd married Wallis Simpson at the Château de Candé in France, loaned to them by Charles Bedaux, a French-born American citizen. Bedaux was a blatant supporter of the Third Reich and had played the duke towards Hitler. He was also an economic adviser to the Nazis and masterminded shipments of, among other things, looted Dutch Guianan gold. He had been introduced to Sir Harry Oakes by the duke in Nassau. The avarice-driven Harold Christie, who had a police record for fraud in Massachusetts, was also at their meetings and they'd talked about financial investments in Mexico. That could all cause difficulties, bring untoward conclusions, for who knew which way the war might go. The death of Sir Harry had to be dealt with quickly, quietly and without too many questions about the British royal family, the Nazis, gold bullion and other personal matters that might become inconveniently pertinent.

The former king had been feted by the authorities in Florida and had elevated contacts there; contrary to Colonial Office convention, he called Miami officers instead of Scotland Yard. He pointed the finger at Sir Harry's son-in-law, the strikingly handsome Mauritian playboy Alfred Fouquereaux de Marigny, who'd eloped with 18-year-old heiress Nancy Oakes. When he died, Sir Harry's wife, Eunice, their three sons and daughter Shirley were at the family home in Bar Harbor, Maine. Surprisingly, the recently married Nancy was spending the summer in Vermont, apart from her husband, who had stayed in Nassau and hosted a dinner party on 7 July.

The politically aware Miami policemen, Otto Barker, a sharpshooter and captain of detectives, and Captain Edward Melchen, the head of the Miami murder squad, followed the duke's finger, not protocol. They'd worked with the duke before, as his personal security during visits to the mainland. They knew he liked things done his way. They arrived promptly, within a day of his telephone call to them, and by Friday, 9 July they were applying their none-too-subtle third degree to Marigny at the Cable Beach murder house. Yet their suspect was kindly given a glass of water and an unopened, cellophaned packet of Lucky Strike cigarettes. To much astonishment, the Duke of Windsor appeared at the scene and talked to his detective friends privately for half an hour. Afterwards, all was calmer in the house.

Alfred Fouquereaux de Marigny was charged with his father-in-law's murder a couple of hours later. Marigny's alibi for the time of the murder was flawed, and what was more one of his fingerprints had been discovered by Captain Barker on a screen in Sir Harry's bedroom. It looked like the Mauritian playboy was for the hangman's noose, and quickly, too.

The trial was a sell-out. Servants lined up to book seats for their bosses, society ladies twittered, it was all very much a sensation. A fresh rope to hang the accused was on order. However, the case against Marigny appeared to be that nobody liked him. He was tall and amusing but, well, not the right sort of people. It wasn't really evidence. When it was shown that officers Barker and Melchen had, inexplicably, forgotten their technical fingerprint equipment, the prosecution case was buffeted.

It soon became even more apparent that Marigny didn't exactly need Perry Mason, although his creator, lawyer Erle Stanley Gardner, was in the courtroom. The fingerprint evidence was exposed, revealed as a plant. The print had been neatly lifted by Captain Barker from Marigny's water glass and transferred to the window screen near Sir Harry's deathbed.

The all-white jury – the foreman was the lawyer Stafford Sands – took a little less than two hours to acquit Alfred Fouquereaux de Marigny by a majority. Yet they said he should be deported from the Bahamas. The Duke of Windsor, who had been in America during the trial, made the deportation order on his return four days later.

No more questions were asked of the duke, or indeed of anyone. Sir Harry Oakes was dead and a spot of bother had gone away. Frank Carbo had told Captain Barker they would need more solid evidence if Marigny was to be easily convicted. He'd suggested a convenient suicide, but that was ruled out as too obvious. And with the islands' Governor pressing for a quick guilty verdict, why not let the trial play out?

In the end, the not-guilty verdict didn't matter, for Carbo and his hit team were not mentioned in the aftermath of the case, as there was no aftermath, no decent official investigation into the murder. With political intrigue smothering the case, the killing of Sir Harry Oakes was bound in paperwork and locked away in a dark-green filing cabinet.

On the Friday of Sir Harry's death, Harold Christie had arranged a lunchtime meeting with him and the men from Miami. Lansky had ordered Frank Carbo down from Miami, instructing him to resolve the situation. Other arrangements were being made and Sir Harry couldn't rip them off for a million dollars and stay alive. It wasn't good business.

Carbo and two reliable associates, one young and strongly built, had arrived in Nassau on a power-equipped yacht that could sleep six. They idled just across the water, off Hog Island, and then chugged over in a Sunburst for their appointment. Sir Harry turned up with Christie and, believing it was just another business meeting, aggressively said he was not cooperating. Carbo smiled and nodded at one of his men. A winch handle with four prongs rattled across Sir Harry's head. He fell to the deck. Harold Christie panicked but was told that Sir Harry was only unconscious.

The killers loaded Sir Harry's body into the boot of his car. At Cable Beach, the stiffening corpse was stripped and gently worked into Sir Harry's blue silk pyjamas; the voodoo touch was added and the bed and Sir Harry were set on fire. Harold Christie stayed away, by the docks – he was seen in Nassau town that evening, giving the lie to his witness statement that he'd never left the house – and only returned to 'discover' the sad death of Sir Harry.

It was a good result, although the botched attempt to get Marigny convicted had left a mystery; that failure took a lump of cash out of Captain Otto Barker's weekly extracurricular stipend.

With Florida flourishing, Lansky kept the Caribbean low key for the time being and set about expanding other United States interests, in the jazzy New Orleans, through the Midwest and up and across to the coast. He contacted Benny Siegel in Los Angeles.

In Havana, Lansky had witnessed the benefits of hassle-free, government-approved gambling. It was why he was so intent on getting, and so furiously disappointed to have failed to get, an above-the-line set-up in the Bahamas. He never forgot that, but he thought forward at all times. He told Ben Siegel to drive out and have a look around, especially at that place north on the bad road from Barstow, the stagepost over from Death Valley in Nevada where gaming was legal. Bugsy told his friend he was nuts.

Lansky insisted. They *would* do a little something with Las Vegas.

4

THE HARDER THEY FALL

'There's No Business Like Show Business',
Ethel Merman, 1946

'What happens if their tits wobble?' asked Boy Boon, with what seemed like genuine concern.

'Jiggle!' said Benny Huntman. 'They get the law on 'em if they jiggle.'

Benny Huntman and the fighter whose talent had helped propel them into the West End of London were standing outside the office they shared with Jack Solomons at 41 Great Windmill Street, 20 yards and a couple of steps up Shaftesbury Avenue from Piccadilly Circus.

Across the street, off to the east, an early-afternoon crowd (the theatre opened at 2.30 p.m.) was gathering for the day's first presentation – 'performance' would be way too active a word – of the delights of the Windmill girls. The identikit girls, with faces layered from the same make-up pot, displayed nude bodies that had not wilted on wartime rations. They were built for comfort – and motion, but that was against the law. The Lord Chamberlain, Lord Cromer, had acknowledged the argument that naked statues could not be called obscene and prosecuted. The Windmill Theatre could present its ladies in motionless poses. The law: if something moves – it's rude.

The audiences paid to view the glamorous girls arranged with some care in exotic *tableaux vivants*, living statues. This was artistic material and the shows were themed. The mermaids were an obvious choice; the Annie Oakley *tableau* featuring the Wild West firecracker and friends was inspired.

'But,' said Boy Boon, shaking his head, 'what happens if their tits, you know, move? How does anyone know?'

'The police are there till closing time,' said Benny. 'They get

67

a good front seat and a nice drink by midnight. There's never been any problems.'

Around Great Windmill Street, you could get most things accomplished for a 'jack' ('jack's alive', five pounds), but top assignments could reach a 'pony' (twenty-five pounds). Murder was getting so expensive in London that some said it was cheaper to do it yourself. The capital was a city of dark corners, of double-barrelled names and shotguns, of bohemian Soho with its spivs, pubs and clubs, and joints where tinsel and morality were casually stripped off. Each territory had its own rules and risks, but unusual connections were often made. Many people were suffering post-war deprivation; an extraordinary mix of others – the aristocracy, the landowners and the villains – were rolling in cash. Apart from the pure pleasure of having lots of money, the toffs and spivs also shared a great enthusiasm for gambling and boxing. They spent and enjoyed themselves because they could.

Which was why it was never easy to climb the stairs to the third-floor Great Windmill Street offices of Solomons Promotions. If you got past the temptations of the tea and billiards on the second floor, there were still rival matchmakers, managers and fighters' representatives crowding around.

Boy Boon had wanted to turn the disused billiard hall into a boxing gym for himself to run, but the rent had been higher than his hopes. Jack Solomons took over the slack and most of the premises. Solomons also wanted to take over the boxing world. He'd had success matchmaking in France immediately after the war, but America wasn't interested. When they thought of British boxing, they saw contenders like Phaintin' Phil Scott, which was never an uplifting sight. He was only one of the British fighters they regarded as little better than fan dancers.

Solomons Promotions required some big-name action. Benny Huntman was in touch with Frankie Carbo, but an impatient Solomons flew to New York to try and get the light heavyweight champion of the world, Gus Lesnevich, to defend his title against Britain's heavyweight champ, Bruce Woodcock. However, Woodcock was the problem. He had a contest scheduled on 17 May 1946 at Madison Square Garden, just over the road from Frankie Carbo's 'office'. The London fight was set for 14 May 1946 at Harringay Arena. Solomons telephoned Ted Broadribb, the manager of the entertaining and capable Freddie Mills. Yes, he'd go for the title, and he also signed up to meet Woodcock at the same venue on 4 June 1946 for the heavyweight title.

Mills, having served in the RAF, had only been back in England a short time after a two-year tour of India with cricketer Denis Compton and other athletes in Compton's Circus, entertaining Allied troops. Post-war, much had changed. Mills had enjoyed a lively and lucky working-class childhood on the English south coast. He was born just after the First World War, on 26 June 1919, near Poole in Dorset. His father, Tom, and brother Charlie were boxing fans and soon so was Freddie Mills, who didn't go many rounds as an apprentice milkman. A booth fighter, he toured with Chipperfield's Circus and got the guidance of William 'Gipsy' Daniels, a very quick and smart Welsh lightweight who was a master of ducking and diving. Mills may have received generous advice from Gipsy but he didn't get all of his cut of the silver from their shared purses. The lessons were effective. Mills learned some street smarts and ring craft. He had immense determination, eagerness more than skill, and the power of an impressive and painful left hook to the body. By the start of the Second World War, he had a solid reputation as an instinctive if a crash-bang-wallop boxer, but even sports fans were by then more interested in the front pages.

Mills fought on in the RAF and in the ring. He beat middleweight champion Jock McAvoy on points in the summer of 1940, and the following year outpointed heavyweight Jack London. He beat McAvoy again in February 1942, which earned him a light heavyweight title fight with champion Len Harvey at Spurs football team's ground, White Hart Lane, Tottenham, on 20 June the same year. It established Mills in London and up and down Britain. He charged into Harvey in the second round and knocked him out with a left hook. The match also propelled Harvey out of the ring. Before sailing for India, Mills lost on points to the bigger, longer-reaching Jack London in a match for the British heavyweight title.

Now he was back and under the guidance of the canny but often difficult Ted Broadribb, who might use his knuckles as adjectives when pressing a point. He was fond of Mills, who was now 'Freddie' to most people. He was never going to be 'Mr Mills'; he was too much one of the lads, a joking, unmistakably English man with a naughty charm. He had a music-hall act for a personality. Gus Lesnevich was grasping for some of that, which is not to say that he wasn't a nice guy. Still, he was most certainly intent on beating all kinds of today, yesterday and tomorrow out of Freddie.

The spin machine to promote the fight hadn't needed to turn very fast. All the tickets, 20 guineas for ringside, were sold many weeks in advance. Gus Lesnevich sounded very New Jersey when he opened up his training camp at the Pelham Arms Gym in Brighton to fans, and that hyped up the fight even more as an America v. Britain contest. The loudspeakers hailed it as such on the night at Harringay Stadium. Freddie appeared to 'There'll Always Be an England' and Lesnevich strode to the ring to 'The Star-Spangled Banner'. They should have given him a fanfare.

Gus Lesnevich got out there twirling like a ballet dancer, not a boxer. It was a spectacular display of speed and precision, and all Freddie could do was keep as many body parts out of the way as he could. Cruelly, in the second round, he allowed a perfect right to his chin, which floored him to a count of eight. When he got up, he kept going down again in a barrage of severe punishment. How he stood up, apparently semi-conscious, for the third round wasn't the miracle; what he did next was. He used Lesnevich as a punchbag, bashing him all around the ring, breaking his nose and turning his always vulnerable left eye into a mass of bleeding, pulped flesh. With the sounds of voyeuristic hysteria echoing around the stadium, Freddie got and stayed ahead on points and looked the winner, landing one damaging blow after another.

Lesnevich, like a wounded bull, got back in charge in the tenth round, swerved under Freddie's left lead and delivered a right-hander that had Freddie shaking his head to clear the flashing stars and cloud of pain he'd been hit with. The count got to nine but Freddie made it to his feet. Another right and another sent him into the ringside, roped like a rodeo bronco. He was hit and down three more times before finally the referee, Eugene Henderson, lifted up Gus Lesnevich's arm. It was a severe, savage and convincing beating. Freddie's next fight was three weeks away.

The billboards were advertising his contest at Harringay Arena with Bruce Woodcock, the tickets had been sold and Solomons Promotions would have been out much money had the fight not happened. It did and went all the way to twelve rounds, despite Freddie hitting the canvas in the fourth round. Woodcock won on points. Freddie got a holiday.

He and Ted Broadribb flew with Jack Solomons to New York, where they mixed with the Madison Square Garden crowd. Benny Huntman, who'd arranged the Lesnevich promotion, nevertheless stayed in Great Windmill Street as the London trio met the boys and had drinks with Jack Dempsey. Frankie Carbo was around, as was Doc Kearns, who was managing the interests of an Italian fighter whose mum back in Cleveland, Ohio, knew him as Giuseppe Antonio Berardinelli. Doc called him 'Joey Maxim', named for the Maxim automatic machine gun. The young boxer had served as a military policeman, working closely with the Miami Police Department from 1942 to 1945. He was tall (just over 6 ft) and good-looking; he was a contender, and everybody said what a nice guy he was.

Joey Maxim and the visitors were at the ringside at Yankee Stadium on 19 June 1946 when Joe Louis knocked out Billy Conn in the eighth round to retain the heavyweight championship. Freddie met the fight followers and some friends of the boys, Frank Sinatra, George Raft, Tyrone Power and Pat O'Brien, who'd played the understanding priest opposite Cagney's tough guy in that movie Benny Huntman liked, *Angels With Dirty Faces*. They had bourbon and sirloin steaks and baked potatoes stuffed with sour cream and chives at Dempsey's and never saw a bill. They were ferried around Manhattan in a shiny Cadillac, their way prepared by crisp $20 bills that appeared as if by magic.

There was certainly a lot of money around the fight game in New York; everyone wore fine suits and rich hats and had a clean, freshly laundered look, like the dollars. And Madison Square Garden was the temple. Freddie carried a silly smile on his shepherd's pie face and took great, childish glee in the carnival of it all, the celebrities and the atmosphere. He was addicted to fame. He always wanted the ball. He never wanted to be left out; he'd get annoyed if he wasn't included in what was happening. Ted Broadribb was his usual self, miserable.

Jack Solomons found himself popular. He was doing business and had a list of management names he'd written out with Benny Huntman, including that of Nate Wolfson, who was pushing his heavyweight Joe Baksi. As the superbly self-confident puppet Solomons was negotiating with the boxers' managers, so Benny Huntman was matchmaking with Frankie Carbo, who watched over it all from his reserved corner table at Jack Dempsey's. Usually four times a year, Benny would fly privately to New York or Miami for meetings with Frankie Carbo.

As soon as a contract was signed, the behind-the-scenes deal dictated that 5 per cent of the American fighter's money went to Carbo and the Mob in a direct arrangement with the manager. Like an Italian real-estate lawyer, the fighter didn't handle money and wasn't present at any exchange: seeing brown envelopes was harmful to the eyesight. The Mob also got 7.5 per cent gross of the gate of fights in Britain and the rest of Europe. Spin-off matchmaking was extra but always on the gross.

With the championship bouts Benny Huntman was arranging, that was a great deal of tempting cash. Jack Solomons' ego was warmed to discover an extraordinary number of American fighters were keen to do battle in Europe. He never made mention of, acknowledged or fussed about the AWOL percentages, which were buried in his books as expenses. He was a millionaire. You had to spend money to make money.

It was a neat and very profitable transatlantic set-up. There was the big-money bonus globally of huge revenue in betting coups if the fights were bent and the winner assured. A sure thing could be created, the odds against the challenger sent soaring to the limit, and pay day was worth celebrating. Frank Carbo and the boys made a mint by putting their money on Billy Fox, who was favourite to lose to Jake LaMotta at Madison Square Garden on 14 November 1947. In, being kind, a haphazard contest, LaMotta went down in the fourth round in a Carbo deal. As part of the arrangement, 'the Raging Bull' also paid $20,000 to the Carbo crowd for the opportunity to take on the wonderful and fluid French fighter Marcel Cerdan. Benny Huntman negotiated the deal with Cerdan's management in Paris, which included in the complex financial arrangements the delivery of American heavyweight Lee Savold to box in London. Early in his career, Savold had caused one of the great boxing upsets in America with a surprise knockout of odds-on favourite Lou Nova.

It was a tightly drawn and finely fashioned web of a world they inhabited, with today's deal always looking on to tomorrow's. A has-been in Detroit was a contender in downtown Sacramento or Barcelona, which was why the Italian giant Primo Carnera, who had his first fight in 1928 and was minus a kidney, was sent from America to work, profitably, with Benny Huntman in Europe.

You couldn't always plan for luck, good or bad. You could take revenge for it, but not legislate for it. Freddie Mills discovered that when he returned to Britain from New York. It quickly became apparent that he didn't have many tomorrows in the ring. After a series of happenstances gave him the challenge, it was pushed hard that he had a chance against the big and strong Joe Baksi, the former coal miner, barroom bouncer and overall monster man. Yeah, said Solomons' salesmen, but Freddie looked a good prospect in the gym and posing for the newspapers with a lion cub.

It was Baksi who sparked on Bonfire Night 1946. He ripped all kinds of stuffing out of Freddie for six rounds. Freddie's eyes, two cuts under the right, three beneath the left, were so damaged in the mismatched massacre that he conceded. He got the goodwill benefit of that uneven contest, but even his greatest fans had to wonder, after he was knocked out by Lloyd Marshall on a 1947 summer evening at Harringay Arena, if his boxing life was finished.

Yet Freddie was proud-to-be-British popular and he was plucky. He was box office and Solomons Promotions understood the value of that. Benny Huntman's better matchmaking or life's elusive luck saw him beat three European fighters, all of whom carried baggage and question marks. That gave him at chance at Scotland's Ken Shaw, whom he took out, and that created a rematch with Gus Lesnevich. The open-air meeting at White City Stadium in west London on 26 July 1948 was for the light heavyweight championship of the world. It gathered more than 46,000 paying customers, with the majority chanting for a British champ.

Freddie held back his eagerness as a boxer and this kept him away from Lesnevich's punches, which, when they connected, were tired. Freddie quickly marked up Lesnevich's face (so ferociously that the American's wife, Jan, fled the stadium) and pursued a damaging agenda. He put Lesnevich, his eyes blurred by blood, down twice for counts of nine and never gave up scoring points. He won the decision and was the world champion, the first British holder of such a title for nearly 50 years. In austerity Britain, it was, however rose-tinted, a triumph of faith that 'British was Best', even against the Yanks.

It seemed the most popular British sportsman was getting it all together, professionally and personally. Only a few weeks later, on 30 September, to some surprise, Freddie married in the Methodist Church at Herne Hill, London. His wife, at thirty-six, was seven years older than him, divorced from South African heavyweight champion Don McCorkindale, and Ted Broadribb's daughter. Chrissie Broadribb McCorkindale was now Mrs Freddie Mills. She had a young son, Donny. Her ex-husband went on honeymoon with them, which induced the lace-curtain prim to struggle for that French phrase *ménage à trois*.

The close Mills family all went off to South Africa, where Benny Huntman was doing business. Solomons Promotions had arranged for Freddie to fight Johnny Ralph, a much-rated young heavyweight boxer, at Wembley Stadium in Johannesburg in November. While Freddie was told everything he wanted to hear by his fans and companion cheerleaders, Benny was keeping up with Norbert Erleigh, a gambler in boxing, horse racing and gold mines. There was much American investment interest in Erleigh's affairs because of seed money that had been provided by gangland cash from Chicago.

When Freddie arrived in South Africa, the incorrigible and enterprising Erleigh was about to begin a second year of hard labour, albeit velvet-cushioned by his vast available funds, in Johannesburg Central Prison. He'd been convicted with his former partner Joseph Milne on a total of 63 counts of fraud and theft. Their New Union Goldfields Ltd, which had controlled 160 companies, was, said the judge, really 'a gambling house'. Indeed it was, and with the conjuring of assets, paying one business to pay another, the gold-mining corporation collapsed, with investors out by £14 million. The money owing was never traced and Erleigh was not as crushed as his empire, even by his silent partners. From prison, he bought advertising for his new stock promotion, Union Gold & Base Metals Corp. Ltd, which he developed from jail. And investors, driven by greedy gullibility, still bought shares.

With Benny Huntman, the fantastical Norbert Erleigh also promoted fights, some of which were investigated by Natal boxing authorities. In Asia, they worked with another promoter, known as 'Sad Sam Itchy Nose', who had influence over all kinds of thrills in Manila and throughout the Philippines. Benny Huntman reported back to America on the feasibility of casino investments in South Africa and buy-ins in Asia. Lansky and company had hungry money.

Freddie's appetite for fame was equally as great. He was a performer. He put his money in the Freddie Mills Chinese Restaurant on Charing Cross Road and expected his personality to be as appealing as the chicken fried rice. In boxing, he did the business with Johnny Ralph, knocking him out in the eighth round in Johannesburg. He should have left it there, but the lure of centre stage and the financial interests of Solomons Promotions made for further obligations.

His encounter with Yorkshireman Bruce Woodcock for the British and Empire heavyweight championships on 2 June 1949 at White City was quite an event. Jack Solomons declared himself a winner whatever the result; he'd sold more than 40,000 seats. Freddie was paid £15,000 to absorb a tremendous beating. Woodcock was too big, too heavyweight, for him. Freddie endured much pain all the way to the fourteenth round when he only made it onto one knee at the count. The puzzle was whether to have a post-mortem on Freddie or the matchmaking. Norbert Erleigh cabled from South Africa to say the rumour there was Freddie was dead. The resurrection took six months.

Ten days after Freddie Mills was clearly outboxed by Woodcock and crumbled to the canvas, the championship path paved by the Frankie Carbo dollar led Jake LaMotta to the Briggs Stadium in Detroit, Michigan, for his fully paid middleweight fight with Marcel Cerdan. The charismatic

Frenchman, the lover of Édith Piaf, a superb boxer and athlete, was knocked over in the first round. He never properly got back into battle and LaMotta was the champion by the tenth round. Cerdan had dislocated his shoulder; a rematch was fixed but tragically never happened. He was flying to New York to see his lover singing when his Air France L-749 Constellation crashed in the Azores, killing everyone on board. Piaf wrote the haunting tribute song '*Hymne à l'amour*' ('Hymn to Love') for him. It was an unlikely anthem for a boxer, but maybe not so much for the romantic Cerdan.

With LaMotta paid off, the always busy Frankie Carbo had organised a fight for Joey Maxim in London. Doc Kearns would take him over to tackle Freddie Mills in the New Year, the start of another decade, the 1950s. On 24 January, at Earls Court Empress Hall Exhibition Centre, they met to dispute the world light heavyweight championship. Freddie lost five front teeth (from a series of left jabs to his jaw) and the fight in the tenth round. A ring second found three of his teeth embedded in the former military cop's left glove. For Freddie, aged 31, the knockout took away the championship shrewd management had achieved for him. It was a boost to Joey Maxim's already intriguing law-enforcement career.

At Great Windmill Street, Benny Huntman was awaiting delivery of the remaining part of the Carbo/LaMotta package, the one-time carnival fighter and bronco buster Lee Savold. Although he was the betting underdog, he'd achieved the record for the fastest main-event knockout, of Italian Gino Buonvino, at Madison Square Garden two years earlier. On 6 June 1950, he took four rounds to finish Bruce Woodcock at White City for the BBBC (British Boxing Board of Control) world heavyweight title. More than 50,000 boxing fans paid to see it. The luck appeared to be flowing Benny Huntman's way. He was picking winners and managing promising fighters like Danny O'Sullivan, Billy Thompson and Tommy McGovern, who were all box office.

Benny presented an amiable face to the world but, as with any Faustian arrangement, there was always the stress of having to think for yourself and worry about what others think. It can play with the personality; not being your own man can foster paranoia. Experience and mental juggling did much to protect Benny, but at one boxing exhibition his mask slipped. He was in the corner of one of his fighters who was expected to win easily. The betting boys had hefty money on Benny's fighter to win and started shouting abuse at Benny when he clearly wasn't. Benny snarled at the crowd – before he jumped from the ring and started fighting with them. A cornerman acted as referee and stopped the punch-up. The fracas was brushed away from the ringside pressmen when the bottles were brought out, the optics discarded and the newspapermen treated to endless rounds of big drinks.

Champagne and cocktails were flowing around Benny at the start of the '50s. He was the darling of café society, with many intrigued to meet the American fighters they'd only seen flickering on black-and-white newsreels. Mae Huntman wasn't fond of the spotlight but was happy to welcome guests to their home, in a block of flats called North Gate opposite Regent's Park. Jack and Fay Solomons, Mae's great friend, had followed them to the area and moved in next door, in an identical block of apartments. Among the many regulars at the parties at Flat 49 was Freddie Mills.

Since his title-fight win against Gus Lesnevich, the boxer and Benny Huntman had become friends. They went to dinner together, did the town, their families met. Freddie was a household name, a celebrity in a time when there were fewer around, and was always good value at the parties. He'd enjoy a drink and a laugh with some of Britain's leading entertainers. Comics like Charlie Chester, Arthur Askey, Tommy Trinder and Bud Flanagan were always telling stories, as was veteran MP and major Labour Party figure Manny Shinwell, a close family friend of Benny's. Boy Boon was usually there and liked looking at and listening to the statuesque actress Diana Dors: she made him breathless, short of words. Albert Dimes talked cricket with Denis Compton and the band leader Joe Loss, who lived with his wife in the same apartment complex. Loss would arrange for members of his band to play and headline singers such as Frankie Vaughan would entertain with them.

Some nights, the bands got bigger than the party when Jack Hylton, trying to please Benny, called up his troops of performers. Jack Hylton and His Orchestra had been the first British band to broadcast to America in 1931, and two decades later Hylton was a great impresario – 'Think champagne and you'll be champagne' – dominating London's theatreland and much of British light entertainment. He owned the Palace Theatre in the Strand and the Victoria Palace. He had a string of acts, including the hugely popular Crazy Gang, under contract. He was Mr Show Business.

He was also obsessively in love with Benny Huntman's sister-in-law Pat Pope. She was in the chorus line, dancing as Pat Taylor, when the man Roger Huntman knew as 'Uncle Jack' began helping her career and started going out with her. It was an intense affair and they had a son, John, who lived with his mother in The Cottage in St John's Wood; their expansive garden backed on to the gardens of North Gate. Young John Hylton (he was given the Hylton name, although his parents never married) and Benny and Mae's son Roger would often play there together with other children from the flats. On school holidays, a driver would take the pre-teen cousins away for the day.

One late morning in April 1951, John Hylton called on his cousin Roger Huntman and they were driven to the Colony Club in Berkeley Square, Mayfair, to watch Judy Garland rehearse. The Colony Club and restaurant were owned by wily businessman Thomas William Parker; the catering was done that day by Silvio and Giovanni Tolaini, the West End restaurateur brothers. The much-liked Tolainis owned the Latin Quarter at 13 Wardour Street, Soho, which had been named by Mae Huntman and largely financed by her husband and phantom partner Benny, who used it for quiet meetings. Judy Garland had a new husband, Sid Luft, and was beginning a four-month tour of the UK, including her first appearance at the London Palladium. The fragile entertainer was nervous.

Before she and her entourage arrived, the boys played the bongos in the supper club and fooled around. The rehearsals were a triumph, as were the Palladium appearances, with the nerves and fear well medicated. It was superstar time and Judy Garland was a pot of gold for them all. Al Burnett asked Benny to get Jack Hylton to bring Judy to the Pigalle nightclub to sing 'a couple of songs'. It was like asking the Queen for 'only one' of the Crown jewels. Yet Benny delivered. That evening, Burnett got up on stage to praise and thank Judy Garland for her appearance. He then turned the spotlight on

Jack Hylton's table to applaud him. The great impresario was fast asleep.

He had many interests that tapped his energy. On another trip, Uncle Jack took Roger and John to his own home at Albany House in Mayfair to meet Lord Mountbatten. The showman was also friendly with the society osteopath Stephen Ward, who was his personal physician and treated him at his clinic in Cavendish Square, just off Harley Street. They were all members of the Thursday Club, a heavy-drinking group including the actor James Robertson Justice and the media character Gilbert Harding. They met at a Wheeler's in Soho and drank champagne and always had to have oysters – good for the libido. Jack Hylton was a popular member; he often paid the bill and owned one of the largest *classical* pornography collections in Europe.

Such expensive peccadilloes and the jiggling or not of tits across the road at the Windmill Theatre were never much of a concern for Benny Huntman. He had other matters to dwell on. Frankie Carbo had him on standby: there had been a lot of heat in America for months, with government hearings into his American friends' activities. And there might, in turn, need to be developments in the UK, especially with Winston Churchill and the Conservative Party back in power. Gambling, the legal variety so beloved by Meyer Lansky, might be on the way in Britain.

What had tantalised the weary mobsters in America who were fighting the rise of the post-war white-picket-fence lobby was the just released Royal Commission report into most forms of gambling. As it stood, the law in effect prohibited all commercial gaming of any significance:

> Anyone who plays, elsewhere than in a private house, any gaming in which there is an element of chance for money or money's worth runs a grave risk of committing a penal offence. Indeed there are certain games, such as roulette, which it is illegal to play even in a private house.

Yet the Royal Commission held out a spoon for the gambling gravy train: it ruled the gaming laws were 'obscure, illogical and difficult to enforce'. It recommended the simplification and clarification of a code. It didn't believe gaming within 'reasonable bounds' threatened serious harm to individuals or the community.

The Commission also said that any new legislation should interfere as little as possible with individual liberty to indulge in gambling but establish ways to restrict excessive gambling. The happy words for the global gamblers were:

> Gambling as a factor in the economic life of the country, or as a cause of crime is of little significance, and its effects on social behaviour, insofar as they are a suitable object for legislation, are in the great majority of cases less important than has been suggested.

As Lansky and company read it, the 1951 Royal Commission recognised the need for carpet joints, for casinos: what they described as 'a facility for commercial gaming'. The Commission had stipulated the need for a legal charge, a membership or an entrance fee, for the punters to play the tables. This was a licence to print money. It was simply a question of when to cash in, rather than if.

Bingo! Benny was told the boys could be coming to town sooner than expected, for America had been experiencing its own, far more public inquiry into gambling and gangsters.

Although most people didn't own their own sets, the American public was loving the new medium of television. They'd crowd into homes and shops to watch their favourite programme, the cumbersomely titled Senate Special Committee to Investigate Crime in Interstate Commerce. It was hosted by a Davy Crockett-type character from Tennessee called Estes Kefauver, a frontiersman-politician who wanted answers about crime and specifically gambling, the other booming post-war economy in America. It was a roadshow, a travelling sideshow, with hearings held across America. The public, through television, were introduced week after week to the idea of the Mafia. It was an exciting eye-opener into the dark secrets of a criminal organisation; a close-up of a deadly group, with Sicilian antecedents, that their FBI director, J. Edgar Hoover, had told them didn't exist.

The Mafia certainly did exist in the public consciousness, as it always had in reality, after the Kefauver Committee. The televised hearings helped Estes Kefauver make a name for himself – he'd steal a Democratic vice-presidential nomination from young Senator John F. Kennedy – but didn't seriously harm the corporate Mob, although they brought much unwelcome attention. Meyer Lansky and Frank Costello and many, many others were quizzed under subpoena but kept calm and played back the interrogation. It did force some junior operatives to learn to count to five and take the Fifth Amendment, a phrase that established itself in the lexicon at the hearings. Jake 'Greasy Thumb' Guzik was the important pay-off man out of Chicago who spearheaded the corruption of politicians and the police: his hands really got dirty and sticky counting so much cash. He pleaded the Fifth because he didn't want his answers to 'discriminate against me'.

In truth, it was a scandalous but wonderful entertainment, a carnival of criminality. It was Runyon without the romance, yet the shorthand writers would have kept going at a mention of 'the Lemon Drop Kid' or 'Meyer Marmalade', for it was that sort of theatre. There were stories of gunsels like Sam 'Golf Bag' Hunt, who carried his machine gun in a golf bag rather than the more elegant violin case. Corrupt fat-cat officials said they did not crack down on gambling as it would cost decent people in their districts jobs. The man they dubbed 'the richest cop in America', Chicago State Attorney's chief investigator Captain Dan Gilbert, agreed he'd done nothing about gambling dens for a decade. His fabulous wealth? He was something of a whizz playing the stock market. *What's My Line*, about contestants with unusual jobs, had begun broadcasting on American television but had to compete with the antics of the boys, of Golf Bag and Greasy Thumb, whose occupations were more sinister than the comedy of their names.

The officials, police chiefs, detectives and those chasing high political office locally and nationally, like hawks after sparrows, were shown to be earning a comparative pittance and yet to have hundreds of thousands in cash and property. The engaging Longie Zwillman had helped one Governor of New Jersey get elected and offered $300,000 to aid another; all he wanted in return was to choose the Attorney General, the state's lawmaker. Longie Zwillman felt he was being generous. He could have asked to choose all the legislature.

The leading lady of the Kefauver Follies was Virginia Hill,

of whom Zwillman said she 'didn't look too hard to know'. By the time she testified, she'd had 'relationship associations' with a long charge sheet of top-tier mobsters, including Lansky, Luciano and Costello. She'd also had four husbands, the Mexican rumba dancer, the present Austrian ski instructor and two others whose employment details she'd forgotten. Her one steady relationship was with money, especially the hundreds of thousands of dollars she'd carried as a bag-woman for the syndicate. Still, there was never enough.

The Committee's Senator Charley Tobey from New Hampshire was mightily challenged as to how Miss Hill made, as it were, ends meet. She was a feisty woman, a little cavalier in attitude and hats; she wore a rakish, wide-brimmed black number and a mink stole, set off by an attitude of boredom with it all. Senator Tobey kept being puzzled as to why so many men gave her money and presents: 'Why would they do it?'

Virginia evaded the question. The Senator kept repeating it. He was especially intrigued as to why an ageing bookmaker in Chicago, Joe Epstein, a man old enough to be her father, maintained regular payments. He persisted. 'Why?' Gosh, he did go on. 'Young lady, why?

'You *really* want to know why?'

'I *really* want to know why.'

'Senator, I'm the best goddamned cocksucker in America.'

Yes, she had some renown, but for the executive mobsters her most gratifying skill was moving money around the world without detection. Virginia Hill wore availability as if Chanel made it; that was effective at customs and immigration in London and Rome and Paris, downright enchanting in Zurich and Geneva.

She wasn't all eyelashes, easy-to-know eyes, blushing and coy and charming, that day in New York. Outside the hearing, following Senator Tobey's questions, she was confronted by Miss Marjorie Farnsworth of the *New York Journal American*, leading the newspaper corps into action. Miss Farnsworth got thumped in the face, a vicious right hook. An intrepid man from the *New York Times* tried to intervene and was kicked in the shins.

Miss Virginia Hill, irrepressible lover of mobsters and money, strode off down the corridor signing off with, 'I hope a fucking atom bomb falls on y'all.'

Virginia Hill typified the disdain many on the wrong side of the law felt for what they regarded as a flying circus. What was most astonishing during the hearings, from June 1950 to September 1951, when *I Love Lucy* took over entertaining America, was the arrogance of the gangsters. Greed tripped up the corrupt of the upper world, but the professional gamblers and thieves had a focus, a plan, and would do all that was necessary to prevent being overmastered. Without fear, they did business the way they wanted, pay-as-you-go. They'd kill if it was necessary. It was never personal. Only business. The gangsters might pray on different days, but profit was their common deity. It was always business that led the decision-making.

5

DEATH VALLEY

'Don't Fence Me In', Bing Crosby with the
Andrews Sisters, 1945

Benny Siegel died to order after a veal dinner for being bad at business. It was a bad business. Lots of people had liked Benny. OK, he'd been a pain in the ass at times, but, hey, that was Bugsy, the way he acted, the pistolero that he was.

Frankie Carbo used a US Army rifle to take him down as he sat by a curtainless window at Virginia Hill's place in North Linden Drive, up from Santa Monica Boulevard and in the richer reaches of Beverly Hills. Bugsy was contentedly reading Braven Dyer on baseball in the *Los Angeles Times* sports pages when he was killed.

Two pinpoint-accurate .30 bullets shattered Bugsy's face. The close-up fireplay by Carbo's two regular associates that followed was redundant and made needless, extra mess of Bugsy and the living room. It was instructions: there was to be no lingering in his death. One steel-jacket shell crushed his nose at the right eye. The other went straight through his right cheek and out his neck. The instant, intense internal pressure punched his right eye from its socket, like a passenger being sucked out of a punctured jet plane. It was found nearly 15 ft away from his body when the police discovered him sprawled, thrown back by the impact of the bullets, on a sofa, a shiny chintz luxury Virginia Hill had bought from a store at the corner of Beverly and Wilshire boulevards.

Hill was conveniently out of town. She was in Europe. She said she'd had a lovers' tiff with Bugsy, gone to stay with her generous friend Joe Epstein, the bookmaker in Chicago, and then flown to France 'for the fashions'. She was travelling with a full four-set of luggage and a wardrobe trunk. She'd gone from Paris to Zurich on a specific schedule set by Meyer

Lansky. Virginia Hill was in everything she did for money, not love. She, like Lansky, knew that if Ben Siegel had to die he would and it was business. Happily, she could afford to mourn her lover in some style. The Los Angeles Coroner's Report 37448 said he'd died of a cerebral hemorrhage, but she knew the cause of death was Bugsy's megalomania.

When Meyer Lansky had insisted Siegel take a look around Las Vegas, it was part of his empire-building. The syndicate had strong operations along the East Coast, in the Midwest and in Florida. Cuba was slowly being created as a Mafia-controlled island. He had political connections directly and indirectly worldwide. His contacts with all the puppet-masters of crime, the men who pulled the strings, were impeccable. He was feared by many people but admired by many more. Nobody could ignore him, not even Ben Siegel. Especially not Benny, whose psychotic impulses his childhood friend had controlled for a long, long time.

One great revenue enhancer for the syndicate was 'the wire', a radio-transmission horse-racing service that fed results to illegal bookies and their customers. When he'd first arrived in Los Angeles, the star-struck Bugsy had teamed up with another face from his past, George Raft. The two joked that during the day they played the horses at Santa Anita Racetrack and in the evenings rode the fillies along Sunset Boulevard. They were a colourful, chauvinistic double act.

Bugsy loved the girls and the horses. He'd been sent to the coast to build the syndicate's gambling business. He'd done that in Los Angeles, worked the rackets with the Hollywood unions, buttoned down the race-wire service and sorted out a live-and-let-kill relationship with the Sicilian-born leader of the California Mafia, Jack Dragna. The East Coast didn't rate Dragna, a man everybody said thought small. He was clearly told to allow Bugsy to make the running. Dragna's main heavy, Mickey Cohen, became Bugsy's bodyguard.

With Dragna as his organiser and triggerman in Los Angeles, there was time to investigate around US Highway 91. Downtown Las Vegas would have suited George Sadlo; it looked as if Pancho Villa had just ridden into the sunset. There were gambling joints and sad cafés that matched the look of the weary cattle-train cowboys and a thousand thousand acres of sand. You just had to cough to start a sandstorm. In business, mostly slot machines, were the Golden Nugget, the Frontier Club and the El Cortez, where Bugsy took a room.

It was the ponies not the poker that had first taken Bugsy to Nevada. Although gambling was legal, the race wire was given state approval only in 1941. Legal gambling, the holy grail – yet he'd looked around and seen only desert. Now, with his corporate instructions, he had to join in the forward thinking. Crooked business had high overheads; being honest meant more profit. Moe Sedway, who'd run booze with the Bugs and Meyer Mob during Prohibition and carpet joints with Jimmy Blue Eyes in Florida, was sent in as a point man in Vegas.

'Handsome' Johnny Roselli was the Chicago Mob's man in town. To the mafiosi, he was Don Giovanni, while on the emerging Vegas strip he was a mover and shaker. The manners, the politeness were a veneer covering the street killer within; he was a man with that perfect shade of tan who'd dealt heroin and made his name in an often bloody way. He'd started out with the Capone outfit, killing as Francesco Sacco, but he'd dropped that birth name before moving out to the coast, where he looked good working with the lacklustre Dragna. His first speciality was Hollywood and the movies, which he ripped off for more than a million dollars. He extorted the money by threatening to use a Mafia-controlled union of stagehands to slow down or kill off productions through the unions he controlled. He was smart and careful, a suitable combination for ensuring his Midwest masters got their proper profit share from the latest El Dorado.

There was easy money being made in downtown Las Vegas at the Nugget and the other joints, but off Highway 91, at the start of a strip of road running gun-barrel straight out into the desert, was the El Rancho Vegas, more of a big-city-style carpet joint. Bugsy tried to buy in to the El Rancho, but his reputation went in the door before him. He blustered and blamed people as other investors created the Hotel Last Frontier, which was the future, a resort with a swimming pool and tennis and, miracle of miracles, air-conditioned rooms.

There were many illegal fortunes heading for Vegas, looking for legality and respectability, and most were simply passing through, having a wash and brush-up, and moving on for more of the same. There was even much talk of clean investment. Hell, the movie cowboy Roy Rogers and Trigger were going to open a dude ranch, Mae West was going to invite people to come up and see her in Vegas, and Sinatra and Tommy Dorsey were interested in buying land along the Strip.

Bugsy had to get in gear. He bought the El Cortez with investments from Meyer Lansky, his trusted associate Moe Sedway and a dozen or so of the boys across America. Bugsy and Sedway were operating it in person by Christmas 1945 and, as post-war America enjoyed an economic upsurge and Vegas real estate went skywards, sold it for a huge profit, at $600,000, seven months later. Happenstance then connived against Benny Siegel. Billy Wilkerson, who owned clubs along Sunset Boulevard and was connected socially throughout Hollywood, had run out of cash in his development of the Flamingo Hotel and Casino.

Wilkerson envisaged a hotel-casino of wall-to-wall starlets, Hollywood stars and big shots from all over, glitter and glamour and headline entertainers, so much going on there was no time – no clocks even to tell you the time – for the hordes flying in on the new airline schedules to realise how much they were losing at the tables.

Bugsy was in heaven. He'd been born for this moment. He and his syndicate partners bought 67 per cent of the Flamingo project for $650,000. The money vanished fast. So did the next investment, as building costs rose uncontrollably. Contractor after contractor walked in the front door of the Flamingo and drove a Cadillac out the back. Bugsy spent money wildly. He had a fourth-floor master suite with side exits, three-foot-thick concrete walls, trapdoors in the wardrobes leading to the basement garage and his always fully fuelled getaway car.

He had Virginia Hill in the master suite with him, Italian countess Dorothy di Frasso in another room, actress and warm wartime pin-up Marie 'The Body' McDonald in another. Along the corridor was Wendy Barrie, fresh from the madcap movie world of Lucille Ball, her co-star in *Five Came Back*. A sought-after star, the English actress, who'd worked with Basil Rathbone as Holmes in *The Hound of the Baskervilles*, put up with a great deal from her lover – and from his other lover Virginia, who'd never made it in acting other than in the bedroom. When the two women met in the lobby of the Flamingo, Hill used her useful right hook to dislocate her rival's jaw.

Bugsy's business life was even more complicated than his bedroom one. It wasn't just a personal spending spree that was doing runaway arithmetic with the construction budget. He was paying top dollar because of hangover wartime shortages. He'd get black-market material delivered in the day, stolen in the night and sold back to him again the next day. It was all a nonsense, but a deadly one.

By October 1946, the money spent stood at more than $4 million. Four weeks later, the boys asked for project accounting. Bugsy panicked, raised money on non-existent stock and spent more and more, to a final upfront total of $6 million, to have the Flamingo open for Christmas and the holiday season. Still the rooms wouldn't be ready for occupancy. Gamblers would come – and go somewhere else to spend the night and their money. It was bad business – with other people's investments. There are few stronger bonds than childhood friendships, and Bugsy and his friends Frank Costello, Meyer Lansky and Charlie Luciano had stayed close and built an empire together. They were blood brothers. Yet business held the trump card.

Ten years earlier, Charlie Luciano, syndicate siren and racketeer, involved in extortion, murder and other such things, had gone down for a sentence of thirty to fifty years on politically conjured prostitution charges brought by crusadingly ambitious special prosecutor Thomas Dewey. Lansky soldiered on with their global gambling plans without the considerable asset of a free Luciano; Frank Costello took over the nine-to-five running of the syndicate. Luciano was an absentee boss – 'away at college', in the patois – but continued to have great influence and receive equally great payments. He 'consulted' from Dannemora Penitentiary in far-upstate New York, where his favourite Sicilian dishes were prepared for him.

Luciano then got truly lucky. American military intelligence ruled that, with his Sicilian connections, he could help in the war effort and supply intelligence that could thwart enemy attacks. He was moved to Great Meadow Prison in Comstock, near Albany, New York, and it was agreed that at an appropriate time he'd be freed. With the war over, 4 January 1946 was fixed as the date of his release, and the man who had put him away, the White House aspirant and now Governor Thomas Dewey of New York, commuted his sentence.

The stinger was that Charles 'Lucky' Luciano was going home, to Italy, back to Sicily, where he'd started nearly 50 years earlier as Salvatore Lucania. Luciano and Lansky and the boys found that that detail was not negotiable. But Luciano had some cheer about the deal, for he and Lansky had mapped out Cuba, and that was only 90 miles from mainland America. Charlie Luciano had been on a road trip around Italy following his return to Palermo. After Rome, he moved on to Naples, and it was there that he received a rallying call, a note reading: 'December, Hotel Nacional.'

Which is where he was on 22 December that year. He'd bed-hopped around Venezuela, gone from Caracas to Mexico City and then Aerovias Q Airlines had taken him to Havana. He was met by Meyer Lansky. The two men were playing host to some of the giant gangster figures of the world, about two dozen of them, including clever killer Albert Anastasia and New York boss Joseph Bonanno. Moe Dalitz, Doc Stacher and syndicate member Longie Zwillman led the hugely influential Jewish mobsters. Also very present were Carlos Marcello out of New Orleans and Santo Trafficante Jr, who'd moved to Cuba from Tampa, Florida, that year to watch over his family's slice of the island's gambling action, carved out by his father. All the major Mafia families were represented at the official meetings on the top two floors of the Hotel Nacional. It was like a reformatory school reunion amid the intriguing architecture on the spectacular Havana oceanfront – with extracurricular explicit personal entertainment, sex and menace. And a singer: Frank Sinatra.

Sinatra was the cover for the Havana Conference. The story was that the guys had got together simply to hear him sing. It almost went sour from the start. Sinatra had arranged for a friend, showgirl and aspiring actress Dorothy Lyma, who called herself Alora Gooding, to meet him there. Sinatra was 31 years old and cockily confident but not so much as to refuse to appear for the wiseguys. But he wanted some fun, too, and Alora, who had spent time in joints around Reno, Nevada, was a lot of fun. She'd worked for Bugsy Siegel and been around with some of the boys. She knew how to look after herself, having been brought up by a gun-crazy father in the California farmland. Sinatra had met her on the set of the 1941 film *Las Vegas Nights* when he was singing with Tommy Dorsey's band. Their affair had run around his performance schedule since then. Happy and excited, Alora drove down from her home in Sacramento to Los Angeles and flew from there to Miami and on to Cuba.

There was edgy, newly customised private security around the Hotel Nacional, especially the areas blocked out for the conference. Most of the guards were off-duty policemen or army officers. They had instructions to keep everybody but the VIP American visitors out. Alora was in her suite with Sinatra when a crashing noise made her jump out of bed. She rushed over to the window, which overlooked a large courtyard filled with coconut palms and a mini-forest of soft-leaved vines. The high, black entrance gates were open and two men in jackets and ties were running towards their part of the hotel. They had something in their hands. She yelled at the startled, half-awake Sinatra, 'They've got guns! They're coming to kill us!'

A hunting rifle was leaning against the wall on the other side of the room. Sinatra began scrabbling through a suitcase. He pulled out a revolver, but hadn't turned around when there were shouts in the corridor and the men burst in. Alora had the rifle expertly armed and pointed at the door. She fired. The man on her left, wearing a dark-grey striped suit fell to the floor. A second shot rang out, from behind the intruders, and the other business-suited man fell backwards into the hallway. Both were dead. Now other men in suit pants and dress shirts were suddenly all over the hallway and crowding into the bedroom, which smelled of cordite.

'You killed that guy,' said Sinatra, lighting a cigarette.

Her voice shaking, Alora protested, 'But they had guns. They were coming to kill us.'

'Those weren't guns. They were walkie-talkies.'

Alora collapsed on the floor and began screaming. Sinatra sat on the bed and said nothing. And the two bodies and any fuss were all swept away by the time Alora was moved out of

Havana in the morning to a lifetime of invisibility. Sinatra still had to sing for his supper.

The bizarre incident was not allowed to disrupt the conference schedule. It was not even generally discussed, and when Sinatra started to mention it he was shut up by Doc Stacher, who gently pressed the singer's shoulder and whispered, 'Leave it. Forget about it.'

Luciano was given a 'tribute' from the gathering – $200,000 in crisp bills – and before the talking proper began the delegates were invited to indulge in all the delights of Havana in and around the hotel. The tasty, mild Bacardi rum and the giant cigars put a little pep in the salsa for the crime convention. The idea was for the delegates to see how wide open a town it was, a place for vast investment of time and money, where anything went.

The sex tourism went to the strangest places. You could have a chorus line for the price of dinner, witness supreme depravity and indulge in bestiality for little more. The more sensitive mobsters settled for the top-end showgirls and expensive escorts. Yet even for the most lecherously liberal-minded, the confining heat of the city contributed to a heightened sense of sordidness, the feeling of being tainted by what was extraordinarily excessive. It was intended as and succeeded as a blatant and spelled-out message: this was a city, a land, an island of total opportunity, where the syndicate could do whatever it wanted, legally and without restraint. This was a paradise without social or economic justice. All that had to be done was to be strong and do and take and exploit anything or anyone that was desired.

It was Meyer Lansky's global master plan to create in Cuba a gambling El Dorado, a golden goose of an island. The way he talked, roulette wheels would be spinning in the sky. All the boys had to do was invest and stand by and watch the millions grow and grow into billions. His dollar-hungry audience at the Hotel Nacional de Cuba were enraptured, especially Santo Trafficante, who was acutely aware of the crackerjack potential in a tropical setting only a hop, skip and jump from America.

And they knew Fulgencio Batista was in the wings. The upwardly mobile soldier, after running a series of token presidents, had elected himself President of Cuba in 1940.

He'd left the country in 1944 and moved to America with its blessing. He'd left his countrymen to be robbed blind by someone else, the new members of the Auténtico Party. At the same time, the American government and the Mafia had no wish for incipient revolutionary forces or Communist groups to become a unified force. The simple way was to assassinate the leaders of such groups, which threatened the ambitions of imperialism – and gangsterism. On all this, former president Fulgencio Batista was most helpful.

In exile, he ran his life from a suite at the Waldorf-Astoria in Manhattan and from his home in Dayton Beach, where he lived with his second wife: he'd married a young lover, Marta Fernandez. The Florida hacienda was on a vast estate, with an English garden and the Halifax River connected to it by its own pier. He kept a small boat on the river. He played tennis at the Daytona Beach Bath and Tennis Club (he was very good) and went to the cinema a couple of times a week: he saw Cagney in *White Heat* three times and Sinatra and Gene Kelly in *On the Town* twice. He had 12 personal bodyguards. The US government also supplied a round-the-clock protection team, with four agents on duty at any time.

Batista's mid-distance control of Cuba was aided by his loyal followers. They'd fly out of Havana on Expresso Interamerico, whose flights stopped in Miami, Vero Beach and Daytona Beach. The Trafficante family was welcome. He also hosted Lansky there, as well as other members of the syndicate, Cuban politicians and soldiers, undercover operatives from several governments and secret agents from Americas north and south and central. Some agents worked for the syndicate and the US government. Batista, for all his Little General airs and graces, in reality did too. These agents were willing and able to contract out on special missions.

Lansky ran Batista's life. They would meet in New York or at the Martinique Hotel in Miami Beach, but crucial talks were usually held in outdoor conference along the Halifax River beside Batista's English garden (paid for by the Americans). Such was the Mafia's power and their interest in Batista that he could have retaken power in Cuba at almost any moment of his self-imposed exile.

Everything was in place for Lansky and the syndicate to take their gambling style and money-making machine around the world. The campaign was off. Cuba was ready. Las Vegas was building, but, of course, Bugsy Siegel, original member of the syndicate, was a problem. He'd wasted money and skimmed a fortune in construction-funds cash, which now rested, delivered by Virginia Hill, in the calm of Switzerland. Whatever boyhood loyalties existed in the room at the Hotel Nacional, it was decreed that Bugsy must die and the syndicate's business interests and massive investment be put on a level footing. It was decided to get someone Bugsy knew to do it. It was always sensible to put the victim, especially one as streetwise as Ben Siegel, off guard.

The man these insiders most respected for this kind of work would do it. Frankie Carbo was a safe pair of hands, if it wasn't your throat he was after, and if there was any mishap he was a killer who would never mutter a word to the authorities. To help cover Carbo, hapless Jack Dragna's name was put out in the underworld and leaked to the authorities as that of the probable killer of Ben Siegel; only the most gullible bought that theory, and it did nothing to enhance Dragna's reputation as a hit man or his future business interests.

The flagship Flamingo Hotel opened on Boxing Day 1946, in some of the worst weather Nevada had known. 'It rained in a desert, for Chrissake.' The air conditioning didn't work. George Raft was his faithful self, present amid a few other celebrities and the decorators' debris. In the showroom, Xavier Cugat and his band worked with mob favourite Jimmy Durante. That evening and into 1947, the casino lost $300,000. Bugsy closed down the Flamingo.

He reopened with habitable rooms and the Andrews Sisters as a crowd-pleasing attraction on 1 March 1947. It all began to work, but not in time to save him.

Bugsy Siegel knew it. He'd drive down to Beverly Hills every couple of weeks and on his return have the locks on his Flamingo suite changed. Every time. He had chairs brought and sat in the hotel corridor with Virginia Hill, watching the locksmith complete the work.

Outwardly, he displayed no other tics of fear. The Flamingo was beginning to make money, as he had always said it would. But it was too late and, yes, deep down, he knew it.

Within an hour of Frankie Carbo pulling the trigger, the

safe in Bugsy's suite at the Flamingo was opened and emptied. The intruder had the code for the combination, which was known only to Bugsy and Virginia Hill – but she, of course, was out of town. Now, in a more permanent way, so was Bugsy Siegel.

As fast as the safe was cracked, the new management moved in. Bookmaker Gus Greenbaum, an alumnus of the Lower East Side, operated out of Phoenix, only a short, bumpy cartwheel of a drive away in Arizona. He was unpacked, showered and strolling the casino in a tuxedo before anyone knew there was a new boss. By his side were Morris Rosen and Moe Sedway. They never erected a sign telling gamblers 'Under New Management'.

But the Flamingo, like Las Vegas and Havana, most certainly was. The syndicate gave Gus Greenbaum and his wife, Bess, a few parties and called him a genius for his amazingly quick turnaround of the profits of the Flamingo.

Greenbaum was a sergeant of the Mob's initial command in Las Vegas, with Johnny Roselli very much the executive officer. They had The Thunderbird, where George Sadlo had played the middleman and Rosemary Clooney gave her first Las Vegas performance, The Stardust, the Desert Inn, The Sahara and, if a forensic fiscal glance was taken, a silent piece of every new build before the foundation was laid. Jimmy Hoffa from the Teamsters Union invested in desert developments, gambling many millions of dollars of his members' pension fund. Frank Sinatra was allowed in 1952 to buy a 7.5 per cent interest in the Sands Hotel.

Sinatra's career, however, was floundering and he believed he could reboot it with the role of Maggio in director Fred Zinnemann's upcoming *From Here to Eternity*, a much anticipated 1953 release from the Columbia Studios of Harry Cohn. Sinatra's friend Johnny Roselli 'suggested' to Cohn that Sinatra would be 'just the guy for Maggio'.

In the Las Vegas empire, the Flamingo remained the flagship only because it was the first big investment. The other casinos made riches beyond dreams, which were counted by the hierarchy, with millions skimmed off in suitcases and trunks and even Greyhound-style buses adapted with false compartments for the cash. Jimmy Blue Eyes was a financial partner and kept an eye on the money, as did Dino

Cellini. The gaming maestro was brought in to organise and oversee the casino operations. He also helped with the entertainment at the Mob-controlled hotel-casinos as America travelled into Eisenhower's '50s to a mantra of renewal, and the syndicate felt more strongly than ever the need to bait the 'whales', the high rollers who enjoyed being treated like kings as they lost fortunes, kings' ransoms of cash.

Dino Cellini had grown into an elegant, personable man, broad-shouldered and confident, with panache, a style of his own that gave grace to his authority. This was someone for whom people did things, someone who expected respect, impeccable in manner and demanding the same in return. Over the years, he had bestowed favours on Dino Paul Crocetti, the gambling-den croupier at Rex's Cigar Store in those faintly remembered long-ago days in Steubenville. Now, with his nose fixed, Crocetti was known as Dean Martin and with his comic partner Jerry Lewis was one of the hottest acts in America. Martin and Lewis played Las Vegas. Regularly.

Johnny Roselli, by now very much the Casanova of the West Coast, was a powerful figure. He was needed, for the Chicago Mob had flourishing interests in Las Vegas, with the skim running into more than $10 million a year, on top of real profits. They were behind the scenes in creating the $50-million Tropicana hotel-casino, which was shared out among the American dons, including Carlos Marcello of New Orleans. Marcello was an expert in casinos: since 1947, he'd been into upmarket carpet joints. His Beverly Club, with its crystal chandeliers – and, yes, showgirls did swing from them – in Jefferson Parish outside New Orleans was America's classiest illegal casino, where Sophie Tucker and Tony Martin entertained.

Now the glitz was also outside, in neon on the Strip – and at the movies. Sinatra's Rat Pack, of Dean Martin, Sammy Davis Jr, Peter Lawford, Joey Bishop and unofficial best pals such as Johnny Roselli, scattered stardust around the desert. The pack 'mascots' were Angie Dickinson, Juliet Prowse, Shirley MacLaine and Marilyn Monroe, whom Roselli adored.

Roselli was not as tight with everyone. Gus Greenbaum, who with Mob help had become mayor of Las Vegas, became a tragic example of those who believe their own publicity about performing miracles. He never got to cash in his shares. After he'd turned around the Flamingo, it was decided by Tony Accardo in Chicago that he should control four other syndicate hotels in Vegas, as well as bookmaking operations in Arizona. Roselli then told him he must run the Riviera Hotel for Accardo. Greenbaum refused, believed he was too important for that. His sister-in-law Charlene was murdered.

He took the job but he didn't take notice. Gus Greenbaum ordered hits on two mafiosi, Tony Brancato and Tony Trombino, for robbing an outfit-controlled casino. That was the way it was. Yet Greenbaum's increasing love of wine and women and his addiction to heroin led to him skimming at the Riviera, an easily detected embezzlement, something far more fatal than self-indulgence.

Two hit men from Miami were ordered up by Roselli. They flew in without notice to Arizona. Gus Greenbaum and his wife were bloodily murdered, had their throats cut, during a trip over to their home in Phoenix on 3 December 1958. Their killers left town shortly after the murders. There were no clues, no suspicions and no arrests.

Greenbaum got a good funeral. There were more than 300 mourners, including his friend Senator Barry Goldwater, who had also known the gangster Willie Bioff. There had been history between Bioff and Johnny Roselli: in 1941, the punk gangster had turned informant on the Mafia's dapper if deadly diplomat to the stars, and Roselli had done some jail time. On 4 November 1955, in the driveway of his Phoenix home, Bioff flew around in little bits after his car exploded, a dynamite bomb wired to the starter.

In cavalier style, with chilling omnipotence, Roselli had with Greenbaum's departure now said goodbye to two associates of a man his party were predicting would be President Goldwater. There was no fear of prosecution whatsoever. Hey, they had the White House in the bag. It was all connections, diplomacy, who you knew – which was very much part of the Dino Cellini mantra.

The always polite Cellini was a regular commuter: Las Vegas, Florida and Havana. It was Cuba that was to test exactly how good a gambler he was, in the casinos but also in international politics, for the Cold War was chilling nicely even in the warm sunshine only a speedboat ride from the US mainland. The island was becoming like wartime Lisbon: everyone had an agenda, a specific interest to look after, and truth wasn't a recognised currency.

Dino Cellini also understood the unspoken pressure from above, for Meyer Lansky regarded Cuba as the groundwork for his increasing ambitions for dominance in world gambling. There was already a European connection through the Unione Corse, the French Mafia, in Marseilles and Paris. The Corsicans were moving heroin and cocaine through Cuba, employing the island as a way station en route to the cities of America. It was a key transfer point. Taking American gaming to Europe and beyond, Lansky told Cellini, was simply a sensible, and profitable, cultural exchange.

With a post-war watch on American ports continuing, the lively Mafia city of Montreal also became a favoured conduit for contraband. It was an important connection. The homeland mafiosi in Italy were moving the product and their New World counterparts were distributing it. It was business on two continents and needed delicate handling, for whoever controlled Montreal was a world player. Into this came the loyalties, or otherwise, of the Sicilian Mafia and the 'Ndrangheta from Calabria, who were never subtle in their demands or vendettas. In the Mafia, as in most things, Canada had not moved as fast as its next-door neighbour. It valued the past, and all things, including murder and money, were dealt with by old-school rules.

Such politics played a turbulent part in the syndicate's dealings in Havana and Meyer Lansky was at his clever, sophisticated best. He apportioned shares in all kinds of racketeering, all the time focused on gambling and its future. Always, he sought the legalised life; perhaps he subconsciously believed that it could make him civilised, too.

He allied with Santo Trafficante Jr, who was connected to the Cotroni family, who'd won the battle for domination in Montreal. Dino Cellini, who'd proved his value in Las Vegas, massaging the egos and finances of the New York and Chicago families who'd piled into the profit paradise, was brought in as man-about-town. He'd handshake and pay his way around Havana, both charming and intimidating the Cuban authorities, so open to corruption they wore their chicanery like medals, and listening to which Mob guys were making out selling guns and ammunition to the young guerilla leader Fidel Castro.

Castro was seen as nothing more than a nuisance, a bedtime story for anarchists. The hold card for the operation was Fulgencio Batista y Zaldívar, and Lansky and Cellini knew how to play it. They even got paid for calling it.

6

ACE IN THE HOLE

'Mambo Italiano', Rosemary Clooney, 1954

Cuba grew tobacco, sugar cane and – away from the serried ranks of slot machines and the perfumed factories of hookers, away from the hubris of Havana, where the poor concerned themselves with survival, not pleasure – much dissent. Yet a little revolution, the occasional outrage, can be helpful, for it proves you need a strong man, a dictator, in charge. The political philosophy that whoever is in power, in control of the army, the security of the state, is open to private enterprise, often to the highest bidder, is indigenous to Central America and the Caribbean. It's a turbulent zone where individuals make events and not vice versa, and so Meyer Lansky did just that, in his normal businesslike way, with nearly a half a million American dollars.

With that cash comfortable in his private Geneva account, in the early days of the leap year of 1952 the President of Cuba, Carlos Prío Socarrás, opened the way for the return of Batista. It was all going to be wonderfully democratic, with a three-way election involving the former army sergeant and president, Roberto Agramonte of the Ortodoxos Party and Dr Carlos Hevia running as the contender for the Auténtico Party.

Batista was running on behalf of the Mafia Party, but that didn't appear on his electioneering materials, which involved dollar bills clasped in fists attached to strong arms, and voters could take that any way they wanted. Still, the Mob's unswerving support for the return of the prodigal son did not enthuse the constituency and their man was a poor third in the polls.

On 10 March 1952, the impatient Batista brutally engaged his own enterprise, cancelled the upcoming elections and, with army support, took over police and military commands and the radio and television stations. He installed himself as 'provisional' president and forced out Carlos Prío Socarrás, '*El presidente cordial*', who left with a shrug as ineffectual as his self-enriching regime.

With him went much money, his second wife, María Dolores Tarrero-Serrano, and their two children, María Antonieta and María Elena, his foreign minister and his minister of the interior. The group's departure is freeze-framed: a photograph shows Señora de Prío in a silk suit and a hat with black fishnet veiling, gloves and earrings and immaculate make-up. Her husband, the President of Cuba earlier in the day, is in suit and tie, carrying in his arms a briefcase and his youngest daughter, María Elena. This scene in the Cuban opera appears as richly cordial as circumstances allowed.

As was the return of the gambling boom to Havana. Batista – the US acknowledged the legitimacy of his leadership within two weeks – appointed a minister of gambling with a stipend of 25,000 American dollars a year. Meyer Lansky quietly accepted the non-Cabinet post and in turn appointed his Mr Dino Cellini as his leading assistant.

Cellini was part of an invitation-only 'war cabinet', comprising himself, Meyer Lansky, Jimmy Blue Eyes, George Sadlo and Dusty Peters, tasked with masterminding control of Cuba. Ripping off a nation, even a small one, was always a thrill. They didn't rush at it, made themselves the sideshow, not the main event.

Quietly, they washed out the grifters and con men operating in all forms of gaming: some card sharps ended up in the Caribbean, others were shoved into the overcrowded, disease-ridden jails or deported. An unequivocal warning was issued to the casino operators to run clean houses, straight games, or face the consequences. Those being talked to knew by whom they were being warned.

In turn, syndicate associates were allowed, if not welcomed, to join in: a gentleman always pays his gambling debts, no matter what the game being played. Tommy 'Three-Finger Brown' Lucchese, whose family controlled Frankie Carbo, had interests and operators in town, but that was all part of the share-out. Santo Trafficante Jr, who attracted gamblers seven miles out from Havana to his Sans Souci casino-club with headline attractions – Liberace for a week, Marlene Dietrich for another – was accommodated by Lansky for his dignified crookery, his power and powerful connections in Cuba.

The Tampa mob controller had imported Handsome Johnny Roselli across America from Nevada to run the Sans Souci casino. Roselli, dapper, debonair, the dedicated fortune hunter, in every sense, was a perfect fit for the role. He could deal with the customers, the stars and the gambling: he knew how they all worked. He had all the Tinseltown tactics and had produced two film noirs: *Canyon City* (1948), about a mass escape from Colorado State Penitentiary, and *He Walked by Night* (1948), a murder-hunt police procedural about a cop killer; the good guys triumphed in both films, which was an outcome Roselli only ever championed on celluloid. With Roselli's connections, *He Walked by Night*, a low-budget B-picture, which had the former-serviceman killer hiding his rifle in a blanket, received the attention of a blockbuster, including a huge picture spread in *Life* magazine.

In turn, the reviews were considerable and good, but Roselli had more important masters than the critics, and one in particular, Tony 'Joe Batters' Accardo, who'd achieved early status working with his baseball bat as an enforcer for Al Capone. When Accardo took over Chicago, he moved his activities west into Nevada and California in power-sharing deals with Meyer Lansky and others. In exchange for this all-for-one-one-for-all arrangement, the Chicago machine also operated in Florida and throughout the Caribbean. With their extended influence, Accardo promoted a young soldier, Salvatore 'Sam' Giancana, also known as 'Momo', in his mob's hierarchy. He became the control man with Roselli, with Hollywood and up and over into Nevada and across the US to Cuba.

The reach of Mob power in Hollywood went all the way to the top. Harry 'White Fang' Cohn ran Columbia Pictures with an autocratic arrogance; he had grabbed control of the studio with the help of Chicago Mob influence and New Jersey's Longie Zwillman, who'd bankrolled the buy-out of a founding partner. Cohn supposedly always got his own way, but he knew better than to defy Johnny Roselli when he insisted, on behalf of Tony Accardo, that Columbia Pictures sign up a new girl for a high-earning three-movie deal. Which was how

Marilyn Monroe got started in the movies and along the way met Sam Giancana. And why many stars flew down to entertain in Havana.

For the tourists, it all added to the fun in the sun. For the FBI and the CIA, it was spook heaven, the great game of East versus West, Communism versus Freedom.

The come-on for Cuba, from the National Tourism Corporation set up by Batista to the vast audience of America so few miles away, a $39 Pan Am round-trip from Miami, was of value-for-money sun and beaches, incredible food and drink, of sensational sights, of the 'foreign' feel, the hogsheads of molasses and sugar, the stalks of bananas and the entertainment. Indeed, the subliminal message was that it was all Carmen Miranda with extra maracas; how sensational it could all be was up to the visitor to discover.

That wasn't difficult for the tourists. Havana has the smell of the southern states of America, a coffee aroma like New Orleans, but spiked with the Spanish, the *café cortado*, the scented air from the olive oil cooking the potato-and-onion-rich omlettes and sizzling spicy sausage, flavouring the bread toasting on the grills, the street-stall shrimp somersaulting on the trays of ice while their big brothers, *gambas*, *langostinos*, *cigalas*, *carabineros* and *santiaguinos* fight for space with soles and turbots and cod, short, silvery eels, blue-backed sea bass, oysters, crab, mussels and a catalogue of clams.

The other charms of Cuban hospitality were as exotic. Visitors, fuelled by Cuba libres from the maestro Mr Bacardi and the indulgent Coca-Cola Company, were quick to shed their inhibitions and put on racier outfits. Which was where the sex from and at any angle became instantly available, a sexual algebra of inventive equations.

While Batista's appointed henchmen plundered the profits of that business, Lansky and Cellini followed the big money. In the not-too-distant past, there had been signs on the dirt roads around Havana, sort of advance warnings from the highwaymen, reading: 'Money or Mutilation'. The casinos of Havana had better public relations: credit. They also had presidential approval stamped all over them. There were new laws to make casino construction easier, tax breaks were available on asking, visas waived, sins forgiven. Havana was the new Lourdes: miracles happened.

It wasn't just the bad guys following the cash. The upper-world private sector knew a good thing when it saw it, too. The airlines increased schedules, cruise liners made Havana a regular stop and clever shipping companies began car-transport ferries from along the Florida coast. Many crew cuts driving bulldog Buicks and brightly coloured and tail-finned Chevrolets, Oldsmobiles and Plymouths rolled into Cuba and along the Malecón, the brash sea-wall boulevard along the Caribbean on the northern edge of the profit promise that was Havana.

There was a price, of course, for providing the temptation. Initially, it was upwards of $50,000 for a gaming licence for a mid-sized casino. Some managed to chisel officials down to $25,000, which fed the police and lower-echelon holders of government office their bonuses. With the profits involved, it was a financial flea-bite. It got better for those with a million or more dollars to invest in a hotel, or with a quarter of a million for a club. The operation licence was gratis. The Government also provided matching funds, tax incentives and free import of construction equipment. The tiger bite came later, with a giant lump-sum payback to Batista after construction and an ongoing percentage of profits. With Lansky, the president was almost a full partner, getting 30 per cent, counted each evening by Dino Cellini or George Sadlo or Meyer Lansky or his brother Jake and collected by Batista's bagman. There was plenty to go around. The slot-machine money, about $1 million annually, even the cash from the parking meters, went to Batista's brother-in-law. There was no need for skimming; this was as straightforward as printing money. All the boys liked Havana, and why not? All the obstacles appeared to have been dealt with.

One evening, Dino Cellini, who'd been joined by his brothers Eddie, Bobby and Goffredo, all efficient in the world of gaming, picked up a week-old copy of a Florida newspaper left by a visitor in December 1952. It reported:

> James Otto Barker, formerly of the Miami Police Department, was found shot dead in a fishing boat in the Everglades. He was involved with the Sir Harry Oakes murder and was purportedly the first person to utilize fingerprinting to solve the case. However, evidence was

103

not used as it incriminated the 'wrong' person.

Another report suggested that Barker had been shot dead by a family member. It was established that the former senior policeman had died violently, but files in the case had gone missing,

Around the same time, as a brutal winter fog (which was becoming commonly known as 'smog') took the lives of hundreds of Londoners, a leading member of the city's social set escaped the threat and holidayed in Menton on the Côte d'Azur with Sir Harry's son Pitt. Pitt Oakes was in reflective mood following his marriage to the English model Eunice Bailey and asked if his friend had known what really happened to his father.

'I wouldn't know. I was only nine at the time.'

'Bloody lucky for you. If it weren't for the gambling crowd, Dad would still be alive.'

It serves as a reminder that unsolved murders never truly die. A secret is only that if it remains hidden. Time can solve as well as salve. But the past was something Lansky and Cellini rarely thought about, taunted by memory only, perhaps, in the night by their sleeping minds – always, always, focused on the future.

They took over the gaming at the Montmartre Club, where their experts knew how to treat and respond to the needs of serious gamblers, the high rollers who had to be convinced they were playing in a straight environment. That way, they happily lost money, often as much as $30,000. It was all so desperately simple – if outside interests didn't interfere, didn't bully the set-up.

Meyer Lansky went about his empire-building. The Montmartre Club was close to the Moorish-style Hotel Nacional, which was owned by the Cuban government. When a casino complex with cabaret room, the Club Parisien, and bar-restaurant was created within the walls of the Nacional, it was sublet to Lansky. Santo Trafficante's International Amusements Corporation (IAC) provided the entertainment, and on opening night Eartha Kitt, at her feline prime as a sex kitten, was the star. The IAC booked talent for the casinos – the much-favoured Nat King Cole, Johnny Mathis and Ella Fitzgerald, the premier names of jazz and cool. Every which way, the boys were earning. It was exquisite daiquiri diplomacy. They had casinos attached to the Capri, the Sevilla-Biltmore, the Commodoro, the Deauville, and it was all supervised by Dino Cellini and his team, who kept these ocean-front money machines in around-the-clock working order.

They also ran the gambling at the Tropicana, which was a Busby Berkeley cabaret all by itself in the jungle on the outskirts of town. The showgirls were startlingly good-looking and the best dancers, with endless legs and smiles. The high kicks could induce vertigo. On offer was an escape into fantasy, a world where, for a price, all desires could be provided for. Dino Cellini ran the gaming room personally for a time, and then Lewis McWillie, who'd dealt blackjack in Las Vegas and killed a few people back East, took over. He was visited by his friend Jack Ruby, who owned a nightclub in Dallas and who also spent some time with Dino Cellini. McWillie regularly flew up to Miami to make bank deposits.

He sometimes travelled with Martin Fox, who looked like Robert Mitchum in a 1940s RKO film noir, all muscle, wearing a linen suit and .38 Smith and Wesson. Fox and his bisexual wife Ofelia would connect through Miami to New York for a few days away from the pressure of owning the Tropicana in partnership with the boys. Fox was an honours graduate from the Cuban gambling rackets and had established the Tropicana, 'Paradise Under the Stars', as a major attraction. It certainly attracted Lansky and Santo Trafficante.

Like Potatoes Kaufman and so many others before him, Martin Fox, tough, street-smart veteran of Cuban lottery gambling, saw the benefit of being open to sharing. In return, he and his wife were lavishly treated; everyone got a good share of the action. With Lansky presiding, business was parcelled out. In New York, the Foxes were taken to the most popular Broadway shows and the showplace restaurants. If there was a world-class boxing match at Madison Square Garden, they had the best seats – which was not difficult, for their host for all this VIP treatment was Frankie Carbo.

Carbo, acting on direct instructions from Meyer Lansky, was to show the couple 'the best time they're ever going to have anywhere'. It worked, for Ofelia Fox, who in the city wore the silver-grey mink coat given to her by Santo Trafficante Jr, said she was treated like a princess. They had an open pleasure passport to New York while they looked around town and visited their money, invested in 5th Avenue apartments. In return, they hosted boxing's Mr Fixit in Havana, which was the place to be.

You can't want to take over even a small portion of the world without a smattering of megalomania. It wouldn't have been right for Meyer Lansky not to want to; he fitted the role of a little man grasping for the top, for his personal kingdom, so well. It was uncanny natural casting. He saw his castle as the Riviera hotel-casino, a pedestal for him overlooking the Malecón.

In 1955, Batista, safely in Lansky's back pocket and with the gangster's voice in his good right ear, introduced Hotel Law 2074, with which his government went into partnership with the boys. Lansky planned to build a monument to his ambition, with the Riviera reaching a couple of dozen floors of double-bedroom suites into the sky. He had his team in place: Dusty Peters, financial courier-in-chief, long-time partner George Sadlo, casino wizards the Cellini brothers and the sports bookmakers Frank Ritter, Max Courtney and Charles Brudner, who'd worked with him in the starting-gate days in Saratoga Springs. The casino floor men were the best: Hickey Kamm, Al Jacobs, Dave Geiger, Abe Schwartz, Tony Tabasso, Roy Bell, Jim Baker, Jack Metler and Ricky Ricardo.

Meyer Lansky *did* want to rule the gambling world. He also saw the Riviera as a repayment for the messy enterprise in Las Vegas when Bugsy Siegel over-extended everyone's patience with his grandiose behaviour at the Flamingo Hotel. Yet Lansky was equally ambitious. This was to be a jewel, a monumental achievement, a reflection of elegant Monte Carlo and luxury Las Vegas, the most upmarket carpet joint of them all.

Batista's contribution to the Riviera was around $6 million. Lansky and his investors – 'We're all going to make a profit' – plunged in another $11 million. It was a big bet. Everything from the bedding to the food and especially the gambling had to be completely taken care of. He relied on Dino Cellini to recruit the proper staff. He wanted good professionals, and Cuban croupiers and dealers for the 'foreign' ambience and public relations for Batista. Dino Cellini opened a croupier school off the Malecón at the Ambar Motors building complex in the commercial centre. The Cellini brothers ran the school.

Ralph Rubio, an American-born son of a Cuban immigrant, was working as a Las Vegas croupier when, speaking Spanish and English, he became a favoured candidate and accepted an invitation to join the Havana operation. He was happy with Eddie Cellini, but found his brother much, much more demanding. Rubio had a personality conflict with Dino Cellini, whom he found stubborn about everything being done his way. He also believed him to be 'an absolute genius in the casino business'.

And nothing was to interfere with business. Yet Albert Anastasia was doing just that. The legendary 'Lord High Executioner' of Murder, Inc. had retained his intemperate ways. He still liked killing people. He liked money almost as much and was disenchanted with the profits tumbling out of Cuba, where he had no action. He complained in a serious way to Meyer Lansky about it. He would not be told that he must remain quiet, stay out of the way and 'let things develop for a time'.

Anastasia's timing was way out. He not only made the mistake of irritating Lansky and then upsetting Lansky, but he also did the unforgivable and did not listen to Lansky. That was too much. Lansky told Anastasia that there was no room for him on the island. It got worse. Anastasia began talking to the Cuban developers of the Hilton Hotel being planned for Havana. He would partner with them. The Hilton's architectural drawings showed it had some two hundred rooms more than Lansky's Riviera.

Albert Anastasia was splattered all over the barbershop of the Park Sheraton Hotel on New York's 55th Street shortly after 10 a.m. on 25 October 1957.

He'd left the Warwick Hotel, where he kept an apartment, and been taken there by Gino Merico, his bodyguard/driver, who dropped his boss off, parked in the hotel's underground garage and went for a convenient stroll. At the same time, regular customer and big tipper Anastasia, who was known to the understandably friendly barbers as 'Don Umberto', climbed into the chair for his usual wet shave and trim round the ears and nostrils.

Into the hotel, which many New Yorkers knew as the Park Central, where Arnold Rothstein had taken a bullet through his monogrammed shirt just short of three decades earlier, two gunmen strode through the double glass doors of the barbershop. They were most efficient.

Anastasia was dozing like a hibernating bear in the leather chair, his eyes closed, as the masked men pushed Franco, his barber, out of the way and shot the man who himself had so often killed to order. The bullets didn't seem to bother Anastasia and he got up and went for his attackers; he reached towards their images in the mirror, desperately trying to grab them. From behind came more gunfire from the assassins.

The Lord High Executioner fell to the floor, as did a discarded handgun. The professional hit – Anastasia would have approved of its expert implementation – was complete. The seven Italian barbers on duty couldn't help the police in any significant way with their enquiries.

Albert Anastasia had tried to cut in on Meyer Lansky's gambling plans and that was not something to be allowed. Anastasia's underboss, the quiet and traditionalist executive hoodlum Carlo Gambino, was standing not far off this violent stage. Gambino was an important friend of Lansky's from the early days and was now only a murder or two from the top job. Santo Trafficante Jr had been staying at the Warwick Hotel the evening prior to Anastasia's violent passing. He'd left early in the morning for Idlewild Airport and a flight south.

He was in Havana for the grand opening of the Riviera on 10 December 1957, planned just in time for the holidays. This parcel of razzmatazz was cheap and aggressive, all veneer, much like those who had created it, much like Cuba's capital. Yet thousands were expected to be flying down to see Ginger Rogers as the extravaganza nightclub act. Lansky told Trafficante that Rogers couldn't sing to save herself. Happily, she redeemed herself by 'wiggling her ass real good'.

Entertainment stars of the moment came out every night at the Riviera's Copa Room. Santo Trafficante's company provided eclectic attractions, from the very American Abbott and Costello to the Mexican funnyman Cantinflas and conservative cabarets headlined by chart singers such as Vic Damone.

The gamblers could have been on the original Riviera, in the south of France, for this Riviera was the venue where the high rollers came out in their finery. The jewels would have made Raffles' eyes pop, the gowns were from European design houses, the tuxedos bespoke, the patent evening shoes handmade. This totally Mob-operated hotel and casino was the most respectable of places. Everything, including, most importantly, the gambling, was straight.

Yet the cross-cultural immensity of Cuba wasn't totally disguised. Visitors came to Havana to do and see things they couldn't or wouldn't do at home, for the lavish decadence. There were vast profits for Batista's henchmen in sex tourism. Taxi drivers would offer pre-teen virgins or cute little boys, and the hookers were hanging out the windows or cantering around corners. The casinos would treat high rollers, politicians with the right connections (like Massachusetts senator John F. Kennedy) and visiting, friendly mobsters to the various offerings.

Senator Kennedy, who was not a casino gambler, did the rounds in Havana with Senator George Smathers from Florida, who was friends with Meyer Lansky and close to Santo Trafficante Jr. Trafficante ran the Commodoro Hotel on the beach and set Kennedy up there for an afternoon with three gorgeous Cuban girls and a two-way mirror. Trafficante did not have the clairvoyance to film Kennedy relaxing.

For the casino VIPs and wealthy tourists, the more 'sophisticated' sex was in nightclubs, where customers could decide on any combination of men and women, boys and girls, to perform live sex acts. Girl-on-girl action was always the most popular – other than the legendary 'Superman' who boasted a 14-in.-long penis, which he'd display alongside an extended row of a dozen silver dollars before showing that it worked. At the Shanghai nightclub, where he was a headliner, if that's the correct term, the tall, lean Cuban was a curiosity for New York gangsters and little ladies from Milwaukee who'd heard the gossip over dinner at their hotel. Superman, or 'El Toro', was a tourist must-see, and no one ever complained or mentioned trades-description disappointment.

There were also efforts to make the sex into a show, into entertainment, and routines from stage shows and Hollywood movies were adapted. One was a Marx Brothers number in which Harpo played a magical waiter pulling tableware from thin air. In the Shanghai version, a couple at a restaurant table order coffee. From nowhere, cups and saucers and spoons appear and then a pot of black coffee is poured. 'Where is the cream?' the woman enquires. The waiter pulls out his penis and, with a little encouragement from the señora's fingers and lips, ejaculates into the cup.

The casinos, nightclubs, sexual shenanigans, off and on stage, delivered golden results. The Mob hotels in Havana all made money. Charles 'Charlie the Blade' Tourine out of Miami came in to run the casino at the Hotel Capri. They had Roaring Twenties gangster chic there, with the hand-stitched tailored George Raft superbly playing the part of a meeter and greeter. Raft, who'd been brought there by Santo Trafficante Jr, was a cool front man. He was a quiet operator, wanted his comforts and not to be bothered. He was a man who took his afternoon nap no matter what was happening. He didn't like or cater for surprises and said as much when he talked to you, always with his eyes on your eyes. He'd played it that way in Hollywood when any career stretch was too much to trouble with.

George Raft favoured the status quo; he'd survived, prospered, by not rocking the boat. He rolled out the tuxedo and the patter, slicked back someone else's hair (it was a 'natural' toupee), put on the welcome smile and went to work. For others, he was his own attraction at what was the world's most sought-after playground. It intrigued many: Sarah Vaughan and Tony Martin sang, José Greco danced, Errol Flynn was the debauched adventurer who flirted with the rebels, Marlon Brando the young actor who was going to be the best method man ever, Hemingway was in residence, Ava Gardner and Elizabeth Taylor brought glamour and looked for fun, and Graham Greene came for the cocaine, bordellos and material for *Our Man in Havana*.

It's difficult to imagine that the burlesque of Havana kept anyone ignorant of the endemic corruption of Cuba, unless it was purposely avoided. The exploitation of the nation was what Fidel Castro used in his campaign against Batista in the process of building his own legend. Batista couldn't see it; the ultimate capitalist thought that with so much money around the bearded jungle habitué would have no appeal. He had Castro in jail but freed him in a public-relations manoeuvre to reflect his benevolent dictatorship. PR worked both ways. It was put around that Castro had died in a jungle shoot-out.

The interview and photograph on the front page of the *New York Times* that followed pretty much rebutted that – and fanned the ever-growing myth of Fidel Castro, aka Messiah. The guerilla manifesto tilted against the *desfalcadores*, the embezzling carpetbaggers, chiefly Lansky and the boys, responsible for the vivisection of Cuba. Castro was seriously outraged that the name of José Martí, nineteenth-century freedom fighter and Castro hero, was on a street-corner strip club. Indeed, it was a malignant symbol of Cuba being stripped bare.

The gap between the haves and the have-nots was a chasm and widening every day. Dissidents, non-believers in profit, casino skimmers, thieves, presumed hooligans of any hue who affronted the easy-going notion of 'anything goes' were swiftly moved out of the way. They became target practice or were squeezed into prisons, and if there wasn't room they were just hung up from trees or lamp posts as behavioural instruction. Those who got lucky were simply killed and not tortured or barbecued for fun first. It was a rule of terror by the kleptocrats and did nothing but fuel the revolutionary zeal of Castro and his followers. Every Batista atrocity added more hate and discontent. That reaction brought reaction, more torture and firing squads and myriad barbaric acts that were executions in all but government terminology. It was evil, and so much so that even America could no longer look away from the brutality. Could they?

Still, amazingly, while outside Havana the dissent grew with the sugar cane in the fields and in the neighbouring villages, the casino mob kept hitting the jackpot. Each day, the ever-reliable Dusty Peters took the early-morning flight to Miami and had the previous evening's gamblers' cheques express cleared in city banks or at their account-holding branches in Miami Beach, Palm Beach and sometimes Fort Lauderdale. The FBI watched every Havana flight, counted Dusty Peters out and counted him in. Dusty Peters knew all manner of assistant presidents and vice presidents in all kinds of air-conditioned financial institutions. After a quiet lunch, clam chowder and a salad, he'd fly back to Havana and the cavalcade of cash would start all over again. People were working hard; the money had to do that, too.

The profits delivered to Florida were swiftly reinvested

with the help of a Canadian entrepreneur, who, like Sir Harry Oakes, had made his money in mining and saw a future in the Bahamas. Louis Arthur Chesler looked like a full-grown cherub, a 20-stone lump of rounded pink who was known accurately as 'Big Lou' and, for his wildlife-style habits – he liked to pee in the woods and in public – as 'Moose'. He made his first big money in mining stock and then many millions in real estate, particularly in Florida, with several associates who included Meyer Lansky and his friends. Lou Chesler had been engaged with gangsters for nearly 20 years, working after the war with a former Prohibition bootlegger, John Pullman, who was also born in Ontario. In jail on booze hijacking charges, Pullman had met the Midwest mob leader 'Yiddy' Bloom, who had the connection to Meyer Lansky.

The ever-careful Lansky admired professionals, and Chesler was good, especially at handling stolen stock securities, which he moved through Switzerland. Chesler was the money magician; he could perform all sorts of tricks and no one would ever know the secret. He was an important part of the gambling expansion plans. Lansky wanted to legitimise the many millions of dollars being skimmed from the Havana and Vegas casinos. There were also huge revenues from the drug trade, heroin and increasingly cocaine, 'the power powder', being shipped by infamous international couriers like Giuseppe de Giorgio. The profits were being shared out and invested internationally.

What was constantly needed was somewhere to put all this money, capital investments. While others concerned themselves with making and stealing money, Chesler and Pullman used it to establish companies, to found and fold them again and again, so that by the time anyone tried to follow the money it had gone shopping, around the houses, taken a holiday, and then returned to base as an upstanding blue-chip organisation. When construction began in 1958 on the Miami International Airport Hotel, the majority of the investment capital was skimmed gambling money from Havana and similar funds from the Sands Hotel and the Freemont Hotel in Las Vegas. Other investment came from a group of Los Angeles lawyers and from international entrepreneur Jack Cooper, who held much stock in the West Flagler Dog Track in Miami and the baseball team the Miami

Marlins. Cooper sold a squadron of P-51 jet fighter planes to the Dominican Republic and ran a casino at the Jaragua Hotel in Santa Domingo. J. Edgar Hoover and the powers of law and order had little notion of the corporate structure being established in front of their binoculars.

The US Government's concerns for Cuba were not righteous; they despised Batista, but they feared Castro and that newly coined 'domino principle' flicking through the islands so close to their shores. It was not a domestic political issue for America: everybody who was anti-Communist was a friend. Eisenhower's vice president, Richard Nixon, toured the Caribbean in 1955. He laid it on: Batista was a reincarnation of Abraham Lincoln; Generalissimo Rafael Trujillo, the butcher who wept for the men he killed, was Nixon's best friend. In Haiti, the hapless Nixon tried to be a man of the people. He talked to a peasant woman who snapped, 'Tell this coconut to get out of the way.' This was translated as 'Nice to meet you', which was all the encouragement America's vice president required: 'What is the donkey called?' The reply: 'He's crazy. It's called a donkey.' It was a trifle in the ongoing perils of diplomacy.

The conundrum was whether the Mob were their allies or enemies. Meyer Lansky's political peripheral vision, his usually acute antennae, wasn't working too well. He was focused on what was his life – the deals – and on gambling, and he was relentless, he wanted more. He envisaged the Havana operation replicated throughout the Caribbean, especially in the Bahamas, and he was in the process of making this a reality, with Lou Chesler as his point man. He sent Dino Cellini to Haiti, where they took a financial interest in a casino in Port-au-Prince, an altogether different voodoo economics on madman 'Papa Doc' Duvalier's island.

With Jack Cooper's help, Charlie the Blade organised talks in the Dominican Republic with the American marines-trained dictator's dictator Rafael Trujillo and won some casino concessions. Trujillo was evil, a twentieth-century Caligula. As an army officer, he had discovered a penchant for rape; when he took power in 1930 and became president he ordered a constant supply of virgins for his bedchamber. He would humiliate his government officers by demanding they sacrifice the virginity of their daughters. When people attacked or

113

even mildly criticised his regime, they vanished. When he got angry with the President of Venezuela, he didn't bother with letters of protest in the diplomatic pouch. He tried to blow him up. He broke off with the Vatican and got a Dominican sorcerer to attempt to kill the Pope with the evil eye. Yet Trujillo ranted against the Communists and cleverly advertised which side he supported in the Cold War. So, for America, he was politically acceptable, an *anti-Communist* degenerate, with a member of the diplomatic corps explaining to a member of the Senate Overseas Committee: 'The fact that they murder their enemies or torture them doesn't usually come up over coffee cups.'

What was good enough for the White House was fine for Lansky. He really would sup with the Devil, no matter what guise he took. Batista had grown chubby, yet all that flesh couldn't conceal the horns, the satanic black holes where his eyes once were. He'd been dealing dirty with this country for such a long time. His Havana comprised streets driven by greed while all around the island so many more were motivated by poverty and the resulting desperate need and had nothing to lose in taking up arms with Fidel Castro. Batista's secret police, the SIM, watched and murdered them. The CIA and FBI were monitoring it with haphazard vigilance. The revolution was the only movement with a proper purpose. At least they knew something: they wanted change.

The FBI surveillance noted many meetings. One involved Dino Cellini and Amleto Battisti who had a disdainful demeanour that disguised a gentle humour and an aggressive business sense. Amleto Battisti was Old World Mafia, a Corsican who owned the Hotel Sevilla in Havana and ran the Casino de la Playa. His money had for years come from racketeering, specifically the *bolita* (little ball), which he ran in parallel with the National Lottery, taking bets and paying out on the official numbers. The outcome could be prearranged and he did that well and often enough to own his own bank, Banco de Creditos y Inversiones.

Battisti was a long-time associate of Charlie Luciano and Meyer Lansky. With Luciano, he'd set up the French connection, shipping heroin processed in Europe into America through Cuban ports. He knew about the import/ export business. Battisti, more wary of Castro, more cognisant of the dissent building throughout Cuba than the mobsters (who, compared with him, were newcomers), wanted to invest overseas, in gambling in Europe. He had the people; the Corsicans were the best croupiers in the world. Dino Cellini heard all this out on 12 October 1958. The following week, the Limey received a call in London telling him to report to Miami. Dino Cellini, Jimmy Blue Eyes and a couple of others would meet him at their usual restaurant out at the Beach for dinner. Benny Huntman was a regular at Joe's Stone Crab.

It was a miraculous place, Miami Beach, home to sunshine arithmetic, for when Benny left for his flight to London he'd usually leave the always crowded and busy Joe's, even after paying the bill, with much more cash than he'd arrived with. What the boys called 'the investment' was always more than the £50 allowed in and out of Britain by currency regulations, but the quietly attractive brunette who took the same flight and could for all the world have been Benny's wife was never stopped or her ivory-coloured hand luggage opened. It all moved along smoothly.

George Raft was also on the move. When the summer season brought down the heat and business at the Hotel Capri declined, he'd taken leave to make a movie. He was going to film for sixteen weeks at Universal Studios in Los Angeles and on location a two-hour drive (with a stop for coffee at Laguna Beach) down the Pacific Coast Highway, at the Hotel del Coronado on Coronado Island, across the curving high-wire act of a bridge from San Diego. It was a Billy Wilder picture called, amusingly to Raft, *Some Like It Hot*. His co-stars were Tony Curtis, Jack Lemmon and Marilyn Monroe. Curtis and Lemmon witness Raft, as gangster 'Spats' Colombo, involved in a St Valentine's Day-style massacre and have to go on the run in drag with an all-girl band, which includes Monroe's lisping wonderment girl Sugar. George Raft played his scenes perfectly – the delivery, the timing. He should have stuck with the movies. He returned to the Hotel Capri on Christmas Eve 1958 and began playing George Raft. The act, the posture and silk tuxedo were impeccable. The timing was not.

Fifteen days earlier, President Eisenhower's personal envoy had told Batista that if he stood down immediately there would be sanctuary for him back at his peaceful home by the

Halifax River in Daytona Beach, Florida. A week before Christmas Day, he was given another message from 'Ike' Eisenhower with somewhat more edge: America would no longer support his government or give him asylum.

Meyer Lansky was in Florida at the time, but with a black cat's bad timing he flew back for the noisy and boisterous New Year's Eve party at the Riviera. None of the revellers heard the news on Radio Rebelde that Castro and Che Guevara were doorstepping them.

The president knew. For his Hogmanay celebrations, Batista folded his dictator's hand, took the money, about $300 million, and ran. It was 2.44 a.m. on New Year's morning in 1959 when Fulgencio Batista flew for the last time from Havana, on an Aerovias Q Douglas DC4 to the Dominican Republic. He wore his uniform and the women with him the evening dresses they'd put on for a sumptuous sit-down New Year's Eve banquet. The flight from the military base Camp Columbia took Batista and his runaway entourage into the black night out over Cuba and to the east, beneath the clouds, which could never hide the detritus of his years in power, his lethal and louche legacy as Présidente de la République de Cuba. Four transport planes followed him, bringing along the spoils of his dictatorship.

On the ground, the rebel forces were a few hundred miles from Havana, where there was dancing in the streets, a zany jubilation like no other for a long, long time. As the people celebrated and the absentee Batista's loyal army tried to figure out what to do, the mobsters who'd played such a part in events, in the corruption that had led to this moment, were considering how much it might cost to pay off this guy Fidel Castro.

The prescient Lansky regarded Castro as another dictator in waiting, albeit one, like his followers, who didn't care for soap but followed a doctrine. Castro was culturally the opposite of Batista, but strip away the rhetoric and they were twin-like, nakedly ambitious, greedy for power, and once again a choice weapon in the quest for regime change was arbitrary killing. This time, though, the executions were for politics, not casino profits. As that first day of 1959 moved on, the charismatic Che Guevara led a rebel victory at the Battle of Santa Clara as Fidel Castro's 26 July Movement began to take power.

The rebel troops weren't so successful when they invaded the Salon Rojo, the Red Room, of the Hotel Capri. They met a tough guy in a tuxedo. The revolution had interrupted George Raft's routine and his sex life. He didn't like that. He was just getting excited.

As the New Year's Eve festivities had settled towards dawn, he'd sent his lady for the evening, a former Cuban beauty queen, to his room. He'd given her a gentle kiss and told her to wait for him. She did, between silk sheets, and when he got there the invitation to join her was enthusiastic. He was doing just that when, as he whispered, '*Feliz Año Neuvo*,' machine-gun fire began rattling around the lobby of the hotel. He called the front desk but screams and shouts and gunfire deafened him to any sense that might have been made. He did hear, 'Mr Raft, the revolution is here.' He took the time to put on his George Raft tuxedo uniform and headed for the trouble.

He was greeted by shouts about bandits, and madcap confusion, and from nowhere he thought about the Keystone Kops, but that was as far as the comedy went. The gunfire in the streets was real and he saw people collapsing dead. A mob of rioting youngsters turned the hotel into a target for their bricks and bottles. Next, the revolution was right in front of him, with around 100 Castro patriots charging into the hotel. One or two sprayed machine-gun bullets around the bar.

George Raft knew the scene. He'd played variations on it. He climbed up on a table and cried at them to calm down. They did. In the silence, a girl pointed at him: 'It's George Raft, the movie star.' It was a good day to find a fan. Raft, wishing he had a script to follow, said that he and the hotel were neutral and if everyone just behaved food and drink would be made available. It turned the revolutionaries quite docile. Some did what Raft thought of as 'lightweight looting', but others quietly drank Coca-Cola and looked for bottles of Bacardi. He'd saved himself and the hotel. He went back to his routine and the former Miss Cuba, who, happily for him, found all the excitement exciting.

As the revolution's first week took shape, the Riviera Hotel was not so lucky in its treatment. It became crowded by the people and their farm animals, and particularly messy were the pigs. It's a colourful incongruity, an *Animal Farm* image:

the fat, pink animals freely indulging themselves amid all the shiny glass and marble and pretension of the hotel lobby, restaurants and casino. Shit, of course, happens – and shit was what Lansky and the Riviera were in.

PART 2

FULL HOUSE

'The Twist', Chubby Checker, 1960

7

THE FACTS OF LIFE

'All Shook Up', Elvis Presley, 1957

With his private education at Harrow, the eminent British public school, Peter Wilson, with the trademark cartoon moustache familiar to readers of the sports pages of England's *Daily Mirror*, was armed with a wonderful vocabulary of bluster. Benny Huntman was holding the semi-automatic Luger. He was pointing the German pistol in the face of the writer promoted as 'the man they can't gag', but Benny was not one to pay attention to other people's advertising. 'If you ever give me problems again, this gun is going to go off with a bang, bang. Do you understand? Bang, bang! Understand?'

Wilson nodded and nodded again to Benny, who was flanked by his son Roger and a couple of his muscled staff in the training room one floor up in Joe Bloom's Gym on Earlham Street, over on the Covent Garden side of Cambridge Circus. Benny's face was all premeditated fury. He'd been working himself up to this moment for years. For Wilson, master of hyperbole, this truly for once could be 'the fight of the century'. He knew Benny Huntman wasn't being amusing. He'd taken not too long a walk up from Piccadilly Circus after a lunch that had enhanced his demeanour and his waistline with the promise of a scoop. This information was more exclusive than he'd hoped for.

The bombastic sportswriter, who enjoyed a huge readership, had for a long time raised an editorial eyebrow at some of the antics of the boxing world: the mismatches, the surprising outcomes, the number of visiting Americans who fell down on the job. Benny Huntman didn't want any more attention – there was a greater game afoot – but Wilson had continued to needle him in print. There were regular innuendoes in his

Daily Mirror column, which was followed by Wilson's friends at the British Boxing Board of Control.

The animosity went back a dozen years, to a Solomons and Huntman promotion in London of a much-heralded 1948 fight between Bruce Woodcock, Freddie Mills's nemesis, and the well-regarded heavyweight Lee Oma. In New York, they thought Oma should win, but they'd had the word and bet Woodcock. Oma said he 'didn't feel too good' the day before the contest and those good with boxing dialect knew what that meant. He certainly didn't look too good a few flurries into the fourth round at Harringay Arena. Woodcock caught Oma with a right-hand blow and the American, who hadn't rehearsed, swayed and took a little time to lie flat on the canvas and roll from side to side. There was no ovation, only pennies thrown into the ring by the disgruntled crowd, and a crackerjack headline in the next day's *Daily Mirror* above Peter Wilson's report, 'OMA! AROMA! COMA!', which led to a commotion and Lee Oma's purse being withheld by the BBBC. Over the years, arrangements had been made to stop such interference, but now things were far too serious not to warn off Peter Wilson, who got the message.

Benny had chosen his life and the pace of it. He was one of life's aggressors, brash, confident, willing to stand up to any confrontation, eyeball life's snake charmers and magicians. He knew them better than they did themselves. Benny loved a fight. Publicly, he arranged, promoted, bought and sold some of the most famous international boxing contests of the twentieth century. Privately, he worked for and with the most influential criminal of the time, Meyer Lansky. In that job, he was just as diligent. For there were always contracts of one sort or another.

Joe Bloom's Gym was now Benny Huntman's headquarters. He'd moved from Great Windmill Street following a turbulent transatlantic decade. He, press sniping aside, had almost stayed below the boxing-control radar, but his New York partner Frankie Carbo had been constantly hassled by a handbook of acronyms, including the FBI, the CIA and the NYPD. It was a cloudy start to the decade.

In his personal stable, Benny had plenty of contenders, including three champion 1950s fighters, bantamweight Danny O'Sullivan and lightweights Billy Thompson and

Tommy McGovern. What upfront attention Benny had from the British Board of Boxing Control was about the management of the two lightweights when they were matched for the BBBC British lightweight title. Yet he escaped fuss when Thompson retained the title on points against McGovern at The Stadium, Staffordshire, on 11 July 1950. This allowed him to keep his Lonsdale belt, one of the last to be made of gold, and Thompson took his glory on the *Queen Mary* from Southampton to fight world lightweight champion Ike Williams in New York. Williams was one of the greatest all-time punchers, with a much lauded right hand, but he also used it to take money from the Mob. Billy Thompson was sidelined; he had a good time in Manhattan and other, more lucrative arrangements were made for Williams through his manager Frank 'Blinky' Palermo.

Blinky, who, with his eyebrows pointing skywards, always appeared to be in shock, was an uptown legend in his home city of Philadelphia in the days before he became the most powerful under-the-counter boxing manager in America as the number-two man to Frankie Carbo. Blinky didn't like crooks. In his bookmaking days in Philadelphia, he'd been ripped off by a gunman on a 75-cent wager. He was out for a handful of dollars, but that wasn't the point. He gave chase, firing his pistol non-stop. The resulting gun battle only stalled when the police sirens got real close. Ike Williams said Blinky only forced him to fake one fight but took *all* his winning purses. 'There was no arguin' with Blinky.'

Palermo was Frankie Carbo's main point man in American boxing. There were others, management men, muscle men and good-and-evil double acts training fighters and lifting their wallets simultaneously. With the fanfare gone after a boxing extravaganza at Madison Square Garden, the hucksters led by Carbo would begin manipulating the market. Even as the defeated fighters, and often the winners, too, lay cut up, battered and bruised, on New York treatment tables, they were being repackaged in Chicago or Philadelphia or Los Angeles. Carbo and company did not want their boys being exploited by anyone but them. A name was a name, a name was a brand and you sold the brand to the seductive jingle of the cash registers until the time-worn shelves finally fell in or your boy got 'too punchy'.

While Benny Huntman and Frankie Carbo, who'd become known to him as 'the Cousin', operated throughout the '50s, it was known by some in America that Carbo was the strongman fixer for the International Boxing Club (IBC) of every significant boxing match in the US. Some of the detail became public during government hearings. The IBC founder and president, James Norris, a second-generation multimillionaire industrialist and equestrian enthusiast, explained Carbo away as 'one of the facts of life' in boxing, as did the IBC secretary, Truman K. Gibson Jr, who for three years was a member of President Harry S. Truman's Committee on Religion and Welfare in the Armed Forces, an upstanding citizen.

Norris owned the Chicago Stadium in his home town, the Detroit Olympia and the St Louis Arena and a healthy percentage of Madison Square Garden. He also followed real-estate investment advice from Lou Chesler, mainly in the Florida area. He found Truman Gibson, a black Southerner and highly effective lawyer, a good man to work with. Gibson had practised law in Chicago and was close to Joe Louis when he was coming through as a fighter; he did the champ's tax returns. Norris said Carbo was, in turn, a 'heavy trial', and had 'even embarrassed me with my horses'. Not, it seemed, with one stallion, which Norris, with deference, named Mr Gray.

These heavyweight citizens were in thrall to Carbo and his management team. To meet their contractual commitments with the US television networks, the IBC needed 1,200 boxers available every year. Norris, the face of American television boxing, explained that Frankie Carbo was a 'convincer' in getting major promotions for the IBC. In turn, the IBC paid Viola Masters, Mrs Carbo, who was living in Biscayne Bay down in Florida, near one of Meyer Lansky's homes, $45,000 a year. That fee was for her husband's 'goodwill' in getting the fights and to 'maintain a free flow of fighters without interference'. The IBC also paid $90,000 to Blinky Palermo for his 'kindness', and it was agreed by one investigating committee that 'every leading manager or promoter in the US is either closely associated with or controlled by Frankie Carbo in some degree'.

It was beginning to sound like a monopoly – in a most strange, strange world. One witness, Hymie 'The Mink'

Wallman, who was also a major boxing manager, said he'd known Carbo since his days of being called 'Jimmy the Wop'.

'Spell that,' he was told.

The New York furrier was precise: 'W.' Pause. 'O.' Pause. 'P.'

However you spelled it, Carbo's name was poison to purity in any of life's pursuits. Carbo had 'persuaded' Felix Bocchicchio, a gambler known as 'the Man o' War' and the manager of the fighter 'Jersey' Joe Walcott, to sign for a heavyweight championship rematch with Rocky Marciano in Chicago in May 1953. Walcott had lost the title to Marciano in Philadelphia a year earlier. He lost again, another KO, and Marciano held his unbeaten record. Marciano hung on to that record into his retirement after retaining the world heavyweight championship against Archie Moore in the Bronx on 21 September 1955. It was Marciano's last fight, and it was arranged by Carbo and Blinky Palermo that Archie Moore would go down, take a dive, so Marciano could retire unbeaten. Moore's manager was Doc Kearns, who was kept in the dark about that fix and at a meeting after the event shouted at Moore, 'You dirty son of a bitch! Why didn't you tell me?' The answer was that Doc was getting older – he was 79 – and talking a lot. No one knew about the Archie Moore dive, but he sure lived in a nice place in San Diego, right along from the singer Frankie Laine, an expensive neighbourhood.

Nothing was said openly about that particular fight, but Kearns was getting very vocal by the time questions were being asked publicly about boxing, and he offered, 'James Norris and Carbo run everything in boxing, and when they feel like it, they throw you a bone every once in a while.' That was an extraordinary remark, for Truman Gibson said the IBC had given Kearns, acting as well as dressing the clown now, a little more than $130,000 for the 'goodwill' of his small guild of boxing managers. Still, there wasn't much of that about. Hymie the Mink said he bought the contract of welterweight champion Johnny Bratton after a conference with Norris, Carbo and Gibson; the money for the deal was provided by the IBC. He said Billy Brown, who was the IBC matchmaker in Madison Square Garden from 1952 to 1958, worked for Carbo and that almost all of the IBC fights in New York were arranged by Carbo through Brown.

Carbo, Palermo, Norris and others also had their claws in

one of the most fearsome profit prospects of them all, the bear-man ton of bricks Sonny Liston. Liston – born Arkansas, no date of birth known, former convict, Mob muscle and, with Teamsters associate Big Barney Baker, helper in fragile negotiations – was a popular guy. John Vitale, the main gangster in Liston's adopted home town of St Louis, with fifty-eight arrests but only three misdemeanour convictions for speeding, owned 12 per cent of him. Blinky had another 12 per cent and two anonymous businessmen had 12 per cent each. Frankie Carbo had the remaining and controlling 52 per cent. You didn't need a calculator to see there wasn't much left for Sonny in these arrangements. Others were made. He moved on to Philadelphia, where he bought his first home on a mortgage arranged by Blinky Palermo. Control was all.

Carbo *was* an extraordinary fact of life. The fighters he controlled included famous names, sporting heroes: Marciano, Kid Gavilán, Jake LaMotta, Johnny Saxton, Jimmy Carter, Rocky Graziano, Floyd Patterson, Ike Williams, Virgil Akins and Tami Mauriello. He put Primo Carnera on his US 'tank tour' (all the big guy's opponents fell down, tanked), before shipping him off to Benny Huntman and Europe. The boxing world, the boys from the newspaper back pages, could find him any time: 'Looking for Frankie is like standing on the corner of 5th Avenue and 34th Street and looking for the Empire State Building.' Still, the cops could never seem to trace him. Most times, he gave himself up to get on with it, get the legal mouthpiece to play the get-out-of-jail card. Where it was dealt from depended on the police precinct location.

The Mink always acted as a link between Carbo and crooked referees and boxing judges. This allowed for huge betting-coup investments, using cash skimmed off from the gambling in Las Vegas and Cuba. Boxing was never, ever about the fighting; the excitement was the deal, the sure thing – talking the deal, dreaming it, making it, doing it, loving it.

Carbo employed syndicate muscle Joe Sica and Lou Dragna, nephew of Benny Siegel's stepping stone Jack Dragna of Los Angeles and a man who enjoyed his job across America. Dragna was involved in heavy work in the contest for the world welterweight title between Carbo's Virgil Akins and Californian Don Jordan, who had the audacity to be independent of the Mob. Violence and extortion followed Jordan's taking of the title on 5 December 1958, at the Olympic Auditorium in downtown Los Angeles. Jordan's manager, Jackie Leonard, was savagely beaten and told by Carbo: 'Nobody has ever said no to us and got away with it. The same thing could happen to you that happened to Ray Arcel.' Arcel had been found beaten to the point of death five hours after turning down Carbo's request to give him a share of the television payments for one of his boxers.

Manager Mel Cooke tried to resist the boys moving in on his world bantamweight champion Eddie 'Cannonball' Martin. The response was for Cooke's face to be razor-slashed to a raw mess. In hospital a few days later, he gave part-ownership of Martin to Carbo's connected cousin.

Other managers, like Irving Cohen, who ran Rocky Graziano, gave proper ownership to Carbo and his associate made man Eddie Coco, who was given a glowing reference by IBC leader James Norris as 'a man of his word, well liked and highly respected by his many friends'. Coco didn't manage for long, as he went to jail for murder.

Cus D'Amato, Floyd Patterson's manager, avoided the fixers and being drawn into the intimidation conspiracy and sailed off to Puerto Rico under the assumed name 'Mr Dudley'.

In this boom era for boxing, the operation was going on everywhere, especially in fight centres like Philadelphia, Boston, Detroit, Milwaukee, St Louis, Minneapolis, Cleveland and San Francisco. And it was all controlled from Mr Gray's 'office' at Jack Dempsey's, from where he also ran his New York bookmaking racket. Frankie Carbo was banking about $200,000 a week in regular accounts, while suitcases of dollars were driven down to Miami for transport to London and Switzerland. Three accounts, access by code not name, were also set up in Frankfurt. Some European banks would make 'accommodations' and not declare deposits, taking a percentage for their discretion. Lou Chesler's partner John Pullman was in the process of founding another dollar sanctuary, the International Credit Bank of Geneva. Chesler had a team of Canadian accountants conducting research on establishing offshore banking in the Bahamas.

Benny Huntman was doing his own feasibility studies,

following a plan that had been mapped out for a long, long time. Benny's task was to ease the way for American gambling in London and then throughout the UK and into Europe. There had already been talks with connections in Belgrade, Amsterdam and Brussels. Corsican croupiers and casino staff from Paris via the Unione Corse were on standby. Powerhouse Carlo Gambino, the Mafia's 'little old man' who'd kill you for being disrespectful, had invested some people in London.

Through the '50s, Benny had met Carbo in New York, sometimes in Miami if their trips to Jimmy Blue Eyes coincided, but more and more he was told to concentrate on the upcoming gambling invasion. When in 1955 he got word that the British Boxing Board of Control were looking into his matchmaking, the wily Benny decided to make himself bankrupt. As such, he could not legally hold a boxing manager's licence; he couldn't even hold a trainer's sponge. No licence, no investigation; no cheques and therefore no checks on him or his movements. Benny quietly went about his work. There were meetings that year with nightclub owners, including his long-time friend Al Burnett, who ran the Stork Club in Mayfair. His customers, crowding into the 200-capacity room, were often elite names: Harold Macmillan, John Profumo, Frank Sinatra, Ava Gardner, Lana Turner, Bette Davis and Elizabeth Taylor. Al Burnett gloried in it all, telling everyone who would listen:

> King Hussein of Jordan is here when he's in London. He jumps on stage and takes over the drums. Jean Simmons always takes off her shoes and dances with me in her stockinged feet, but that's nothing compared with what some of my customers do.

Burnett, with his business partner Bill Ofner, also found the funds in 1955 to buy the Pigalle Club at 196 Piccadilly, opposite the Piccadilly Hotel, for £75,000. It became the place to go, to be seen, with lavish floor shows, one involving eighteen chorus girls in £6,000 white fox furs bought outright for a thirty-second appearance. There was a little-known private exit from the Pigalle, which could take guests discreetly into the anonymity of Jermyn Street. When he bought the Pigalle, Al Burnett also completed a £25,000 arrangement to reopen the Society Restaurant on Jermyn Street, which had closed down a year earlier. It had a concealed door to a passageway that led through the kitchens, dressing-rooms and storerooms and then straight on for a few yards into the Pigalle. Halfway along, there was a private elevator, which could whisk the coy and their special guests into the night – or luxury surroundings. Berkeley Square was on the corner, and the Mayfair Hotel met it at Stratton Street.

The club owner had good friends in the entertainment world, including the enterprising showman Bernard Delfont, who when he was a struggling businessman was helped by Burnett:

> Friends helped me out. When I needed ready cash to pay the bills, Al Burnett, who went on to run a couple of nightclubs in the West End, would collect a bundle of money from his night's takings, put it in a bag and deliver it in the middle of the night to where I was living. I'd wake up in the morning to find the mat by the front door strewn with fivers.

The Pigalle was a playground for London society, European and Arabian royalty and Hollywood movie stars, where Princess Margaret might meet Peter Sellers or Richard Burton, Audrey Hepburn, Marlene Dietrich and Gary Cooper, or greet the Maharaja of Baroda, Sir Pratap Singh Gaekwad. Everywhere you turned, you were following money – or girls. Some guests would have bedroom entertainment sent into the Pigalle, and if they were acceptable the next stop was a suite at the Mayfair.

Close by, off Bond Street and over the half-moon driveway at the Westbury Hotel, in a fourth-floor room, young gambler John Aspinall, accustomed to fleecing unsuspecting players at chemin de fer – known as 'chemmy', a game utterly extravagant in its madness – would be playing high-stakes poker. Or he might be going around town with his partner John Burke and hosting illegal chemmy games in private houses in Mayfair and Belgravia and at the same time challenging the outdated gambling laws. The police, certainly in the West End, generally turned away from illegal gaming as long as it did not disturb, did not draw notice to itself. It was a superficial society, the sort of Waugh-ish world where when the veneer was stripped away all that was there was more veneer. For the majority, it was all jolly fun; for Aspinall, it was a deadly serious business. He needed the money and this was where it was. There was a giant jackpot waiting to be won – by whoever dared. He wasn't the only interested party.

The gambling scene in London was changing rapidly. Benny knew that all preparations had to be ready when Las Vegas quietly came to town, when American gaming, the craps and blackjack, arrived alongside legalised gambling in the UK, which Lansky and his group were furiously lobbying for. They'd already spent plenty of money paying their way. MPs from all parties had no idea who was really entertaining them, but they recognised that the treatment was lavish. Home Office officials were on 'advice retainers' and senior Metropolitan Police officers were thinking about moving out to nice homes in Surrey. Benny had been asked about his activities, his American connections, but that came to nothing, as he used the Lansky method with the police: he paid them off, including high-ranking members of the Flying Squad, whom he'd meet for drinks and brown envelopes at the Howard Hotel down from the back of the Savoy on the Thames. He was totally loyal to the Mob, who had adopted him in New York and set him on the path of plenty, if not of righteousness. Benny knew who he was.

It wasn't often that he lost his temper as he had with Peter Wilson. There was the moment he almost drove down a business rival on the way to Petticoat Lane with Roger. He'd seen his despised boxing competitor Jarvis Astaire walking across the road and only braked when the red mist of his anger suddenly cleared. He'd planned to have Astaire murdered by the young Krays, Ron and Reg. He'd worked out a deal with their older brother Charlie in which Benny would sort out boxing promoter Mickey Duff, who was proving a stubborn obstacle to the twins' empire-building, as he had no fear of them and would not be intimidated. The problems had resolved themselves, and there was no point in killing for the sake of it, only when business demanded it. Benny had no fear; he had certainty.

Mae Huntman, however, had no inkling of her husband's Mafia connections and his role in the Lansky master plan. His boxing career allowed for the late nights, the quick trips, the sudden meetings, the flights to America. 'A bit of business' was always the explanation that cleared away any questions. It got so Mae didn't ask.

Others were more aware. On holiday in Cannes with Jack Solomons and his wife, the Huntmans were at dinner with the Regent of Iraq when Benny said about himself, 'Not bad for a Jewish kid from the East End of London, to be having dinner with an Arab prince, Your Highness.'

The Regent replied, 'Yes, for an Arab and Jew to sit and eat together . . . you make anything possible. You could probably get away with murder.'

'Yes, I could. I could,' said Benny.

The table fell silent; the Regent looked at Benny and laughed. Jack and Fay Solomons didn't even smile. The Solomons knew the unknown Benny better than most.

Benny Huntman kept in contact with the Regent of Iraq up until the prince, always accompanied by beautiful women when he met Benny, was murdered, along with most of the royal family, on 14 July 1958, in a *coup d'état* that ended the Iraqi monarchy. His body was trailed along al-Rashid Street and cut into pieces. It was the brutal end of one era and the turbulent start of another. And also the reason for the delay, for that moment, of Mafia intrusion into gambling in the Middle East, where there was a lot of interesting talk going on about oil exploration.

With Batista gone from Cuba and Castro in edgy control, Benny had met Jimmy Blue Eyes and Meyer Lansky in Florida in 1959. They had been joined a day later by Dino Cellini, who, like Santo Trafficante and Jake Lansky, had been briefly jailed in Havana in Triscornia Detention Camp, the immigration holding pen. They'd been visited there by Jack Ruby, who made three other trips to Cuba in 1959, accompanied by Lewis McWillie. The inside word was they were working on an arms deal. But for whom?

The transatlantic mob began hands-on arrangements for establishing their own casinos in the Bahamas and London. High on the agenda was top-class gaming staff for the casinos. The best way was to establish a Havana-type croupier school in London and from there feed the other European and Caribbean casinos. The Cellini brothers, the mechanics led by the master Dino Cellini, would be in charge. The move would also get around some early London and Washington objections to the gambling in the Bahamas; it had been leaked that officials were nervous about Las Vegas workers, believing they would be Mob employees.

Jimmy Blue Eyes would act and speak, as always, as though he were Lansky himself. At the meeting it was also agreed that Jimmy was to work directly with Benny in opening up London to Mafia gambling. Moves had already been made to get favourable treatment from Prime Minister Harold Macmillan's Conservative government, which was working on new UK gambling laws, in dealing with the British Governor and Executive Council legislators in the Bahamas. Contacts at the American Embassy in Grosvenor Square had been established. Hell, the Yanks were already in the middle of Mayfair. The aroma of profit was in the air; they could smell the money, and they were hungry for a taste of it.

Lansky knew all it would take *was* money. With him, there was always money. He was on the books as the kitchen manager of the Hotel Riviera, but his personal share in the enterprise was upwards of $4 million. It was his loss, and that of his investment associates, when Castro and the pigs took over, but he repeated to all who asked that there is always a risk in business. And Cuba was business.

The Mafia's financial wizard had led the way in numbered accounts and corporate investment, had legitimised, laundered, a fortune for decades before Castro took power, embraced Moscow and shut off America. He'd been forced to fold his hand in Cuba and he was pissed off enough to offer $1 million cash for Castro to be dead, but that was not just anger, it was also business. With Castro gone, the casinos 'the bearded bastard' had nationalised would be open again. It was Lansky's way, logical – revenge and a business result. Castro, meanwhile, got friendlier with Nikita Khrushchev just as John Fitzgerald Kennedy, Prohibition big shot Joe Kennedy's boy, was elected the 44th President of the United States.

Yes, said Lansky, he'd 'crapped out' when he left Havana, but that was a past deal. He'd lost a battle, not the war. When he met Benny in Miami and London, he seemed a happy man. 'We're on a new roll.' Lansky's health wasn't great, but he lived for the next move – 'Deals pump the blood to my heart' – and he had a portfolio of assets to bankroll it. As always, he was driving the destiny-mobile.

The slight snag was that gambling was illegal in the Bahamas. And so was the kind of brash, bonanza gaming they dreamed of setting up in London. But that was the point of the Limey, and he'd done well. He had many friends. He could help deliver the islands and London. On cue, the Betting and Gaming Bill was introduced to the British Parliament on 16 November 1959 by the unsuspecting Home Secretary, Mr Rab Butler. The House of Lords got it six months later.

Benny was helped in his lobbying of backbench MPs and Cabinet members by parliamentary contacts like Manny Shinwell, who was able to single out MPs of value in this particular quest. There was also an intriguing selection of others working for the same result. Among them were slumlord Peter Rachman, pilloried in the press for exploitation of his tenants, and his partner Raymond Nash. They lucratively employed the MP and lawyer Billy Rees-Davies, who'd lost an arm in the Second World War (and, yes, he was known as 'the One-Armed Bandit'), to help put through the Gaming Act. 'He cleverly talked it up to MPs,' said Nash. They also used the Labour MP Tom Driberg. Nash, who ran chemmy evenings, fronting clubs for Rachman, found Driberg unpleasant, always in need of protection, but 'he did the job for us'.

They all did. On 29 July 1960, the Betting and Gaming Act became law in a nation with an under-the-counter gambling turnover of nearly £700 million. In London and the rest of the country, it was open season for bingo halls, betting shops, casinos and clubs; Britain was pioneer country and Hellfire Club culture was back. Benny and the boys didn't rush at it; better to let some others lead the way and test for troubles.

The tall former boxer and Polish immigrant John Mills started Government-approved gaming at Les Ambassadeurs; Crockford's and old and new clubs, like John Aspinall's Clermont Club in Berkeley Square, followed. There was Al Burnett's Pigalle Club in Piccadilly and linked nightclubs like Mark Birley's Annabel's, which, located below the Clermont, brought in big money and celebrity. The gently affable, quietly spoken Birley, purveyor to the gentry of impeccable manners and taste, defined the secret of the club's success: 'It has to have exclusivity and lots of cunt around.'

Dino Cellini told Benny that when he and his brothers were growing up in Steubenville, the girls were 'fifty cents a crack and one dollar on Saturdays'. The casino charmer laughed, 'If you went early Sunday, you could get two for the price of one.'

Everything was going to cost much more in Paradise. But first, they had to play some hardball.

8

THE BANK OF MONTE CARLO

'Halfway to Paradise', Billy Fury, 1961

Christopher Columbus got to the Bahamas before any of them, but Meyer Lansky and Dino Cellini were more in the vampire tradition of buccaneer Henry Morgan and the monstrous pirate Blackbeard, who had the skull and crossbones tattooed on his heart. The islands were an unfairly uncared for fragment of the British Empire, which took a rather Duke of Windsor view of them, but at least they were left more or less alone. Others with interests there, however, preferred bloodsucking colonialism, which upped the ante. Whatever colours they flew, the pirates had never sailed away altogether.

When the incongruous Wallace Groves, convicted fraudster and multimillionaire (a phrase that always makes heads shake and invites wonder), first arrived in the Bahamas in the early 1930s, much of the islands were wilderness. He saw commercial potential for retail development and for tourism. He also went to see Stafford Sands, a character out of *King Solomon's Mines*. Sands was a giant of a man, with a huge girth and glass where his left eye had been. He and his career had prospered since the murder of Sir Harry Oakes. He was an especially clever politician, a devious genius some said, and his work had allowed the white-majority United Bahamian Party (UBP) to rise to power in the islands, while he became a member of the Government's Executive Council. Groves explained his idea: he had gone into the lumber business and explored the northern island of Grand Bahama, and there was much fresh water, with the potential for construction of a deep-water port. They could bring in tourists and there was always the possibility – just a possibility, mind you – of gambling, which was 'working out very well' in Cuba.

The Hawksbill Creek Act of 1955, created by Stafford Sands, did the dirty deal between Sands, acting for and as the government, and Wallace Groves for the sale of 150,000 acres of land at $2.80 an acre. Groves was given total power to levy licence fees on anyone who wanted to do business on Grand Bahama and could deport without explanation anyone he didn't particularly like. There would be no Bahamian taxes imposed for 99 years. It was a wonderful arrangement, a blank cheque, and easy to shake hands on.

The tax-free city of Freeport came into being and Groves was the boss of everything. He created companies with his friends in the UBP and with the merchants in Nassau, the influential business group the Bay Street Boys. If the name sounded like a bunch of gangsters, it wasn't too far off. They got 10 per cent of the place – the land, the harbour, the airport, the public utilities, the taxi company, the gross receipts of supermarkets and cinemas. Any other business? That'll be 10 per cent.

All the arrangements were legally looked after by Stafford Sands, who was getting more than 10 per cent. His fees were in the millions of dollars. The duplicitous dealings, involving Sands and Wallace Groves' Grand Bahama Development Company, and the many dovetailing corporate partners he created, had the full attention of the FBI.

Their investigations of the conniving and corruption were driven by fear of casino gambling in the self-governing British colony. It was a perfect location, offshore, tax happy, and only 70 miles from the Florida coastline. Indeed, Lou Chesler had suddenly appeared with $12 million and had teamed up with Groves and the Grand Bahama Development Company to sell building lots in Freeport. This was a legitimate business enterprise, but it did not go as well as the new 50–50 partners had planned. Certainly, that was what the financial books suggested.

Although not one word was intentionally publicly spoken, the cash machine for all this enterprise for the greater good, profit, was to be gambling, specifically the Lucayan Beach Hotel and Monte Carlo Casino at Freeport on Grand Bahama. That was decided in Miami in 1960 at a closed meeting between Lansky and Dino Cellini, Chesler and Max Orovitz, a Miami Beach money manager for Lansky and Chesler. The

Mafia would invest the start-up money for the casino, about $600,000. The rest was classic Mob, sure and safe and secure: everyone was paid, no one cheated, and the only ones who got hurt, physically or financially, were either foolish or greedy, and usually both. There was also talk of a move against Castro: spooks from the CIA had been all over the Cuban colony in Miami, Little Havana. 'They were looking for more than black-bean soup.'

The Grand Bahama Development Company continued, according to the bookkeeping, not to prosper as well as had been predicted. More incentive was needed, and the Executive Council and London were told this. A year on, Wallace Groves and the big men, Chesler and Sands, who avoided elevators together, hosted a private meeting with the islands' power brokers about starting legal gambling on Grand Bahama to bring tourists and much-needed money to the islands.

Premier Sir Roland Symonette, Attorney General Lionel Orr, Treasurer William Sweeting, their wives, and Colonial Secretary Kenneth Walmsley were told of the absolute necessity of gambling to boost their economy. The meeting, at the Fontainebleau Hotel in Miami Beach on 26 September 1961, was part of the soft sell.

When the influential guests had gone, one of the Bay Street Boys brought up the problem of the Bahamian government's anti-gambling stance and the coyness of the American and British governments. 'Always exceptions, proves the rule,' indicated the totally confident *Sir* Stafford Sands. (The knighthood had been bestowed in return for services to the empire or some such thing. He kept the citation with his collection of antique paperweights.)

Sir Stafford's confidence was, unsurprisingly, shared by Lansky. The gangster kept his offices at the Singapore Hotel, Miami, private from all but his intimates. It was at the favoured Fontainebleau Hotel (which had particularly large safe-deposit boxes in the manager's office) that, at the start of 1962, he met with his brother Jake, Dino Cellini, Charlie 'The Blade' Tourine, Michael 'Trigger Mike' Coppola and the bookmakers Max Courtney and Frank Ritter. At that meeting, they discussed expansion plans for Europe, as well as gambling in the Bahamas. Charlie the Blade's friend and partner Joe Nesline, who was the crime boss of Washington

DC, was in on the London deal and would travel there with Lansky to meet with Benny Huntman. Nesline had been born in Washington but raised in the shadowland breeding ground of Steubenville. His enforcer, Ralph 'Dum Dum' De Mark, was also from the Ohio town where the Cellini brothers had started out. Freddie Ayoub, another alumnus of Rex's Cigar Store, was also to be operative in London.

The Lansky syndicate front men and Lansky himself met with the Unione Corse in Paris, from where they were masterminding drug-trafficking from their heroin headquarters in Marseilles. There were also early plans for sex clubs in Amsterdam and throughout West Germany – 'they like that sort of thing' – all bankrolled by the gambling profits.

When gambling returned to the agenda, they agreed that Benny Huntman would find a location for the croupier school in London as soon as possible. Benny's efforts had been concentrated on the Mafia's gambling strategy, but he'd got back his boxing licence so that he could once again officially help with the transatlantic ring trade.

His skills and experience were needed, as all the years of eluding punishment had ended for Frankie Carbo. After what Federal Judge George Boldt, sitting in Los Angeles Superior Court on 2 December 1961, described as 'more than 40 years of violent crime', the emotionless Frankie, the Mr Gray of boxing, got 25 years in the slammer. He was sent to 'the Island', to the secure but spectacular Alcatraz in San Francisco Bay. The evidence against him had been expertly presented by the new president's brother, US Attorney General Robert Kennedy, such that Carbo was convicted of extortion and conspiracy for muscling in on the earnings of welterweight champion Don Jordan. On the same charges, Blinky Palermo got 15 years and the gunsel Joe Sica the same as his boss Carbo. Lou Dragna had a better lawyer and got five years, overturned on appeal.

Some months after the convictions, an enquiry was made as to who was running boxing with mastermind Mr Gray in the penitentiary. 'Frankie's organising everything from inside the pen, making the deals.' Nothing was allowed to prevent business being done. Mr Gray was still to be in charge of Sonny Liston, the dollar machine, the Great Greenback Hope.

To get business traction and ensure quick success in the Bahamas, Lansky offered Sir Stafford Sands an upfront $2 million, but the astute politician, who'd been around this track before, avoided being 'bought for life'. It clearly felt far better being rented; he said he would accept the money in legal fees, for making the necessary arrangements, which went ahead, as did the construction of the Lucayan Beach property.

Before ground was broken, Lansky, Dino Cellini and the Lucayan Beach architects met, and part of the building, 9,000 sq. ft in total on the drawings, was marked out as space for squash courts, what they called 'hardball courts'. Dino Cellini himself was in charge of designing this sports area, with precise places reserved for slot machines and craps tables and all the other accoutrements of gaming. The boys talked the hardball code, but their minds saw the Monte Carlo Casino.

No one else must. Any public opposition to large-scale gambling had to be stifled, as it had been in the early days in Florida and then in Nevada. Schools were built, church roofs repaired, regular contributions made to all manner of civic endeavours. God worked in his mysterious ways and one church even got a 999-year land lease. It was, in a fabulous display of faith, renewable.

Newspaper owner Sir Étienne Dupuch had protested against the evil of gambling since 1955, but as the Lucayan Beach foundations were laid, he became a $1,400-a-month consultant to the Grand Bahama Development Company, which supplied him with $50,000 of advertising. His attitude changed. Several others, including Sir Roland Symonette and his son Robert, Speaker of the House, also became consultants, on fees ranging from $14,000 to $68,000 a year. Lou Chesler wrote these payments off as 'softeners'. A monthly fee of $10,000 was also paid to Sir Roland's UBP, disguised as Sir Stafford Sands' legal retainer. On record, Sands had received $1,090,000 for his legal services to that point. Another $800,980 was billed for other law work.

As the Grand Bahama Development Company was, on paper, doing so badly, on 20 March 1963, Sands (for another fee, $123,000) set up a new company for the ever-more-flamboyant Wallace Groves, who was by now sporting cufflinks custom-made from Spanish doubloons discovered in the wreck of a pirate galleon. The shares of Bahamas Amusements Ltd were owned 50–50 between Lou Chesler and Groves's wife, Mrs Georgette Groves.

The attorney for Bahamas Amusements Ltd, Sir Stafford Sands, presented to the Executive Council the company's case for a Certificate of Exemption allowing gambling at casinos anywhere on Grand Bahama. If green-lighted, this would in turn be given automatic approval by the British governor, Sir Robert Tapeldon, who'd taken office in 1960. The Executive Council called a closed meeting to discuss the issue and voted 8–3 to grant the gambling licence on 1 April 1963.

It was pointed out, with amusement rather than as a result of serious conflict-of-interest concerns, that Sir Stafford Sands, as attorney for Bahamas Amusements Ltd, had negotiated a licence fee for the casinos with Sir Stafford Sands, the Minister of Finance. All around, he did quite a deal. On top of his already healthy remuneration, he received a further $515,900 in legal fees and a consultancy agreement allowing $50,000 a year for ten years.

There were some conditions. The casinos had to be operated along with hotels with more than 200 rooms. By happy chance, the Lucanyan Beach Hotel had 250 rooms. Wallace Groves, who controlled his affairs from the Grand Bahama Port Building, known to locals as 'the Kremlin', also happily agreed on behalf of the partners to employ only European casino staff. Luckily, training was about to start in London.

Benny Huntman had arranged with a friend, the owner of Selby's Banqueting Rooms in Hanover Street, Mayfair, to open a school for croupiers in the upstairs billiard room. It was to be operated by the London School of Turf Accountancy. A casino expert, Mr Dino Cellini, would oversee. Nigel Morris, the Bahamas Commissioner of Police, allowed a Bahamian identity document to be issued to Max Courtney so that he could travel to London and work with Cellini. He needed the travel document as, being wanted on federal charges in America, he had no valid US passport. Mr Morris argued that the so-called undesirability of Mr Courtney was a 'technical judgment'. Hey, they wanted the best possible croupiers for the Bahamas. The initial investment in the school was a quarter of a million dollars.

What could possibly go wrong in these happy islands with bank secrecy, no corporate or income taxes and legal gambling? The FBI seemed to think it would create 'a laundromat for hot money'. It's all a question of viewpoint. Lansky and company felt they were the men about to break the bank with the Monte Carlo. They'd been halfway there, now they were in Paradise.

The Lucayan Beach Hotel and Monte Carlo Casino were built by Lou Chesler's company Lucayan Beach Hotel and Development. Canadian companies held a majority of shares, but a sizeable portion was held by the family of Frank Nitti, who had taken over running Chicago when Al Capone 'went to college' at Alcatraz. Chesler vacuumed up huge investments from other companies he was involved with and skimmed for torrential-rainstorm days. But he shared the proceeds with his other partners. He knew much better than not to do that.

But he didn't care about another wealthy man, indeed one of the globe's richest men, George Huntington Hartford, who never bothered with his first name as the surname usually had the doors flying open. He was the heir of the Great Atlantic and Pacific Tea Company (the American A&P, the largest supermarket chain in the world) and enjoyed synchronised interests: beauty and young girls. Huntington Hartford was a powering pleasure seeker and saw what he wanted in Hog Island.

The owner, the Duke of Windsor's old friend the now ageing Swedish billionaire Axel Wenner-Gren, sold him a goodly portion for $14 million in 1960. Huntington Hartford, doing what someone should have thought of before, renamed Hog Island as Paradise Island. It was all aesthetics, buildings painted in ice-cream shades and many, many millions of dollars spent from then on. Huntington Hartford also brought in practical infrastructure, water and a sewage system, but chunks of cash went into the exquisite buildings. In Hartford's home, some of the bedrooms were equipped with two-way mirrors. He created the island's Ocean Club, his own Xanadu, from monastic stones that William Randolph Hearst had been unable to use at his epic monument to himself, San Simeon on the California coast, but had lovingly stored in a

Florida warehouse. The Ocean Club was a gem of a nightclub but, although exquisite, too exclusive to make commercial sense. Fiscal thoughts didn't jam Huntington Hartford's thinking until $24 million had gone into the project – with nothing in return.

He knew Salvador Dalí and the Duke and Duchess of Windsor and Richard Nixon. He'd spent time with heiresses Doris Duke and Barbara Hutton, and movie stars Marilyn Monroe ('too pushy, like a high-class hooker') and Lana Turner ('past her prime', he said, when he met her). Huntington Hartford liked prime. Throughout the 1950s, he would have employees approach young women on the street on his behalf. The first of his four wives was Marjorie Steele, an aspiring actress. When they married, she was a teenager. Huntington Hartford pursued his interests everywhere he went.

Charlie Da Silva could hustle anything and anybody. He was the premier confidence man of London and always did his homework. He knew the power the sight of a nubile female frame in a short, tight tennis skirt would have over Huntington Hartford. Da Silva got himself into the good graces of the governor of a girls' reform school in the English countryside and arranged for Huntington Hartford to go there for tea. He told him there was an investment opportunity, but not to mention to the governor about buying it. They had tea and buns, but Da Silva saw Huntington Hartford needed encouragement. He wandered over to the window, which he knew looked out over a tennis court. There were young girls in tennis skirts skipping around. Charlie offered, 'Oh, do have a look at the property.' The supermarket tycoon took a look, finished his tea, left the governor's office and before they got to the car Charlie had a cheque for a great big deposit on the place. Charlie had *sold* him the reform school.

Huntington Hartford had partied with Errol Flynn and done business with Aristotle Onassis and Howard Hughes. Yet when he was in trouble in Paradise, he approached 'the dean of gambling', Meyer Lansky. The plan was for Lansky to intercede regarding Huntington Hartford's application for a gambling licence for his Paradise Island resort in Nassau. It didn't work out, despite his offer to pay 50 per cent of the proceeds to the Government. Lansky, with his intermediary Sir Stafford Sands, had his own game. Huntington Hartford's gaming application was thrown out within 24 hours on 17 April 1963, 16 days after Bahamas Amusements Ltd had been successful. He tried again and again but it was a Wallace Groves consortium that won the gambling certificate of exemption, with no questions asked, only months later. Fed up with being sidelined, Huntington Hartford put Paradise Island up for sale. Almost immediately, it was bought by Mary Carter Paints, a corporation with hard-headed inclinations disguised by a disingenuous name. They took over for $3 million cash, assuming a $9 million mortgage and leaving Huntington Hartford with a quarter interest. Huntington Hartford, as Paradise Island's biggest player, was 'accommodated', but he didn't understand that in Mafia-speak that meant 'cheated'.

Cold War politics were again interfering with the Lansky syndicate plans. The Mob view was that the botched Bay of Pigs invasion of Cuba – 'three days, for fuck's sake' – which they had collaborated with had been 'a fuck-up' mainly because of Kennedy and his lack of aerial support. Angelo Bruno, 'Angie' to the cops in Philadelphia, where he was the Mafia's number one, was incredibly angered by the Kennedy clan. He was one of the eight members of the Mafia's ruling commission, a board member of the syndicate and enjoyed extraordinary influence. Meyer Lansky had met with Tony Varona, the leader of an anti-Castro group in South Florida, at Lansky's home in Miami in 1960, and the gangster had offered the Mafia's continuing support against Castro.

Shortly afterwards, Varona and his group employed the services of Washington lawyer E. Kipper Moss for propaganda and fund-raising. Kipper Moss founded Moss International Inc. in 1954, and through it represented the National Coffee Association and the Bank of America. More importantly, he advised 19 countries on business matters and helped the Democratic National Committee organise conventions. He was a hugely influential and politically connected operator. His mistress was Julia Cellini, sister of the Cellini brothers, whose secretarial-services business at 1025 Connecticut Avenue, Washington DC, was a front for Kipper Moss's activities – one of which was arranging for Dino Cellini to offer $2 million on behalf of the syndicate to Varona to finance operations against the Castro regime. The proviso was the understanding that the syndicate 'would share in the Cuba of the future'.

The Kennedy administration scuppered the plans by pre-empting Varona. The British had supplied intelligence to the White House and the CIA that the anti-Castro support was dismal, but that was ignored and they went for it on 17 April 1961. 'Futile. Stupid,' thought the Mob. The expat Cubans trained up by the CIA were no contest for Castro's men, who'd had years of revolutionary arms experience and received up-to-date help from their Moscow friends.

The CIA, acting without presidential approval, asked the Mob, through Santo Trafficante Jr, to assassinate Castro. Dino Cellini was an 'executive liaison' on the abortive Operation Mongoose. The Mob blamed a dilatory President Kennedy, even though they themselves had skimmed off millions of dollars in CIA funds intended for Cuban plotters. Lansky and company, especially Philadelphia's Angelo Bruno, decided JFK was just like his old man, 'a ratbag double-dealing bastard'. They felt betrayed and a good deal of that resentment had nothing to do with patriotism, but simply with business, with the loss of funds and opportunity in Havana. Lansky and even more so Sam Giancana believed killing Castro would have opened up the golden streets of Havana once again. They truly hated the Kennedy family.

The anger was deepened by US Attorney General Robert Kennedy's public pledge to hound organised crime. 'And we put his brother in the White House.' The Kennedy brothers were playing good cop, bad cop with the Mob. JFK had met with the Mafia to enlist their support in the 1960 election. His mistress Judith Campbell Exner told me in 1976 in Long Beach, California, that she had personally taken money to the influential Mob boss Sam Giancana, with whom she also slept, when she wasn't spending nights with his Mr Fixit, Johnny Roselli. President Kennedy wanted help, but he didn't want to pay for it with influence. Giancana was wiretapped and was heard saying, 'The President will get what he wants out of you, but you won't get anything out of him.'

The Mob were in the middle of this game as icicles were forming all over the Cold War. The Russians had placed missiles in Cuba and at the same time a British political sex scandal had the FBI active in Benny Huntman's London.

They'd opened the file, codenamed 'Bowtie', on the war minister John Profumo, who had slept with model Christine Keeler, who had slept with a Soviet attaché, Yevgeni Ivanov. Their immediate concern was whether the pillow talk had involved atomic secrets.

Christine Keeler had been introduced to Profumo by Stephen Ward, whom Benny Huntman knew through Jack Hylton. This small world was in a whirl; everywhere, the spooks and the cops were spinning about looking for reds under the beds and spies in the skies. All, irritatingly, as Lansky and company made the big moves.

The animosity between Robert Kennedy and the FBI's director-dictator J. Edgar Hoover gave the global gamblers more room, but their movements by commercial plane from the Bahamas to Miami and other cities in Florida were closely monitored. The two-man surveillance teams were surprisingly efficient in doing that: doorstepping in Paradise was a pleasant assignment. Yet they missed the clandestine boat trips and the misdirecting chug-chug of private planes that set off in one direction but carried on the journey in another, taking money and intelligence. The world was on edge; it was buzzing. The chance of tomorrow even arriving was being given odds. And the dice were rolling internationally on behalf of the syndicate.

The Lucayan Beach Hotel and Monte Carlo Casino was under way, with marketing materials advertising exclusive European croupiers and casino staff. The taint of Las Vegas by proxy that an American accent might suggest was not to be permitted. Yet, looking around the embryo Monte Carlo, it could have been Vegas, or Havana, with such a bunch of familiar faces. These were 'necessary and exempted casino experts' and included: Dusty Peters; the evergreen George Sadlo – he'd just turned 80 years old – tempted once more out of retirement; the Cellini brothers; and Frank Ritter, Max Courtney and Charles Brudner, who were now on wanted warrants throughout mainland America. Frank Ritter, aka Frank Reiter, was credit manager, a role vital to the casino profits; most gamblers plan to win, not lose, so they don't empty their bank accounts before take-off. When they lose, as the odds dictate they must, the essential knack is to know how much credit to extend to whom. Frank Ritter knew what most gamblers of the world were worth. He'd bet his mother on it, and said so. Other regular faces included Hickey Kamm, Al Jacobs, Dave Geiger, Abe Schwartz, Tony Tabasso, Roy Bell, Jim Baker, Jack Metler and Ricky Ricardo, the executive corps. But, as promised, the British were coming.

Dino Cellini took his usual room at the London Hilton on Park Lane. He was hiring croupiers. One of the first was Tom Gerard, a good-looking Scot with curly blond hair. He was a barman at the Hilton. He was also an actor and had worked with Stanley Baker, who had produced and starred in a 1960 film, *The Criminal*, as a gangland super-operator modelled on Benny Huntman's friend Albert Dimes. It was at that time that the FBI office in Washington had archived 'Italian Albert' as a Mafia point man in London. Like London buses, fame arrived in a cluster.

Dino Cellini spent much of each day at the croupier school, which officially ran five days a week from 11 a.m. till 11 p.m. It was unlikely he'd discover a mechanic as good as he was, but never say never. With Benny Huntman, he'd imported the American gaming tables into the Selby Rooms, though many extra had arrived in the shipment and were in storage. There had also been consignments of slot machines, the mechanical one-armed bandits that clubs in and around London were being invited to install for an ongoing kickback. It was a duplicate of the manipulated jukebox business on the US East Coast. This time, the contact was with the Bally Company of Chicago, operated by Morris Kleinman, yes, the legendary Jewish gangster Morris Kleinman who ran liquor for Lansky during Prohibition. The geography and the machines might change but not the purpose or, other than because of natural or required passings, the personnel.

Sometimes enthusiasm ran away with the younger elements among the salespeople, those who didn't know their history. Wartime spy and champion safe-breaker Eddie Chapman, a close friend of Britain's gangster overlord Billy Hill, ran a club in Surrey and some pressure was exerted on him to join the fun: 'They came down to see me suggesting I operate their machines. I said no, and that was the end of the argument. They asked about me and were told to behave. Probably wasn't so easy for other clubs.'

At the Selby Rooms, there was that casino hush, as if the

room is holding its breath, punctuated only by the rattle of dice and the gathering of chips in quick-moving craps games. Amid the gamblers were half-moon tables holding blackjack set-ups and roulette wheels. Dino Cellini told visitors that 'the British accent sends the American customers wild'. He was very open in his availability and recruitment. Everything had been approved, the paperwork stamped, by the UK government. The correct departments had been very kind. He said selecting trainees was an instinctive process. 'When you're closed in for so long in such a small room, you soon learn to sort them out.' This was the green baize of opportunity.

Roger Huntman helped his father, arranging this, doing that and setting up the apparatus of the croupier school. He exercised at Joe Bloom's Gym, as did another young guy, David Cornwell, who was working as a £6-a-week delivery boy for the Charles Jourdan shoe shop on Old Bond Street. The two often had lunch together and in the evening went to the clubs that were opening around every corner in London, 'but mostly Soho'. With sharp eyes and a good mind, David Cornwell makes a solid witness.

'Because Roger's father was a fight promoter and a partner of Jack Solomons, the leading boxing promoter in the UK, we went to Joe Bloom's, where all the top fighters from all over the world used to work out. One time, we met Muhammad Ali there with his manager Angelo Dundee.

'We're up at the gym one day and Roger says to me, "Dad wants to meet us downstairs in a restaurant, he wants to introduce us to someone." After we finished up, we went down to this restaurant, it was an Italian, and his dad was with another man, and he said, "Boys, say hello to Dino." We shook hands with this Dino. After some small talk, Benny told us that Dino Cellini was opening a casino on the island of Grand Bahama in the Caribbean. The casino would be a very classy operation and would be located in a top hotel, newly built, named the Lucayan Beach Hotel.

'Benny then said, "Dino is going to train you to be dealers in a casino and take you to the Bahamas."

'I looked at Roger and said, "Is this true or what?"

'The Dino guy just wanted to know, "Are you interested?"

'"You bet. We'll do it."

'We had to go to this school in Hanover Square where

Roger's dad and Dino had converted upstairs into a mini-casino and they had two or three people up there teaching. I had never been in a casino in my life. We were only 18 years or so old. I was living at home with my parents in Highgate. There was about a hundred other guys, mainly Italians, who Dino had approached: "Do you want to go to the Bahamas? I'll teach you to be a dealer."

'It was strict training for six months, so I got a job that started at Covent Garden about 4 a.m., delivering drinks to all the theatres in the West End. I learned how to carry two full crates of Coca-Cola up to the top bars of the theatres. It was hard work and put me in good physical shape very quickly. I was to discover that there were hidden benefits to the job, as the boss of our crew used to give me a tip every week of £4. How this money was made, I didn't ask about. I'd finish about 10 a.m. and go up to the school.

'After enrolment, we were assigned to individual teams and given times we were to attend. The school was run by Dino and Neto [Vincenzo] Spertino, his brother-in-law, who had a background in casinos in Italy. Also, the school was endorsed by the London School of Turf Accountancy, who at graduation distributed diplomas to trained dealers. A lot of very colourful American characters came around the school who obviously knew Dino Cellini well and some had worked with him in Havana.

'I was assigned training in American craps on an East Coast layout. This game is dealt on a large table, as big as a billiard table, and the dealers are on each end, as opposed to a Western Game, which is dealt from the side. We began by getting to know the feel of the chips – a croupier has to be able to sort them into groups by touch alone – and we played the games again and again and again. It was as tense as genuine games.

'As well as Italians training, there were many Jewish kids at the school who had a natural ability for gambling. Roger Huntman and I worked hard and completed the course after six months and were accepted to work in the Bahamas.'

Benny Huntman had really begun to work with his benefactors. He had to be careful; his manipulation of boxers and fights had got him unwanted attention. There must be no interference. His son Roger, a carefully spoken man, was to be his eyes and ears.

'In 1962, my father flew to Miami to meet Jimmy Blue Eyes and Meyer Lansky, and the full extent of Lansky's plans was explained to him. He was to ease the way for American gambling in London and then throughout the country and into Europe and the Middle East. There had already been talks with connections in Belgrade, Amsterdam and Brussels and Beirut. A year later, Dino Cellini came to London to join up with my father. He was a laid-back character, softly spoken and, like most Italian Americans, used his arms demonstrably when speaking; he had a strong personality and spoke with authority and was given the respect he demanded.

'An intense man, with emotions you felt could explode at any time, he was courteous at all times, and oozed sophistication and class, a highly intelligent, focused man, and with my father's connections, they were formidable. They built a bond of trust and friendship. It was open season for gambling in London.

'The Macmillan government had brought in the Gaming Act to "control" the action, but it was like the Wild West. My father arranged with his friend the owner of Selby's to open the croupier school there. The idea was to train British croupiers to learn the American style of gambling to work on Grand Bahama, where only British croupiers could be employed in the casino. That was to keep out American underworld activity coming from Las Vegas and Cuba. They were naive to the extreme.

'Two months before we were due to go to the Bahamas, my father and Dino opened a gambling club called the George Cinq in the Selby Rooms, using the American-style gaming tables. After the croupier school closed each evening, I went along with other dealers to work at the George Cinq, dealing blackjack and running American dice and roulette games way into the night.

'It wasn't for fun. There was a purpose. Over the space of the first few weeks of the club's opening, I was told officials from the Home Office and Foreign Office would come to my table and I was to give them a credit line of up to £5,000. I was told by my father or Dino when that person was in the casino and who it was.

'It happened with three people over a two-week period, twice with one person and the other two just once. Each time,

149

the marked player asked for £300 in chips and played blackjack for about an hour and signed a credit note with me. There was a special blackjack table for these Whitehall and American officials, and I was the only one who dealt for them. The club never gave cash over £1,000 to a customer, but wrote a cheque. My customers never won or lost more than £50 in a sitting. When they had finished playing, I called Dino or my father and handed the credit note over. They went to the cashiers' till, where the credit note was handed back to them and a cheque was written out, which meant that the cheque had to be for £1,000 or more.

'Because they'd been paid by cheque, those British government officials couldn't deny they had received cash from the casino and not deliver, couldn't take the money and run.

'This same business transaction also involved two American Embassy officials. All five were now in the pocket of Dino and my father. The Lucayan Beach Hotel had just been completed and the casino could now open up if there were no last legal difficulties or problems with the British or American governments. That wasn't likely.

'While we were waiting to fly out, Dino asked me to go up to Liverpool to work in a club there. He'd been visiting potential clubs in the Midlands, Manchester, Newcastle and Glasgow. He had talked with the owners of this club in Liverpool, and he was in there. The intent was to get American gaming into every casino in Europe, and if not take over, certainly take a great deal of the action. With the Bahamas up and running, the door would open.'

And destiny, preordained or not, helped as well. America suddenly had greater concerns. President John F. Kennedy was assassinated in Dallas on 22 November 1963.

9

THE TWILIGHT ZONE

'Walk on the Wild Side', Jimmy Smith, 1962

With the shock of Dallas, nobody knew what to think and everybody was being told what to believe. The conspiracy theories began in tandem with the relentless news bulletins. They arrived so fast they were somersaulting over each other. After the Mob-attached Jack Ruby, who as a boxer was known as 'Sparkling' Ruby, gunned down marksman Lee Harvey Oswald two days after JFK's assassination, it took the worldwide conjecture to spectacular heights. As the days and weeks and months went on, the links between lone gunman Oswald, Ruby and the Mafia and the CIA, the anti-Castro movement, Cuba and the Bay of Pigs debacle were whipped up into an incredible confection.

Shadows were darkening every corner, haunting logic out of the way. There *was* much Mob influence within the CIA and the FBI, and as such they could easily be manipulated in the killing of the President. They certainly had motivation, for they believed that President Kennedy and his brother Bobby were traitors who would stop their business expansion. Roger Huntman is adamant, given his feedback, that this was classic Mafia, getting obstacles obliterated to protect future profit.

'I can't emphasise that enough,' he says. 'The Kennedys stood in the way of Lansky and the Mob's gambling ambitions in the Bahamas, London and Europe. While the Kennedys were in business, the Mafia were out of business there. The Bahamas was the Mob's gateway to unimaginable riches. The Kennedys went to war with organised crime after the Mob, with the Teamsters union, helped JFK to win the presidency. Joe Kennedy assured them there would be no investigations into their activities. The main American prosecutor said the assassination had the standout signs of organised crime. You bet.

'Dino Cellini knew Ruby and so did Trafficante. Lansky knew everybody. There's such a thing as coincidence but it's difficult to believe the Mob got lucky and somebody out of the blue, Oswald, assassinated Kennedy and they got the result they needed. Chance doesn't enter their business.

'Bobby Kennedy believed the Mob were behind Kennedy's assassination. Carlos Marcello's personal private investigator, David Ferrie, during the 1950s was pictured with Lee Harvey Oswald. Marcello admits on FBI tapes that he killed JFK. Hundreds of hours of FBI tape were never released. Oswald's uncle was bookmaker for Marcello. Jack Ruby, who had cancer, also worked for Marcello and his loyalty remained. Lansky and Marcello were partners in gambling clubs in and around New Orleans. Lansky had meetings with Marcello at the Shoe Bar Club, in which he had money, in New Orleans. It followed a pattern and always has; look at the murder of Sir Harry Oakes. Don't get in the way. In an act of betrayal, the Kennedy family got in the way and then couldn't escape the power of the Mob.'

Some of the trainees from Dino Cellini's croupier school had gone to the movies on a cold November afternoon and as they left the Odeon, Marble Arch, where they'd seen Albert Finney as Tom Jones, they were met with the news of the assassination in headlines screaming across the front of the London *Evening News*. A couple of them had planned to buy the new, second LP from the Beatles, *With the Beatles*, which had just arrived in the shops. That, along with many other plans, was forgotten.

For Roger Huntman, it was like a green light: 'That was a Friday and on the Monday we were told we were off to Grand Bahama. The world and our world had changed.'

The entire American Mafia syndicate was to profit in some way from Meyer Lansky's mission to run gambling in every corner of the world. There was only one proviso: his ambitions must not be interfered with by anybody else's. This was where the Kennedy family were enraging the Mob: they wouldn't stay out of the picture. John Kennedy, although having the 1960 presidential Mob vote through Joseph Kennedy, had pursued them from 1957, when he sat on the Senate Rackets

Committee chaired by John McClellan of Arkansas. Robert Kennedy was the committee's chief counsel. The brothers fiercely quizzed Carlos Marcello, the Mafia godfather of Louisiana and Texas, Mickey Cohen from Los Angeles and the Teamsters union leader Jimmy Hoffa. These people were all cruel enemies to make.

It got worse. When RFK became US Attorney General in 1961, the Justice Department went after organised crime, indicting 116 members of the Mob. He increased Mob prosecutions more than a dozen times over the previous Eisenhower administration. He waged a personal vendetta against Hoffa and pursued Carlos Marcello, who had been born in Tunisia of Sicilian parents; he'd joined the flow of immigrants to America in 1910. Marcello used a fake Guatemalan birth certificate to avoid deportation to Italy. RFK, well aware Marcello was not a Guatemalan, had immigration agents place him aboard a 78-seat jet as its only passenger and drop him off in Guatemala City. Marcello and his lawyer were later flown to El Salvador, where soldiers dumped the two bespoke-suited men in the wilderness. Marcello fainted three times and broke several ribs before finding his way to a small airport. Secretly back into New Orleans, he promised revenge against the Kennedy brothers: 'You know what they say in Sicily: if you want to kill a dog, you don't cut off the tail, you cut off the head.'

A more evenly worded, and considered, threat came from Santo Trafficante Jr: 'Kennedy's not going to make it to the 1964 election – he's going to be hit.' Trafficante had inside knowledge (according to a US Department of State document uncensored in 2011) that made killing President Kennedy a 'business priority'. A coup to overthrow Castro had been planned for 1 December 1963, at the behest of JFK, ten days after his visit to Dallas. The intention was to intervene, with great force if necessary, to bring democracy American-style to Cuba. Yet this would be a purely US government operation, no dirty tricks, no mobsters. The CIA had decided in 1960 that it would be a grand plan to assassinate Fidel Castro and that the Mafia should be employed to do the deed, as that was their particular area of expertise. This was a conflict of interest with RFK, who was attempting to eradicate the gangsters to whom the CIA wanted to pay suitcases of dollars to whack Castro with extreme prejudice – no questions asked, provide bank account number.

In an absurdly turbulent scenario, the CIA hired the former FBI agent Robert Maheu to contact and contract Hollywood's Handsome Johnny Roselli, the friend of Frank Sinatra, who had played a huge role in President Kennedy's inauguration. Maheu, who worked in Las Vegas for Howard Hughes, said he was representing corporate gambling interests who'd lost a fortune in Cuba. The former spook was led by Roselli to 'Sam Gold', who was Giancana, and a guy called 'Joe', Santo Trafficante Jr. The imaginative CIA agents provided the Mob with poisoned pills and cigars with which to take out Castro. There was no success and there never could have been. The Mob thought the weapons so ridiculous they took the CIA cash and found better use for the poison. Yet the CIA men pushed the Mafia to pursue Castro. Roselli ran a sniper training camp in the Florida Keys and plots evolved on and on until the Cuban Missile Crisis in 1962, when nuclear-warhead envy took over the debate.

A year later, the Kennedy brothers wanted nothing to do with the Mob. Their stated intention, in writing, was to keep organised crime away from the Castro plot being orchestrated. Agents were to make it appear the provocative, Moscow-upsetting action, the State Defense Contingency Plan for a Coup in Cuba, was staged from within the Cuban government. There was more galling information. The Mob were to be banned in perpetuity from reopening their casinos in Havana. And their every movement in the Bahamas was being shadowed by the FBI.

But hang on in there! The deal had been done: with Castro gone, the Mob 'would share in the Cuba of the future'.

Now, however, they were being shut out.

The mobsters, especially those who had invested heavily in the Cuban casinos, couldn't believe it. 'Fuck's sake. *For fuck's sake!*' They'd helped JFK win the White House with their political fixes, they'd connived with the CIA to kill Castro and now the Kennedy brothers were prohibiting them from 'dipping their beaks'. In their world, that was a capital offence. The Mafia were not in business for politics but profit; politicians and their ambitions only mattered when the Mob could cash in. By murdering Kennedy, they could get the Government off their backs and get on with making money.

They had the means and the motive. They also had the connections to Lee Harvey Oswald and his killer Jack Ruby, who by shooting Oswald began an ongoing conspiracy business. If you telescope the extraordinary circumstantial evidence, it gives a painful picture of an angry and disturbed section of America in the early 1960s.

If it is considered against the Mafia's purity of motive – cash profit – it takes on significance. Lee Harvey Oswald was partly raised by Lillian and Charles Murret, his aunt and uncle, in New Orleans. In April 1963, Oswald stayed in New Orleans with the Murrets. Charles Murret was a bookmaker in a gambling operation run by Carlos Marcello; Oswald helped out as a runner collecting wagers for his uncle for a few months, which put him in direct contact with the gangster world of the Big Easy.

Politics followed: that summer Oswald distributed leaflets about the Fair Play for Cuba committee, giving 544 Camp Street as the committee's office. In that building was former FBI agent Guy Banister, who was working as a private detective; his principal client was Carlos Marcello. David Ferrie, a former airline pilot who'd publicly denounced JFK for the failure of the Bay of Pigs invasion, worked for Banister. In 1955, Ferrie ran a New Orleans squadron of the Civil Air Patrol. One of his cadets was Oswald. The two men were pictured together in Clinton, Louisiana, in September 1963. On two weekends before JFK's assassination, Ferrie met Carlos Marcello; on the night of 22 November, David Ferrie drove 350 miles through a rainstorm to Houston; he spent hours making calls from public phones at a skating rink. Had Marcello been using Ferrie to help plot the killing of Kennedy? Was Ferrie's Texas trip to make sure, from telephones beyond Carlos Marcello's immediate domain, that Jack Ruby silenced Oswald? It is seductive material.

Jack Ruby worked for the Chicago outfit, for Tony Accardo and Sam Giancana; he'd moonlighted with Santo Trafficante Jr. Yet in 1963, his closest regular Mob contact was Carlos Marcello, who controlled prostitution, narcotics and slot machines in Dallas. During early November 1963, Ruby made an exceptional number of telephone calls to Jimmy Hoffa's contacts, to crime bosses in Chicago and New Orleans and to Johnny Roselli in Los Angeles.

Frank Sinatra had that year sponsored Johnny Roselli as a member of the Friars' Club, the Hollywood celebrity fraternity of which almost every famous entertainer was a member. Handsome Johnny got in and got lucky with a clever card-cheating operation that took members, including Phil 'Sergeant Bilko' Silvers, Zeppo Marx, himself a spectacular card cheat, and Debbie Reynolds' husband Harry Karl, for hundreds of thousands of dollars. The card caper involved spies in the attic who peered through peepholes to read the cards of the players; they sent coded electronic signals to a member of the ring seated at the table, who picked up the messages on equipment he wore on a girdle beneath his clothes. Why not? It was there for the taking. Roselli couldn't resist, even with the pressure to kill the President of the United States. Money mattered. Money motivated.

And being kept away from it added to the anger that provoked Carlos Marcello to organise the hit on JFK. He worked with Sam Giancana and Johnny Roselli and, arguably, one of the most evil mobsters of them all, Santo Trafficante Jr. Trafficante always seemed a bitter man, a man who was depressed by the success of rivals *and* associates. He didn't have friends. He had a curl of the lip and utter cynicism. He tolerated people like Meyer Lansky when he believed he himself should have been running the Mafia world. He was like a banished Roman general who'd been away hacking at the Gauls for too long, a man willing to do anything for what he wanted, for self-glorification.

Trafficante carried with him an unsettling detachment. The evidence makes him the pivotal behind-the-scenes player in the assassination, with his principal cohorts Carlos Marcello, Sam Giancana and Johnny Roselli. There is a story that a Corsican sniper was offered the JFK assignment but rejected it; he claimed two other shooters took the job and worked alongside Lee Harvey Oswald. If you accept that the Mob killed Kennedy, then you accept that there was no lone gunman. But how many shots were fired and by whom?

Almost half a century on, those six seconds of photographic images from Dallas, on the day a president died and an industry was born, remain freeze-framed in memory, those tragic ticks of time still the most studied and debated in American history: Jackie Kennedy in her pink suit and matching pillbox hat, JFK grinning and waving, the crowds cheering and the gunshots that shattered the world, stopped the Camelot carousel.

The consensus on what happened, from official documents and investigations:

On 22 November 1963 at 12:30 p.m. US central time in Dallas, Texas, as President Kennedy's open-top car entered Dealey Plaza, which included the Texas School Book Depository, the First Lady of Texas, Nellie Connally, turned around to JFK, who was sitting behind her: 'Mr. President, you can't say Dallas doesn't love you.'

When JFK's car turned left, passed the depository and continued down Elm Street, shots were fired at Kennedy; many witnesses heard three shots. Others did not identify the first gunshot blast they heard as a weapon being fired and there was scant reaction from the crowd or the motorcade to the first shot, with many later saying they heard what they first thought to be a firecracker or a car exhaust backfire. Within one second of each other, President Kennedy, Governor Connally and Jacqueline Kennedy all turned abruptly from looking to their left to looking to their right. Connally immediately recognised the sound of a high-powered rifle, then he turned his head and torso rightward, attempting to see President Kennedy behind him. Connally could not see JFK and started to turn forward again, and was hit in his upper right back by a bullet, fired in a gunshot that Connally did not hear the muzzle blast from. He then shouted, 'Oh, no, no, no. My God. They're going to kill us all!'

Mrs Connally heard a first loud, frightening noise that came from somewhere behind her and to her right; she immediately turned towards JFK and saw him with his arms and elbows already raised high with his hands close to his throat. She then heard another gunshot and John Connally started shouting. Mrs Connally then turned away from President Kennedy towards her husband, then another gunshot sounded and she and the limousine's rear interior were now covered with fragments of bone, blood and brain matter. As President Kennedy waved to the crowds on his right with his right arm upraised on the side of the presidential limousine, a shot entered his upper back, penetrated his neck, slightly damaged a spinal vertebra and the top of his right lung, exited his throat just beneath his Adam's apple, then nicked the left side of his suit tie knot. He then raised his elbows and clenched his fists in front of his face and neck, then leaned forward and towards his left. Jackie Kennedy, who was facing her husband, put her arms around him. The same bullet went into Governor Connally's back, causing an oval entry wound, impacted and destroyed four inches of his right, fifth rib bone, exited his chest just below his right nipple, creating a two-and-a-half-inch oval sucking-air chest wound, then entered just above his right wrist, impacted and cleanly fractured his right wrist bone, exited just below the wrist at the inner side of his right palm and entered his left inner thigh.

A fourth bullet, the final shot, entered the rear of President Kennedy's head then exploded out a roughly oval-shaped hole from his head's rear and right side. Head matter, brain, blood and skull fragments, from JFK, covered the interior of the car, the inner and outer surfaces of the front glass windshield and raised sun visors, the front engine hood, the rear trunk lid, the follow-up Secret Service car and its driver's left arm, and motorcycle officers riding on both sides of the President behind him. Jackie Kennedy then reached out onto the rear trunk lid. When she'd crawled back into her car seat, she said, 'They have killed my husband. I have his brains in my hand.' Secret Serviceman Clint Hill was on the left front running board of the back-up car, immediately behind the presidential limousine. Hill heard one shot and jumped off into Elm Street and ran forward to try and get on the limousine and protect the President when he heard two more shots. After JFK was shot in the head, Hill said Jackie Kennedy began to climb out onto the back of the limousine; he thought she was reaching for something, possibly a piece of the President's skull.

When he left the Texas School Book Depository building and collected his revolver at his rooming house, Oswald shot dead policeman J.D. Tippit, who was about to question him. Six witnesses identified Oswald as Tippit's killer. Three watched him discard empty cartridges. The cartridges matched the gun he was carrying when police seized him in a cinema. Fragments of the bullets that hit the President were matched with the rifle found on the sixth floor of the Depository. Oswald's fingerprints were on the rifle barrel. Fibres from the clothes he wore when arrested were caught on the rifle butt. Yet evidence from the crowd and policemen suggests there was another gunman in Dealey Plaza, firing from a grassy knoll in front of the presidential motorcade. An acoustics expert who examined a police Dictabelt recording made of one of the two radio channels used during the motorcade said that sounds on the belt came from an escorting motorcycle with its microphone stuck open, that four shots could be detected on the belt and that there was a 50–50 probability that one of them came from the knoll. Other experts put the probability at 95 per cent. There had been a conspiracy.

With JFK dead, it was suddenly gambling time in the Bahamas. The Lucayan Beach Hotel and Casino complex was to open on 31 December 1963 in a 'Mambo Italiano' moment resonant of Havana. It was fanfared as 'hello, 1964' and advertised as 'the place billionaires go to get away from millionaires'. With tremors of Bugsy Siegel's Flamingo, the accommodations and facilities weren't quite ready. But Lou Chesler's cheap flights for the croupiers were. He'd arranged for them to fly to the Bahamas via Canada, where he'd made special financial and immigration arrangements. It made for a long flight for David Cornwell and the others, who were to encounter some intriguing personnel in their first overseas employment:

'It was a hell of trip via Canada. I was 19 years old and it was a whole new world to me. We'd been told we would be leaving on a chartered flight to open the casino for New Year's Eve 1963. We didn't find this out until after the assassination of John Kennedy. I had no idea how it was linked to the owners of the new casino venture in the Bahamas.

'We landed on Grand Bahama at an airport located on the west of the island. It was not what we'd imagined it would look like. There was nothing there, only miles and miles of flat coral covered in young fir trees; all the old trees had been cut down for lumber by a man called Wallace Groves, a disgraced stockbroker from New York who had promoted the casino project with the Bahamian government.

'We were greeted at the airport by Frank Ritter, one of the casino bosses, and a bunch of Bahamian policemen who proceeded to frisk us. We had to go into a room, up against the wall, and be body searched. I don't know what they thought they were looking for. We were all kids.

'We were then bussed to the "town" on Grand Bahama that comprised one motel, one mini-market, two banks and various small apartment buildings. Talk about a one-horse town . . . I will always remember looking out of this bus and saying, "Where's the bloody palm trees?" There was just nothing there.

'We were put in an apartment building while housing, a village in the middle of the jungle with minimal facilities, was being constructed. The more we heard about this village, the worse we felt, but being young and on an adventure what did we care? I was very green. I shared a small apartment with Roger Huntman but couldn't start work in the casino as the hotel construction was behind schedule. They asked us to work on it.

'After a few weeks, everyone was becoming extremely bored with the situation. You can imagine how a bunch of young virile men from a town like London being marooned on this lump of coral in the Caribbean would feel about this isolation. There was nothing to do at night; this was practically a desert island. There was one bar and restaurant and the Royal Bank of Canada. That was all there was in the whole bloody place. As a distraction, some of the clever Italian guys started organising chemmy games in the apartments, and some of those games got really out of line. Sometimes the money bet was unbelievable. Guys were betting a whole month's salary. Some of the more experienced men made large amounts of money. A pub opened up, eventually. There was television, but it was primitive.

'There was absolutely no female company on the island and a few boys who had money flew over to Miami Beach to relieve the boredom. There was some relief when a group of young cocktail waitresses arrived from Miami to work in the casino, and the juggling and prancing for their attentions was something to behold. I remember one young man called Ronnie Cooper took up with a French girl, then it turned out that he was wanted in London by the police for the murder of a bookmaker and he was promptly extradited. I think he got life, and his girlfriend took it very badly.

'I waited out this period and the casino finally opened on 22 January 1964 with the society-crowd Hope Ball. The casino was full, but the celebrities at the opening were not players, so we didn't do much business. It was a beautiful place, a luxurious hotel with wonderful rooms. The casino was

Benny Huntman (second left) with the legendary Jack Dempsey, who was the catalyst for his American ventures. They're flanked by the popular US dancing duo the Astor Brothers. (courtesy of Roger Huntman)

The sociopath gunsel and Mafia boxing czar Frankie Carbo as he looked when the young Benny Huntman first met him in New York. (© Getty Images)

Benny Huntman was immaculate as ever even when training with the world's first Hispanic boxing champion, Panama Al Brown, in London. (courtesy of Roger Huntman)

The massive bulk of Primo Carnera was too much for many opponents to handle. Here Carnera is gloved up by London manager Benny Huntman before a gym sparring session.

In a dodgy corner: Benny Huntman with one of the Mafia's most exploited fighters, the Italian giant Primo Carnera. (courtesy of Roger Huntman)

Benny Huntman on the town with one of his most talented boxers, the superbly eager Eric 'Boy' Boon, who heralded the rise of Jack Solomons' management empire. (courtesy of Roger Huntman)

Benny Huntman caring for another of his great hopes, Danny O'Sullivan, one of three brothers known as the 'Fighting O'Sullivans', and the great-uncle of snooker champion Ronnie O'Sullivan. (courtesy of Roger Huntman)

Benny and Mae Huntman on a night out at the extremely overweight Teddy Brown's club; he was known, of course, as 'the Thin Man'.
(courtesy of Roger Huntman)

An autographed tribute to 'England's best manager', Benny Huntman, from his American import Gus Lesnevich.
(courtesy of Roger Huntman)

In the shadows: Benny Huntman stands behind Gus Lesnevich at Harringay Arena on 14 May 1946, with Freddie Mills beside them, before the world light heavyweight title fight. Mills lost the match, which was called 'the greatest fight in British boxing history'. (© Getty Images)

Prince Abdul Illah, the Regent of Iraq, between Benny Huntman and Jack Solomons, with companions, in the south of France.
(courtesy of Roger Huntman)

On the town – it was rare for Mae Huntman to join her husband on the social circuit, but when she did she was much admired. (courtesy of Roger Huntman)

Welsh boxer Tommy Farr, Joe Louis and Benny Huntman are caught off guard at the Colony Club gaming tables.
(courtesy of Roger Huntman)

Roger Huntman gets into show business at the Colony Club before Judy Garland begins rehearsals. (courtesy of Roger Huntman)

The 1940s movie-star look: Dino Cellini's wife, Helena, aged 20, around the time she met her future husband. (courtesy of Dino Cellini Jr)

Dino Cellini outside the Colony Club, having been asked to pose by George Raft. (courtesy of Dino Cellini Jr)

Colony Club chips featuring George Raft's image.

A letter from Jack Hylton to Benny Huntman. (courtesy of Roger Huntman)

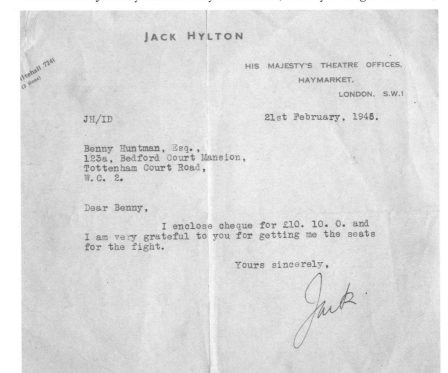

JACK HYLTON

HIS MAJESTY'S THEATRE OFFICES,
HAYMARKET,
LONDON, S.W.1

ltehall 7241
(3 lines)

JH/ID   21st February, 1946.

Benny Huntman, Esq.,
123a, Bedford Court Mansion,
Tottenham Court Road,
W.C. 2.

Dear Benny,

          I enclose cheque for £10. 10. 0. and
I am very grateful to you for getting me the seats
for the fight.

                    Yours sincerely,

                    Jack.

18th December 1964

L | S | T | A

The London School of Turf Accountancy

CROUPIER'S DIPLOMA

No. 15

This is to certify that the holder of this Certificate

Mr. D. CORNWELL of

LONDON, ENGLAND

has undergone a Complete Croupier Course in LONDON

and is now fully efficient in the Game of

GAME   EXAMINER

AMERICAN CRAPS

Dino Cellini
Principal Croupier Tutor   Principal of the L.S.T.A.

David Cornwell's diploma, signed by Dino Cellini before the London trainees left for the Bahamas. (courtesy of David Cornwell)

The card for the Pair of Shoes Club, where David worked for a while.

RECEPTION:
HYDE PARK 1801-2

OFFICE:
HYDE PARK 4397

The Pair of Shoes Club

21, HERTFORD STREET,
LONDON, W.1.

The croupiers at the Lucayan Beach's Monte Carlo Casino, Freeport, in December 1964, with Bobby Cellini in glasses centre stage. Second from his left is David Cornwell. (courtesy of David Cornwell)

Dino and Helena Cellini outside their home in Miami in October 1977, the day after the couple's arrival back in America from Monte Carlo. Dino had been quizzed for four hours by the authorities on his arrival in the States. He was suffering from cancer and died 13 months later. (courtesy of Dino Cellini Jr)

Roger Huntman in 2011. (© Douglas Thompson)

spacious and luxurious in the European style and there were four large craps tables, ten blackjack tables, six roulette tables and two big wheels – a game not for serious gamblers.

'Dino Cellini was the casino manager in charge of the games, but there were also a lot of characters around the casino whose function we were not exactly sure of. Dino's brother Eddie was a pit boss on blackjack and his younger brother Bobby a boxman on the craps tables. Added to these you had George Sadlo, an old-timer from everywhere, Frank Ritter, a bookmaker from New York, and Max Courtney, another bookie from New York. A third bookmaker, called Charlie Brudner, from Miami Beach, was a real animal who constantly chewed Havana cigars and trimmed the end he chewed with a small pair of scissors. These three men were, we learned, the biggest illegal bookmakers in New York and were under federal indictment from the FBI and were hiding out in the Bahamas until the "heat blew over". They went all the way back to Dutch Schultz, to bootlegging. The ultimate boss was Meyer Lansky, who'd moved everything to the Bahamas.

'Some of the American employees in management at the Lucayan casino looked like characters out of Damon Runyon: large cigars, two-tone wing-tipped shoes and monogrammed shirts were everywhere. One of our game inspectors was Irving Perelman, a very nice man who had worked as casino manager for Frank Sinatra when he owned the Cal-Nevada Lodge. Another interesting employee was an ex-fight game journalist, Eddie Borden, who was editor-in-chief of *Boxing Illustrated* in the 1950s. He was a famed world authority on professional boxing whose Canadian Air Force record was so impressive that at the end of the war he was the only non-British citizen to be allowed to operate as a London bookmaker. Eddie got in some trouble because he named Frankie Carbo as Manager of the Year 1959 in his magazine.

'Eddie was a gentleman, a close friend of Benny Huntman, who did not have a background in casino management but looked like he was getting a "favour" job for services rendered in the past. This description served quite a few men working in the Bahamas. Eddie Borden was a loner who worked hard all year, walked to work, spent zero and on an annual two-week holiday blew all his savings betting the limit on the don't side in another casino, smoking a box of Romeo and Juliet cigars a night.

'There was also an ex-world boxing champion working as security in the casino, a guy called Joey Maxim. He had links to Eddie Borden and Frankie Carbo. All those involved in the casino had strong ties to the fight game around the world.

'The casino gradually got busier due to the player connections of the management team and the proximity of Miami Beach to the Bahamas. Cuba was 90 miles offshore, Grand Bahama was even closer, a mere 30 minutes by plane. This was a golden time. Practically all of the New York gambling crowd came to Florida, notably Miami Beach and West Palm Beach, in the winter months, and at that time the amount of illegal gambling in mainland USA was very big, so most of the Bahamas players were involved in these operations. A man called Dusty Peters from Miami arrived in the casino every Friday night and he returned to Miami with cases of cash and cheques from the casino. He had one other night a week, but never the same evening. Another of these agents was Hymie Lazar, who was a courier for other interests in the US. The money went out of the Bahamas pronto!

'Like Las Vegas, somewhere like the Monte Carlo Casino was created by criminals for criminals. They weren't built for the legitimate man in the street, they were built for the people who were in the rackets, who were cheating on income tax, were up to nefarious activities. They were the people that had the cash. Bundles of it. Nobody bothered. There was no reporting. People used to get on a plane with $100,000 in several pockets.

'I took a trip to Miami Beach when I'd been working in the casino for some months and was making good money. I had gone from earning £6 per week in London to $200 per week, a big jump. On the plane back, I saw a player named Artie, who was a bookmaker in Miami Beach and gambled very high in the casino playing craps. He invited me to drink with him and introduced me to the man with him: "Say hello to my friend. He's a lieutenant in the Miami Beach police." I shake the man's hand and Artie says, "Show Dave your gun and badge," which the policeman proceeds to do very proudly. Obviously, the relationship between these two men went beyond that of friendship.

162

'When the plane lands, Artie invites me to share a cab to the casino, where I'm going to change clothes for work. When the cab arrives at the casino, the cabbie asks Artie for $5 to which Artie says, "No way. The fare is always $3," and he proceeds to get into a heated dispute with the cabbie. As I was running late, I excused myself and told Artie I'd see him in the casino. When I went on the table to deal, I saw Artie and he says, "What do ya think about that SOB cabbie trying to cheat me?" I replied that the cabbie had a lot of nerve. Artie played on the tables all night long and proceeded to lose $50,000 like it was nothing, yet he would argue with a cab driver for $2. That's what makes players hard to figure out.

'Eventually, all the dealers had to move out of the comfortable apartments to the village in the middle of nowhere. We moved to make room for American middle management who had been promised these apartments. Life in the dealers' village was like a bachelor holiday camp with very primitive accommodation. However, there was a party on every night and all forms of entertainment, with girls coming and going and card games lasting all hours for not small money. The management were not happy but what did they expect, everyone to live like monks?

'The casino became very busy, especially at weekends and holidays in the winter months, and the dealers were gradually making more and more money through tips received at the tables from players; these tips were given 100 per cent to the dealers. One weekend, a player named Price showed up at the casino and proceeded to play very big on the craps tables. He always wore his hat all the time when playing. Perhaps this was his lucky hat. However, every bet he made for himself, he matched it with a bet for the dealers. We loved this player. In the course of the weekend, the craps tables took $36,000 in tips from this man. Every bet he made, he bet for the boys. He was laying out lots of money. He went broke. He lost all his money. We didn't play it back again. Whereas if he won, he would play the money back again. We just locked our money up. Frank Ritter was pissed. He didn't like it.

'It was so much money, in fact, that the bosses called a meeting to reprimand the dealers for "hustling" the player for the tips, a charge that was not really valid. Price just loved playing this way and created a great atmosphere on the games.

Anyhow, there was nothing that the bosses could do about the matter; it was just something to gripe about. Tips were what made the job interesting and were one of the things that would really sharpen up a dealer's attitude to good service on the tables. We had another guy called McGee who used to come in. He was a jewel thief, a hustler. An old guy, he used to lose a lot of money. Lots of people, bookmakers like my pal Artie especially, came for the fun, for the losing. More than 80 per cent were invited and brought to gamble in the casino. They were provided with girls and God knows what. The girls would come over for a couple of nights at a time.'

The Monte Carlo Casino was an instant success. In Miami Beach, Max Courtney's bookmakers kept a constant check on the credit ratings of high rollers who showed up at Freeport. There were some early-day problems because of the wonky telephone system, which meant that credit checks were delayed. The boxing impresario with the horse called Mr Gray, the convivial Jim Norris, obligingly allowed the radio aboard his yacht, *Black Hawk*, at anchor in Hawksbill Creek, to be used to relay credit information back and forth between Freeport and Florida. By June 1964, around the grandly ironic time Harold Christie, friend and foe of Sir Harry Oakes and doyen of Bahamian real estate, was knighted by the Queen, the Monte Carlo Room had made more than $1 million – on the books. It was on a roll, with never a losing night. Peat, Marwick, Mitchell & Co., the international accounting firm employed to keep the Monte Carlo's books, did not trust those available records and resigned. When a casino employee was questioned about how each evening's money was looked after, it went: 'Who counts it?'

'Mr Lansky.'

'Personally?'

'Yes. Or Mr Sadlo.'

The cash flow was steady and wonderful. Lansky was feeding the money into assorted operations and using it as seed money for his London and Continental plans, as well as paying out to the American Mafia's now established Five Families. Everyone in the so-long-ago-imagined international syndicate got a piece.

As part of their exemption to operate the Monte Carlo, the mobsters had bought into regulatory safeguards: the security system involved routine accounting procedures and inspectors all paid for and controlled by the casino. The security men were pleasant retired colonials, from Singapore and Aden. The New York Criminal Intelligence Bureau noted: 'They're nice old guys who wouldn't recognise a Mafia man if he walked right up and offered to sell them a bag of heroin.'

The FBI attempted to break up the Lansky skimming of the casino's profits but couldn't. It worked at three levels. The kickback: Max Courtney, Frank Ritter and Charles Brudner got giant bonuses of up to $330,000 a time and the money was kicked back to Lansky in Miami. The junket: travel agents and sporting clubs arranged for groups of high rollers with good credit to be sent by charter flights for expenses-paid weekends of gambling on Grand Bahama. When they lost, they paid not the casino but the junket trip manager. The casino profits don't appear on the books, only the expenses, the tax write-off, for lavishly hosting the gamblers for their weekend losing at the tables. The third and most profitable method of moving money was the credit skim: gamblers asked casino managers to extend credit against personal cheques or 'markers'.

They all went with Dusty Peters on his twice-weekly trips to Miami, when he'd usually have coffee and a chat with Meyer Lansky at the Fontainebleau Hotel. One account was used for the credit profits and, helped by banking officials, after being cleared they were moved out of that account in Miami to America's godfathers: Sam Giancana in Chicago, Steve Magaddino in Buffalo, Carlo Gambino in New York and Joe Zerilli in Detroit. Funds from IOUs that were not easily forthcoming were collected locally by enforcers. Blood or cash? That was the invitation.

David Cornwell saw the money-go-round at first hand: 'Frank Ritter and the others were running everything. They had the clients, because of their bookmaking operation. They knew the gamblers. Contacts started to come in, and good players, too. They were customers of the illegal bookmaking. When they were down, they were given credit and it was collected in the States. Some of these guys were quite elderly. The experience showed. They knew what they were doing: things got pretty good. You could work a double shift if you wanted. We worked hard but we made good money. The tips were fantastic. We kept all the tips. George Sadlo was a mysterious guy. He looked like somebody's old uncle but he had form going back to the Mexican revolution. He walked around like a giant. He had a remarkable aura.

'Nobody knew if he was the manager, but he could do whatever he wanted there and he walked around, and this and that. He used to say, "Anyone want to work a double shift?"

'I'd say, "Yeah, I'll work. I'll come in."

'So when you used to come in and do your double shift, you might have knocked off at four o'clock in the morning, but you had to be back at midday to start in the afternoon because they had two shifts. It wasn't twenty hours; it was two shifts. There would be a crew of us, five or six, and he'd come in and he'd say, "Right, there's nothing for the moment. Sit over there, boys." We would sit over there and have a cup of coffee and about an hour later he would come over and say, "It doesn't look like there's anything here today for you," and he'd go in his pocket and bring out a roll of money and say, "Here's $20 each. Go home." That was fantastic. You got paid for your double shift, $20. They didn't need you, but they understood that it had inconvenienced you to come in.

'It was free and easy. There was so much money around. They were clever. And these guys were in total control of it. You could understand why they didn't want anything to get in the way of their business. There was a lot of talk about Kennedy's assassination. When we went to Grand Bahama, it was immediately after the Kennedy killing. The same operators who were active in the Havana casinos were present in the Bahamas and we heard stories about how all expatriate Cubans exiled in Miami blamed JFK for not assisting the Bay of Pigs freedom fighters with promised US air support during their invasion. It is doubtless that if this air support had been forthcoming during the invasion probably Fidel Castro would have been ousted and casinos restored.

'Lansky and his partners had a fortune invested in Cuba. They had just finished building what was the jewel in the crown, the Riviera Hotel, so there was much at stake and the loss of this source of income was a body blow to organised crime in America. Secondly, Bobby Kennedy was being relentless in his pursuit of various Mob figures, causing many of them to cease operations or leave the country for a life in exile. One story went that a good friend of the Cellini brothers got a very heavy prison sentence for merely travelling in a car that had betting receipts discovered in the glove compartment. One of these figures hounded by Robert Kennedy was Carlos Marcello, the kingpin of New Orleans. He was barred from re-entry back into the US after a trip to South America, as he was not officially a US citizen. After much strife, he re-entered the US, but he promised to get rid of those Kennedy brothers.

'When I worked at Lucayan Beach casino, one of the dealers became friendly with a big gambling figure from Baltimore and was invited to visit the city. When the dealer returned, he mentioned how he had visited many illegal casinos in the Baltimore area and had travelled to New Orleans, where he had met the man who had JFK shot. This was in 1964, a few months after the killing, when the name of Carlos Marcello was unknown to the world, so I believe there is some credence to this story. These guys were so in control of making and investing money.'

And much more. In his unique way, Sonny Liston was also en route for the Lucayan Beach Hotel and Casino. Although Frankie Carbo remained resident on Alcatraz, that wasn't an antidote to the contagious Mob connections carried by Liston. Floyd Patterson had retained his world heavyweight championship for a second time against Ingemar Johansson and held it by defeating Tom McNeeley on 4 December 1961. He wouldn't, however, meet Liston, who was clearly the man who should be given his chance at the title. His manager, Cus D'Amato, aka Mr Dudley, wanted nothing to do with the IBC. He'd already been there.

When D'Amato was moved out of the tricky equation, Patterson was up for Liston. The 'ugly bear' won brutally and fast in the first round in Chicago on 25 September 1962, with the third-quickest knockout ever recorded. With screams of a fixed fight, the Patterson halo was bent sideways. He was so ashamed he left Chicago's Comiskey Park in disguise, wearing the hairpiece and fake beard he carried in case he lost. He put them on again after Liston retained the title in just four seconds longer at the Las Vegas Convention Centre on 22 July 1963.

America, rather warily and with some righteous foreboding, was home to the new heavyweight boxing champion of the world. The champ got to show off his crown on the road. At the end of August that summer, he was in Britain with his manager Jack Nilon and some of his team. And his petulant impatience and petty vanities were wonderfully indulged. Along with his peccadilloes, if that's the name for it. He presented a boxing exhibition at Wembley Stadium, organised by British promoter Mickey Duff, who had accommodated Liston at the Piccadilly Hotel in Mayfair. Liston called Duff complaining, 'This place is a morgue.'

Duff told him it was a Sunday, everything was closed.

'How about some broads?'

'That's not my racket.'

Yet Duff, in the interest of harmony, went to a nightclub and explained to a friend the needs of champion boxer Sonny Liston. A tiny, busty Scottish girl said she'd love to meet the champ, look after him. Duff called Liston and told him, for appearances' sake, to order up some room service, whisky and sandwiches, make it look like dinner with this girl.

Duff and a trainer took the girl, Vikki, over to the hotel. At first, Liston had his mitts up: 'Who's the fag she brought with her?'

'No, no. This fellow just came with me. He's leaving. See you tomorrow.'

Duff had arranged for a couple of sportswriters to interview Liston, and the next morning he took them to the suite. The banshee yelling from the room could be heard all down the corridor. It was a furious, maniacal screaming of a withering range of exceptional expletives. They went in and Liston was standing in his robe. The Scottish girl was facing off to him. She turned and shouted, 'He fucked me all night. I got no sleep. He gave me ten quid. Ten fucking quid! Imagine!'

Duff looked at Liston: 'Sonny, that's not a lot of dollars.'

Liston shrugged his giant shoulders: 'Yeah, what about all the sandwiches she ate?'

Fortified, Liston went off on tour. Whatever the reason, he dressed as a 1920s Chicago gangster and rode a white horse through Newcastle. In Glasgow, he wore a kilt and had a go at the bagpipes, which won him a welcome in the city. He said, 'I am warm here because I am among warm people and react to it. When I return to the United States, I will be cold again.'

He also won a little friend, Peter Keenan Jr, the 11-year-old son of the former British bantamweight title holder and winner of the European and Empire championships at 8 st. 6 lb. The lad acted as Sonny Liston's mascot as he toured the city. His father had a solid relationship with the not always genial giant Liston. Peter Keenan was what might be called forthright, and when he felt he was being bullied by the menacing, six stones heavier Liston, he challenged him to continue their argument outside: 'I've never lost a street fight in my life.' Liston refrained and that was the end of it and they remained friends, if at opposite ends of the scales.

It was a topsy-turvy world. When Liston returned to America, he signed to take on Cassius Clay, the noisy brat who'd been shouting at any microphone that would have him about being 'the greatest'. For the world championship fight in Miami on 25 February 1964, the odds-makers had Liston as a 'runaway favourite'. It was an interesting phrase.

Clay's trainer was Angelo Dundee. The fight was being staged by his older brother, the former fighter Chris Dundee (Cristofo Mirena), who had worked as a boxing manager from the Capitol Hotel near Madison Square Garden. That was during the time Frankie Carbo was the lethal power at the IBC, and they lunched most days at Dempsey's.

Some months before the contest, on 29 October 1963, Inter-Continental Promotions signed an apparently absurd $50,000 contract in securing the rights to promote the loud but certain loser Cassius Clay's next fight after the Liston–Clay encounter. Sonny Liston had 47.5 per cent of the stock in recently established Inter-Continental Promotions, while officially Jack Nilon and his three brothers had the same. Bill Cherry, a lawyer, had the remainder. Frankie Carbo was in jail, so surely he or any of his associates couldn't have invested? In the usual roundabout way, they had. Sonny Liston had signed over half his shares in Inter-Continental Promotions to Sam Margolis of Philadelphia who was associated with the city's number-one gangster, Angelo Bruno. Mr Margolis was in the vending machine business but before that had been a partner in the Sansom delicatessen on 39th Street with his son-in-law Carlo Musciano and Blinky Palermo. The group also owned the apartment building next door; Sonny Liston lived there when he first moved to Philadelphia. It was great to have friends.

Before the fight, Cassius Clay was living in Miami; Angelo Dundee ran a gym near his home. Sonny Liston was up in Colorado preparing in Denver. The match wasn't attracting enough excitement, as in paying customers, cash, for the promoters. Sonny Liston was sent out to bang the drum for some business. Although he wasn't loved, he was nevertheless the world champ, but he was a tough sell. Liston represented all that was mean: they said the beast of a man looked nicer than he was. For an America that so shortly before had violently lost its president, he wasn't boxing's Sir Galahad, he wasn't the champ as hero that America wanted.

Sonny Liston was Mr Bad. But he was in a good mood when he arrived at the Lucayan Hotel in the Bahamas 12 days after it opened.

Roger Huntman was in the Monte Carlo Casino when he had a look around: 'He had been in the offices paying his respects to Dino and the others and one of the managers brought him over to meet me. Liston was laughing about coming over to Buckingham Palace, joking around. He was in great spirits, kidding around and joking with me. They'd brought some girls along to do publicity pictures with him and he had a big smile on his face. I had my picture taken with him and he was around for a time.'

The odds had run with Liston from the contract signing. Bookmakers everywhere had him annihilating Cassius Clay. The odds on a Clay surprise were generous when the fight was announced but as 1963 turned into 1964 and January into February there was something in the air. Nothing was so certain any more. Oh, the big, positive money was on Liston but the numbers on the challenger were dropping. By fight day at the Convention Hall at Miami Beach, there wasn't what you'd call a good wager either way – only brave ones, but there are always these. Suddenly, a great deal of money said Clay had a shot at the title. Somebody knew something or somebody knew somebody. Hey, for enough loot, the Mona Lisa would talk.

Sonny Liston hadn't said a thing. Cassius Clay talked a

better battle than General Patton but remained a no-hoper against the champion, who was widely perceived as invincible. Still, what was supposed to be a one-sided fight got to the end of the sixth round with the boxers on even points. They connected – Liston had a bruised right eye and was cut under the other – but AWOL was Liston's ferocious aggression; he looked as if he was sparring with a friend, working out before supper.

By not answering the bell for the seventh round, Sonny Liston also ignored a place in the world and flew to the dark shadows where you build not a future but walls of denial. That way, most of the time, the fear isn't there. But it never truly vanishes, and so paranoia persists. Liston sat in his corner, claiming his left shoulder was damaged, and Clay won by a technical knockout, a TKO. Clay jumped centre stage and performed a victory dance and found his beloved microphones: 'I'm the greatest. I shook up the world!'

Amid the howls of dismay and disbelief over the result, the contract held by Inter-Continental Promotions instantly seemed a very clever piece of business. They didn't have exclamation marks big enough for the furore, amid the howls of dismay and disbelief, over the result, especially among Liston's sucker-punched followers, who'd bet suitcases of cash, and some their homes, on him staying the champion of the world. But that left shoulder did him down, didn't it?

Without being inside Liston's head, the closest you get to the typhoon of torment in there is from matchmaker Teddy Brenner, who was in Liston's dressing-room when the man whom expertise and good sense said could not be vanquished returned from the ring defeated. In his book *Only the Ring Was Square*, he remembered:

> The moment Liston came through the door he reached down with his left hand and picked up an armchair and threw it across the room. The chair must have weighed fifty pounds. Made a terrible racket when it hit the wall. 'Motherfucker!' Liston screamed. The sound of his voice was sharper than the chair smashing against the wall. His rage filled the room and suddenly it seemed crowded, though only a few of his handlers were with him. I walked out. Outside, I was thinking, if Liston had thrown a

punch as hard as he heaved the chair, maybe he would have kept the heavyweight title.

And maybe that display, that dressing-room tantrum, reflected the anguish of the dividing line between the light and the dark. Cassius Clay had no reason to think he was anything but the greatest. The next morning, he celebrated his victory, his membership of the Black Muslim movement and his new name: Muhammad Ali.

Preparations for the lucrative rematch began immediately. Alcatraz penitentiary had closed a year earlier and Frankie Carbo, still the 'commissioner of underworld boxing', had been moved up the coast to McNeil Island Correction Institution in Washington state. He could still reach out across America. He had to go around corners to the Central Maine Youth Centre, a schools hockey park, in Lewiston, Maine. All the usual suspects, Las Vegas, Miami Beach, New York, did not want to entertain Liston–Ali as it now was. Liston achieved an 8–5 favourite rating, which was, in the circumstances, a travesty. Ali, though he didn't know it, was the usually elusive grail, a sure thing.

The fight, on 25 May 1965, was amateur dramatics heightened by inebriated choreography. Liston was pronounced super-fit before he got into the ring. Yet before the fight, he said he didn't feel it. Teddy Brenner was again prime witness to events:

> I walked into his dressing-room with Joe Louis. Louis patted Sonny on the back and said: 'Good luck, Sonny.'
>
> Liston looked him straight in the eye: 'Joe, I don't feel so good.'
>
> 'What do you mean you don't feel so good? You gonna win,' Louis said.
>
> Liston looked down. When he raised his head, he said, 'Just ain't right, Joe.'
>
> We were back in our seats a few minutes later and the fight started and Ali went into his shuffle. Liston flicked a couple of jabs at Ali, but they missed. I saw Ali throw a long right, while he was up on his toes, and it glanced off Liston's jaw. He went down.

But not with a bang. One of the ringside reporters recounted: 'Liston collapsed slowly, like a falling building, piece by piece, rolling onto his back then flat on his stomach, his face pressed against the canvas.'

The crowd protested with shouts of derision, of a fix, of a fake fight. Ali, reckoning it was a display of anti-Black Muslim rhetoric, called his first-round win 'a righteous victory'. Others called his long right 'the phantom punch'. That evening, as summer loomed, there were many phantoms in the arena – and punching above their weight.

Others were haunting London. With the Bahamas an open door, that was the next step for the gambling empire that Lansky envisioned spreading across the Atlantic, to England and on to France, with his associates in the Unione Corse, and on and on like a rolling dice through the Continent and beyond the Iron Curtain, using London as a bridgehead. The capital city, the perfect place to encourage perfidy and casual corruption following contrived changes in the licensing legislation, was a world of gambling, guns and gangsters, a home from home. The Mob, operating like a corporate raider plotting a hostile takeover, was ready to invade wide-open Britain.

Since the Gaming Act (recodified in 1963 without basic changes) Britain had legally indulged in just about every form of gambling. The Government's motive in bringing in the Betting and Gaming Act was simple: to legalise what it could not stamp out. Gambling, it declared, was an instinct impossible to suppress. But what was incredible to the Mafia was that you could put a bet on almost anything: horses, greyhounds and the next prime minister, the odds given in newspapers, the bets taken by telephone or in a high-street betting shop that had never officially existed before.

Bingo was legal: there were more than 12,000 clubs and those counting believed 14 million were playing every week. With bingo, the Government thought it was legalising a church-social pastime; instead, it began an £85-million-a-year commercial game anyone could play, including the blind, using Braille boards.

Also on the right side of the law were gaming clubs where roulette, chemmy and poker were available. Slot machines – there were nearly 25,000 one-armed bandits across the country – were being fed sixpences adding, in the most remarkable arithmetic, to more than £10 million a year. The most significant effect of the Betting and Gaming Act was an upsurge in gambling: from £683 million in 1960 to £853 million in 1962 and in 1964 more than £1,000 million. The popularity of betting shops was extraordinary: 14,388 betting-office licences were issued by June 1963. Betting shops were everywhere: railway stations, holiday resorts and even on a North Sea fishing trawler, taking bets by radio from other fishermen.

The politicians believed they would slow down gambling clubs by banning the 'cagnotte', the house cut, and only allowing a fee for each session of play. It was presumed the fee would be for a whole evening's play, but the clubs, if they charged, often charged £10 for every 'shoe', the tray-box of cards that are run through in around 40 minutes. That made chemmy and roulette, with similar fee-charging ingenuity, hugely profitable.

By the time the Mob were preparing to arrive, there were 23,000 gaming clubs in Britain, from the lavish Clermont Club and Crockford's to run-down but equally legal dives, places like the American 'peanut parlors'. The new gaming laws had changed British society more than just about anything since the Second World War. Now specialists were on the way to lead the revolution.

1 0

SHADOW BOXING

'A Nightingale Sang in Berkeley Square',
Frank Sinatra, 1962

It was one of those days on Grand Bahama a sharp Madison
Avenue man could have invented. Everything was in order,
the sun was high in the sky, the ocean that off-rainbow blue
the Impressionists spent their lives trying to capture. Roger
Huntman walked along the beach in the afternoon pondering
on how good life was. He got along with everyone, enjoyed his
work; his croupier skills were impeccable, his circumstances
comfortable. He got a lot of respect. Paradise wasn't half bad.

There was always plenty of excitement. On a recent evening,
Leonard Firestone, the head of the Californian tyre company,
had walked into the Monte Carlo and asked for a 21 table all
to himself: 'I was the main dealer and this guy was there for
three days and gambling most of the time. He lost a fortune,
many hundreds of thousands of dollars, and he was good for
it and more; the credit guys never blinked. They gave him the
freedom he wanted. It wasn't unusual.'

Yet Roger Huntman missed the buzz of the big city, the
vitality of London. Someone read his thoughts. He arrived at
the Lucayan for a swing shift at the Monte Carlo Casino one
evening in late February 1964 and was called over as he passed
reception.

'Dino Cellini wanted to see me immediately in his office.
There was another person with Dino, who was introduced to
me as Mr Alo, and I was told he was a good friend of my
father. I was told to arrange to go back to London immediately,
where my father would explain everything to me. I was
delighted. Grand Bahama was a great place and I'd enjoyed it,
but it had been long enough for me. I missed London and
wanted to be back and see my parents. My father met me at

175

Heathrow Airport and we drove to our new home at St Georges Court, Brompton Road, Knightsbridge. My father told me that he and Dino wanted to "bring me in".

'They were going to flood London with American gambling, and I must learn from Dino and, above all else, do everything he and Dino asked of me, no questions asked, and for this I would have a life very few people ever dream of. I was ecstatic, happy to agree. This was a chance to work even more closely with my father and with Dino, who many of us regarded as a god in the gambling business. He was the man. I settled in to London pretty quickly. We'd have dinner together, and often with Freddie Mills. He'd become great pals with my father, and Dino, too.

'When Dino Cellini arrived in London in 1963, he said he'd heard Freddie Mills had a club in town and would Benny arrange a meeting with him, which he did. Benny, Dino and Mills had dinner at the Curzon House Club in Mayfair, where Sir Maxwell Joseph, who owned it, also joined them. Dino and Freddie became good friends that night. I got on well with Freddie. We all did; he was easy to like. We were always wandering around Mayfair together, through Berkeley Square and over to Piccadilly. Dino liked to walk; he said it helped him think. He was always on the go. He and Freddie would march along together.'

Freddie Mills was an asset in dealing with Sir Maxwell Joseph. The former boxer was essentially a cheerful man; he wasn't threatening and had a lovable if dopey grin. He was a celebrity before the age of celebrity, had been one of Britain's most adored sportsmen, a hero to millions, a colourful character loved by the headlines and television. He'd made a dozen movies but other than an early couple in the Carry On series, *Carry On Constable* (1960) and *Carry On Regardless* (1961), they were as forgettable as his face was memorable. It didn't matter: everybody wanted to see or hear anything with Freddie Mills involved.

He was on radio comedy and quiz shows, did theatrical tours with the big names of light entertainment; he'd be on the bill with Frankie Howerd or Dickie Henderson, on the receiving end of one-liners from Arthur Askey and Ted Ray. He'd had a weekly national newspaper column, ran his own London nightclub, made a couple of records, was a regular on the teen pop show *Six-Five Special*, advertised electric razors with Benny Hill and Freddie Trueman, and was a 'face' at scores of charity and media events. Few resented his fame and popularity. Everyone, it seemed, loved Freddie Mills.

Certainly Dino Cellini and Benny Huntman seemed to. They saw Sir Maxwell, who'd founded Grand Metropolitan Hotels, as the key to London gambling for the Mafia. They wanted to use the Dorchester, put in American gaming tables, nightly elaborate and expensive floor shows, and establish it as the European flagship for their operation. They believed gamblers would fly to London from around the world, from east and west. They had to show Sir Maxwell, who was answerable to his Grand Metropolitan board and his shareholders, that they could get the numbers. What they wanted was to put a Las Vegas hotel operation in the centre of London, at 53 Park Lane, and start manufacturing money all the way to the principality of Monaco and beyond.

Roger Huntman, young, keen and eager to please, had been placed as a croupier a couple of nights a week at Al Burnett's Pigalle Club, where a casino equipped with American-style gaming tables and walled off by transparent safety glass had been installed. It stood at one end of the room while at the other was one of London's best floor shows; in the middle, the customers could eat and drink and keep their eyes on the high kicks of the dancers or the big bets of the gamblers.

'My father asked me to go to the Pigalle Club and reserve a table for six people and to make sure it was one of the best tables near the floor show for eight o'clock that evening. He told me he and Dino, with Jimmy Blue Eyes, who had both flown in for a few days, would be joined by two others. I looked forward to seeing Dino again after a few months, and Jimmy Alo, and I happily carried out that duty.

'I was working in the casino that evening when my father, Dino, Jimmy Alo, one Italian and two Frenchmen walked in. The Italian's name was Frank Merranzano; one of the Frenchmen was called Paul Sauve; the other name must remain secret. It would be too dangerous otherwise. I was told they were going to introduce American gaming to Europe through Dino, with Dino taking me to Europe with him as his personal assistant and croupier manager.

'I felt that this was an audition to test me, to see if I was the

177

man, when the time came, to assume my father's role in their business in London and Europe, working with Dino. It was exactly what I had dreamed of, and to work alongside Dino Cellini, this was the icing on the cake. What a life I could see in front of me.

'Soon I was working directly for my father and Dino and running two 21 card tables they'd put in at Sir Maxwell's Curzon House Club in Mayfair. The idea was to show him how successful American-style gambling was in London; he was old-fashioned and had stuck to Continental gaming like chemin de fer, which was being overtaken in popularity by American gambling. Benny and Dino asked me to come up with an idea whereby they could control any competition that would challenge them in casino operations in London. I realised then if we unionised casino staff we could shut down any gambling club that might be in competition with us unless that club paid its dues to us. They decided ACE, Association of Casino Employees, was brilliant, but too dangerous as it could bring attention from the police.

'I reported each week either to Dino, who stayed at the Hilton Hotel in Park Lane, or to my father on how the operation was doing at the Curzon. My father and Dino, who was now flying in and out of London from the Bahamas, had a meeting at the Curzon House Club one evening, and it was agreed with Sir Maxwell that Grand Met Hotels' jewel, the Dorchester Hotel in Park Lane, could open a casino and floor show with top American acts being brought over to appear there. Everything was going to plan. Sir Maxwell had to put the proposition to his board. If the deal came off, it would make the Dorchester and gambling one of the most prestigious operations in the world and give Lansky his springboard to Europe. He'd already bought the British officials and unsuspecting politicians he needed.

'Sir Maxwell, with all his genius for business, was very naive, albeit in a worldly sort of way. Did he realise he was dealing with American organised crime? I don't know. He did have a meeting with my father and Dino and two American "company lawyers" at our home in Knightsbridge – my mother cooked a special lunch of fish and chips – with the explicit aim of establishing American gaming in London. It would be run by a new company under the umbrella of

Maxwell's Grand Met Hotels, but the company name would be changed to Grand Met Hotels and Casinos. Everything was being set in place, a legitimate front for the Mafia. Meyer Lansky wasn't going to be named on the board of directors, but in reality he was the CEO of it all.

'Dino and my father wanted to open avenues from Las Vegas to London: they knew they had to organise a membership list of high rollers from Vegas to present to Sir Maxwell to show the potential of a casino at the Dorchester, and they decided that the Victoria Sporting Club on the Edgware Road was the perfect location for trial runs.'

The Victoria Sporting Club, 'the Vic', opened on schedule on 17 December 1964, which was in very good time for the rehearsal. The £250,000 casino went into business right next to Woolworth's on the Edgware Road. It had a 400-seat card room, bridge, poker and kaluki, a version of gin rummy, a gaming room for roulette, five shillings minimum, £150 maximum bet, blackjack, chemmy and baccarat. There were thirty croupiers as the doors opened and five closed-circuit television screens in the manager's office, revealing the crowd that came through them.

In charge was an internationalist, the son of a diamond merchant who had French casino connections. He was a Dutch Jew by birth, born Issac Wijnberg in Amsterdam in 1941, a naturalised American by passport (George Wijnberg) and a habitué of France (Georges Wynberg) and England (George Wynberg) by inclination. A resident alien in England, he could not be paid for tax reasons for running the casino. Instead, he held 699 of the initial 2,000 shares, in the name of Mrs June Wynberg. Half of the shares in Mrs Wynberg's name were held on behalf of other and unnamed parties.

There was some difficulty, possibly reflecting the tangled ownership of the Victoria Sporting Club. Mr Wynberg said a series of violent threats were made by telephone, which was why he surrounded himself and his wife with a team of seven Corsican bodyguards. After three weeks, they were replaced by four former CID detectives who'd worked with Scotland Yard's Flying Squad. In all, Mr Wynberg employed 12 former CID officers.

There seemed to be some other confusions, but Roger Huntman explains how they were cleared up: 'There was a hitch. George Wynberg had a verbal agreement with my father about bringing junkets into the club from Vegas, but a couple of bookmakers who with others financed the Victoria Sporting Club found out about the deal with my father and blocked the arrangement. At the same time, Dino told me he was pulling me out of the Curzon House Club and to go and see George Wynberg personally. I would take control of the 21 tables at the Vic. This was also blocked by the bookmakers when they heard who my father was. There was ongoing business between Sir Maxwell and my father and Dino, and my job had been done at the Curzon House Club. Something or somebody had to give. Or go.

'Two nights before the opening of the Vic, my father told me to be there in my evening suit and to report to George Wynberg. I was also told to pick my own dealers for 21 and make sure they were there on the opening night. Wynberg would give me a contract to sign, which would state that I would receive £35 and 5 per cent of anything over £1,500 in winnings on the tables per week. The bookmakers who had objected had been "approached" and everything was now under control.

'On the opening night, it all went as I was told it would. I saw two men with Wynberg – muscle. One was Pat Stapleton, who had been the all-Ireland heavyweight boxing champion and who my father had managed, and the other was Jimmy Houlihan, a good friend of his who had been the entertainment entrepreneur Robert Stigwood's bodyguard. I went over to Pat to say hello. I had always got on well with him. Pat was about 6 ft 4 in. and built like the proverbial brick house. I don't believe his heart was ever in staying in boxing; he had found his vocation as a bodyguard, and, boy, could he fight.

'I'd watched him in action at a club called the Pair of Clubs in Baker Street, which I think was part-owned by John Bloom, the Rolls Razor washing-machines tycoon, and I was at the bar with Pat when two idiots from the East End started getting well out of order. They didn't look like mugs. Pat knocked out each of them, one punch each, and carried them up the stairs.

'Also there on the opening night of the Vic were three French-Corsican guys, and they definitely were not customers. One of them stood by the cashiers' till flicking a coin. I thought at the time he had seen too many George Raft and

Bogart movies. But they definitely had the look of people you don't mess with. They'd been brought over by the Unione Corse for my father and "French" Henry, who was the union's gambling man in London.

'Some months after the Vic's opening, Benny and Dino started junkets from Las Vegas and eventually turned it around into a London–Vegas junket connection; gamblers deposited a minimum of £10,000, which they guaranteed to gamble, for an all-expenses paid trip to Las Vegas, where the hotels they stayed in were run by the syndicate.

'Sir Maxwell Joseph had come to another meeting at our house where the finances of the America-to-the-Dorchester junkets were decided. It was agreed that gamblers heading for the Dorchester, more than 100 at a time, would guarantee a minimum of £40,000 gambling funds. There was a tremendous amount of money to be made and this was just the start.

'The sterling and dollars were flowing. Benny and Dino were now building the membership list, and I was earning a small fortune. I don't know what was said to those bookmakers, but it certainly worked. We never had a moment's trouble. The trouble came from somewhere totally unexpected.'

It came from Freddie Mills. His star was no longer shining so brightly. The Freddie Mills Nite Spot in Goslett Yard, Soho, off the Charing Cross Road, which he ran with his partner Andy Ho, was a failure. There were serious financial problems. At the same time, Freddie was going on the town with Benny Huntman and Dino Cellini, seeing how the other half spent – spent money he desperately needed. In a wild attempt to solve his cash problems, Freddie Mills tried to blackmail Benny Huntman. It was a fatal mistake. He made his move in the wrong place at the wrong time with the wrong man and the wrong Mob. After that, there was no right move.

Roger Huntman is astonished that he himself survived the period. 'It was like Dodge City. Everything was way over the top: the violence, the gambling and most of all the ambitions. Anything could happen and did. People lived noisily, at a roar, but died as quietly as could be arranged. Every day, there were winners and losers. My father was on the winning side, always had been. He made certain I supported that side, too. He carefully used me in his schemes, drawing me into the web, making me a player in the plans. Only with most of the participants dead do I feel able to talk about it. The Italians say you can only have so much patience, yet I'm still nervous about it. I always will be about the events that shaped my life and underworld history.

'For that history is still being made today. I have spent many years thinking about and calculating the enormity of my father's role in the Mafia's move on London. It was vital. He was single-minded about it. It was only after he arranged and organised the murder of his friend Freddie Mills that the ghosts of all he'd done began preying on him, put a poltergeist in our lives.

'Freddie became a problem out of nowhere. One evening, Dino and my father took Mills to the Vic, where they were importing gamblers on junkets from America. Mills was asking a lot of questions about who owned what and who was connected. He wouldn't shut up about it. It was the start of the trouble. Freddie Mills had got too close to Dino and kept on about the gambling. He wouldn't stop rabbiting on, and Dino especially didn't like that. He was all about control, keeping the balance, holding the nerve and also, very much, holding your tongue.

'Another evening, in the middle of 1965, myself and Benny and Dino were having dinner at the Vic when Freddie stormed in and said he had tried to find Dino at a number of clubs without success. Freddie was in a flushed state, wanting to know why he had not been invited to dine with them. Benny called for a chair and a menu for Freddie, but he said that he had not come to eat but wanted to talk business. Dino took the menu from Freddie, told him this was not the time and that he was embarrassing everyone and to leave the table. There was a look on Dino's face that I'd not seen before. My father went around the table, picked Freddie up by the arm and told him not to make a scene and to phone him at home, and that Mills had to leave right away. Freddie took the hint and left.

'It was early morning the next day that my father took a phone call from Mills. Freddie said that he was desperate to see him right away. My father told him to come to our flat in Knightsbridge at 2 p.m. I let him in. He wasn't the usual cheeky-chappy, happy-go-lucky Freddie. This was not the friendly and flamboyant man I knew so well. He just nodded at me and marched in. He'd arrived early, around 1.45 p.m., which annoyed my father, as he was on the phone.

'When the call ended, Freddie got right into it, didn't wait for a pause, didn't light a cigarette, didn't bother with any pleasantries. My father slowed him down by picking up a cigarette and lighting up. He looked at Freddie, who gushed out the words. He told my father he needed to borrow £2,500 as his club was going bust. He was told it wasn't possible as my father's money was tied up. Freddie then asked if Dino would put in and financially back some American tables at Freddie Mills Nite Spot. Again, my father said this was not possible. Freddie should wait, allow things to settle through the summer, and they'd talk again.

'Freddie became incandescent, shouting that he needed the money right away or he'd lose his club. I thought Freddie was going to explode he was so puffed up. His face was beetroot. He turned on me and asked me to leave the flat as he had something personal to discuss with Benny. My father told him he was the only person who was leaving. In a way, Freddie did blow up. He self-destructed. Freddie said that unless Benny loaned him the £2,500, he would to go to Fleet Street and tell all the newspapers who Dino was and that he knew all about Benny and Dino's business and the Mafia connections.

'My father's face was filled with anger. He told Freddie to get out or he would throw him out. He told him never to contact him or Dino again: "You should never have threatened us."

'I showed Freddie to the door. He was as white as a sheet. He was ashen. His teeth were chattering and he was catching his lips in them, chewing on himself. I'd never seen anyone look like that; there was shock all over his face. He knew he'd gone over the top. He was in a panic. He told me to tell my father he was only joking and to "apologise to Benny for me".

'It was too late for that. He'd intruded at a pivotal moment in the Lansky master plan. His threat was against the whole enterprise. The newspaper would have run with his story; he was a national hero with astonishing information. If the truth had got out, Sir Maxwell Joseph and all the others would have vanished from the deal, the great prize. It would have been too hot to handle. Freddie had just announced himself as a dangerous liability. He'd killed himself.

'When I got back in the room, my father had sat down. He said nothing. He was staring into space and smoking. After a few minutes, he picked up the phone. My father told me to leave the room, but I could hear him on the phone. I could not hear the words, but I now believe that's when he issued Mills's death warrant.

'On a Thursday, 16 July 1965, my father and I went out onto the Brompton Road and a blue Bentley was waiting for us. It wasn't our car, but my father had the keys and drove us to Heathrow. He said his own car wasn't appropriate. We picked up two men off the Pan Am flight from New York. We met them at arrivals and they looked like a couple of Yank tourists. I was introduced to them by my father as his son. He didn't say who they were to me, but he obviously knew them well. He never used any names.

'They were a strange pair, one short, one tall and chubby, and nobody said much except hello, how was the flight, that sort of thing. They only had a couple of cases. We drove into London in almost total silence. I thought they were tired from the flight. We took them to the Piccadilly Hotel, opposite the Pigalle Club in the West End. Nothing much was said during the journey, but when we got there my father told them, "You're booked in under the names of Bennett and Harvey."

'I do not know who the men were. I don't want to. I never want to. I never saw them again. A few days later, my father said he'd changed his mind about Freddie and wanted to help him out. He asked me to go see Freddie at his club to tell him to be there on Saturday night, 24–25 July, when my father would bring the £2,500 loan he'd asked for.

'I went over to the Nite Spot and Freddie wasn't too happy to see me. I was with a friend of my father's, Anthony. Anthony had worked for my father for about 15 years, but I didn't really know him. My father had said to take him "for company".

'Freddie gave me a strange look. I told him I had a message from my father for him. When I told him my father would lend him the money, the £2,500, his demeanour changed completely. He asked when and I said my father would bring it over personally on Saturday. He then got a big smile on his face and started buying drinks for people in the club. There weren't that many, but he wanted to get a night going. He wanted to buy me drinks, but I said I had to work and left him to it. Anthony came with me. After that, I never ever saw Anthony again.

'I always got on well with Freddie and, as I was only 22 and naive, they knew Freddie would trust me with that message. I'm positive they had finally "brought me in". It's the rule: always send someone they know. I unwittingly set Freddie up.

'Around 10 p.m. that Saturday night, when my father was supposed to go and see Freddie at his club, my father walked into the Pigalle Club with some Americans. I asked him if he had been to see Freddie, and he told me he had phoned him and put off their meeting until the following night. Not much later, Freddie walked down the alleyway near his club, where his car was parked, and got in the back seat to have a sleep, which he regularly did. Shortly afterwards, Mills was dead, shot in the head.

'My father and I were having breakfast about 5 a.m. with two Americans, who with some others had been flown in on a junket from Las Vegas. Someone who I had never seen before came over to our table and whispered to my father. The whisperer almost immediately turned and left.

'My father told the table, "Freddie Mills is dead."

'I said something like, "What's happened?"

'The older American leaned over and put his hands on top of my father's hands and patted them. He didn't say anything, didn't raise his eyes; his lips twitched a little in a smile.

'My father said, "It's terrible. I'll put Mills's money back into the bank."

'I don't believe he'd ever taken that cash out of his bank.

'I now believe my father never phoned Freddie Mills.

'I now realise I had been used to set Mills up for the gunmen from America.

'I thought it was strange when my father announced to the Americans that Mills was dead, for I didn't think they'd know who he was.

'The American who was sitting next to me was huge, a bodybuilder, and we had talked about bodybuilding, as I also did some. The second American was slight and much older, and the difference between the two was quite striking. The conversation between this frail-looking American, who was a chain-smoker – the waiter had to come over three times and empty the ashtrays – and my father was virtually all about gambling, which the man-mountain American didn't involve himself in; he was subservient to this older friend.

'Of course, it was Meyer Lansky. Lansky knew when the hit was going to be carried out and he was in exactly the right place at the right time. The Pigalle Club was usually open 24 hours a day when a junket was in town. That night, it closed early. It wasn't out of respect for Freddie.'

11

SUMMERTIME BLUES

'You Really Got Me', The Kinks, 1964

On the last day of his life, Freddie Mills was an uneasy man, but he didn't show it. He'd got used to concealing the increasing business problems that were intruding into every moment of every day. He'd thought the connections with Dino Cellini and Benny Huntman would see him through this tight spot. But they didn't want to know about him or his troubles; they were too busy with themselves, with their own deals. He'd made a mistake fronting up to Benny, and maybe they'd come after him. He'd explain; it would be OK. But maybe he should have protection.

On the Tuesday before he died, he went to Battersea Pleasure Gardens, a leftover attraction, south of the Thames, from the 1951 Festival of Britain, and visited May Ronaldson, who ran the fairground shooting gallery. He'd spent his teenage years fighting in fairground boxing booths and was friendly with Mrs Ronaldson, who looked on him as a son. After they'd talked, he borrowed a Belgian .22 rifle from 'Mum', saying he was going to open a fete the following day and wanted the gun as a prop for his fancy-dress cowboy outfit.

Roger Huntman went to see him the next day, the Wednesday, to tell him about Benny Huntman's change of heart and set up the meeting for late Saturday evening at Freddie's club. On Thursday, Freddie returned the rifle to Mrs Ronaldson, explaining to her that the fete had been cancelled. Then, the dark shadows got into Freddie's corner. In a short time, there were so many they had to squeeze in. The fear, the paranoia, told him he needed the weapon. His other self told him he had a deal with Benny now and need not worry. Yeah, but the rifle wouldn't do any harm; it was insurance.

On Friday, 23 July, he borrowed the rifle again, telling Mrs

Ronaldson the fete had been fixed for the next day. The rifle was from her stock of about 50 weapons; it was a little ancient, she said 'like myself'. She added, 'It was a semi-automatic self-loading rifle. You just pulled the trigger and didn't have to cock it after each shot.' After Freddie left, Mrs Ronaldson noticed that three rounds of the special ammunition used at fairgrounds – the bullets disintegrate on impact – were missing. She didn't think further about it.

Freddie's house in Denmark Hill, south London, was in the centre of unremarkable suburbia. Everybody knew Freddie and Chrissie Mills, who in turn knew the local tradesmen by their first names. Chrissie also knew it took a bit of nagging to get Freddie working in the garden and if there was anything abnormal about that Saturday it was the enthusiasm with which he cut the lawn and tidied the hydrangeas. With the girls, Susan and Amanda, they went to do the weekly shop. After they returned, Freddie said he fancied smoked haddock for a light supper before he went off to his nightclub. His wife and daughters went off to the fishmonger to get it, and Freddie went to bed to prepare for his long night in Soho.

When he got up, at 8 p.m., he had his supper and, with a daughter on each knee, watched *The Morecambe and Wise Show* on television. When it ended, he danced to a Beatles song with the girls and then carried his two protesting daughters upstairs to bed. There was a lot of laughing and then he drove off in his silver-grey Citroën to the Freddie Mills Nite Spot. When he got there, he had more drinks than usual and said he was going out to his car for a sleep.

As normal, Chrissie Mills arrived at the club later in the evening. She'd been a little delayed waiting for her son Donald McCorkindale and daughter-in-law Katie, and it was about 12.55 a.m. on Sunday, 25 July. They were met by Andy Ho. He said Freddie was not well, and led them to Goslett Yard, the cul-de-sac near the nightclub at the end of that dead-end street. Chrissie Mills and her son found Freddie in the near-side back seat of his Citroën dead from a .22-calibre bullet through his right eye. The fairground rifle was resting upright on the outside of Freddie's right leg. He'd died instantaneously; the murder weapon was placed neatly beside him.

The imported Mafia hit men had turned Freddie's protection into the weapon that killed him. Two shots were fired, one into Freddie's head, the other into the near-side front door of the Citroën. Roger Huntman believes Laurel and Hardy simply got lucky: 'They had been given their own weapons but found Freddie asleep and turned the rifle on him. The rifle was a repeater and it was faulty, so the second shot got pumped out in the moment. They left the gun but smudged up the fingerprints, for there's nothing as guilty as a "clean" gun. Anybody could have handled that weapon. It was a perfect hit. It was neat and they made it look as if it just might be a suicide. That was incidental. The job was done and they were off, never heard of again.'

Freddie's death in London's Soho on a cold midsummer weekend in 1965 was a sensation that would run and run. Freddie Mills was loved in that celebrity way as the guy-next-door who had made it, and that was why his sudden, violent death shocked so much. Millions of people thought they knew him personally, all but believed he'd bought them a drink.

His murder provoked a host of lurid theories, yet nothing as cold-blooded as the truth.

Ronnie and Reggie Kray controlled the action north of the Thames; Charlie Richardson and his group managed the South Bank. When Freddie was found dead, it was presumed without any evidence that he had run foul of one or other of the London gangsters. There were claims that he killed himself because he felt guilty about being a secret homosexual in the days when that lifestyle was illegal; others said he'd been unable to cope with the suicide of his close friend, the singer Michael Holliday, with whom it was also claimed he'd had an affair. Others said that he had a secret female lover or that he was a victim of a Chinese Tong involved in opium-dealing in Soho. There was a one-paragraph printed suggestion that the American Mafia were involved, but that was dismissed while the other stories were lubricated, given legs; disinformation was carefully and with intent distributed in the clubs and pubs of Soho and beyond.

No matter what stories were stirred up, it was in the underworld rather than in the offices of Scotland Yard that the majority believed murder had been committed.

Repeatedly, those who were around the clubs and pubs of London heard the phrase 'gangland execution'. Those who had experience in the etiquette of such things said that Freddie's demise, viewed from outside suburbia, had all the hallmarks of a professional hit. The speculation was as endless as it was colourful. It also had a purpose: the more stories, the less certainty.

Most of it followed the Westminster coroner Mr Gavin Thurston's verdict, which ruled that Freddie had committed suicide by shooting himself in the eye with the rifle found in his car. His family always disputed the verdict, as did Jack Solomons, saying it was not in Mills's character: 'If Freddie stood here and said to me, "Jack, I shot myself," I wouldn't believe it.' Certainly, Reg Kray, named in some theories as the culprit, said he didn't believe Freddie had killed himself. He made it clear that he and his brother had had nothing whatsover to do with it.

The most subdued theory was that Freddie had been depressed over money and had decided to end it all. Cash was a worry with no regular income. His work as a boxing promoter had been thought, with a devilment of irony, to be too straight for that game at that time. The BBC had rejected him as a pundit for the Liston–Ali rematch. He was no longer the golden boy. Time had tainted him. There's never much call for a Midas without the touch.

Still, manufactured rumour roared off the conveyor belt. Most flamboyantly, that Freddie was a serial killer of at least eight young women whose naked bodies had been found in or around the River Thames between 1959 and 1965. The teeth had been bashed out of some of the victims' mouths, and three of the bodies had been sprinkled with spots of industrial paint; six had their panties stuffed down their throats. They had all been small women, the tallest standing at 5 ft 2 in. They had all been prostitutes and had died when their killer, dubbed 'Jack the Stripper', had strangled them during sex.

Freddie was a piece that fitted that jigsaw, but only if squeezed effortfully into place; completed, that particular puzzle would still be a false picture. Freddie as a mass murderer didn't go easily, but the tale persisted as a motive for his supposed suicide – all to the aid of his killers.

The Jack the Stripper case began to take shape on 17 June 1959, when Elizabeth Figg, 21, was discovered propped up against a tree in a park in Chiswick in west London; she'd been strangled. It began some months of fear for the working girls of London, who started patrolling each other and carrying knives in the emerging post-war environment of 'help yourself, for no one else will'. Their world, from Soho out to Notting Hill, around many naughty corners and back again, with the louche lifestyles and the Westbourne Grove marijuana minimarts, was genuinely shaken by the violent sex murder of one of their own. Yet there was little sympathy from the police or the public. That changed in November 1963, as so much did.

People found they were living in a very different world; time had not simply gone on, but for many onlookers it had warped, society had metamorphosed, and, for good and bad, we had the shorthand for it in the phrase 'the Swinging Sixties'. In Britain, there were an amazing number of legislative reforms. As the nude musical *Hair* didn't say, it was the age of the new tolerance as well as of Aquarius. The destruction of accepted social structures and rules was compulsory if we were to be *modern*. It created some surprising tricks: with the glory of the Pill, the illegitimacy rate went up; some women complained that taking the contraceptive banished the extra excitement of sex. Of course, as they always point out, you can't legislate for everything – or everyone.

Still, this easing up, this live-and-let-live attitude, was codified into law as, in time, divorce, abortion and homosexuality were dealt with. These were not government initiatives, but reforms driven by MPs sitting way back from centre stage in the Commons. The small-minded were shuttled aside as the brake was eased off accepted morality and the accelerator stamped down towards more abandoned, although ironically more complex, lifestyles.

On the grand stage, we had the Cuban Missile Crisis and for a time it looked, in that familiar refrain, as though we were 'all doomed' – something that concentrates the mind. On 5 June 1963, the Secretary of State for War, John Profumo, resigned from Harold Macmillan's administration, admitting he had lied to Parliament about his relationship with Christine Keeler. The great grandee Macmillan accepted Profumo's

191

going and called it 'a great tragedy'.

Profumo, an ambitious 48-year-old, said he had misled MPs about his sexual liaison with 21-year-old Christine Keeler. It was claimed that Profumo, war secretary since 1960, had assisted in the disappearance of Miss Keeler, who had not appeared at the Old Bailey in London to give evidence against a man accused of possessing a Luger pistol. His letter to Macmillan stated:

> At that time the rumour had charged me with assisting in the disappearance of a witness and with being involved in some possible breach of security. So serious were these charges that I allowed myself to think that my personal association with that witness, which had also been the subject of rumour, was by comparison of minor importance only. In my statement, I said there had been no impropriety in this association. To my very deep regret I have to admit that this was not true, and that I misled you and my colleagues and the House.

The Profumo Affair, one of the greatest scandals of the twentieth century, raged into history that November, a high-proof, intoxicating cocktail of sex and security and the mighty fallen. At times, it seemed they might rewrite the Bible to include this gossip in a gospel – fire and brimstone with great legs. Jack Hylton, then 71 and still perky, who, through his friendship with Stephen Ward, mixed with the society crowd drawn into the entangling web of the Profumo scandal, told Benny Huntman that he knew no more than anyone else. But he would, wouldn't he?

Astonishingly, in the same months another sex scandal was entertaining the people of Britain, from the Court of Session in Edinburgh. The divorce of Margaret, Duchess of Argyll, heard in March 1963, the same month John Profumo lied to the Commons, was the longest and most sensational such case to occur in Britain. Sexually explicit Polaroid photographs were pivotal in the case, brought by the Duke of Argyll against his aristocratic, self-important wife, and became part of a government inquiry, really more of a quiz show, revolving around whose penis was whose. There were many potential candidates in the frame. The Duchess was photographed wearing only a string of pearls and performing fellatio on a lover, and a series of photographs of a man masturbating were discovered in her bedside table. The photograph of the lover was cut off at the neck, and in the media he became 'the headless man'.

Margaret Argyll, the only child of a self-made Scottish millionaire, was a society beauty who, her husband said, had slept with eighty-eight men, including government ministers and three members of the royal family.

With Profumo's sex life causing all manner of problems for Macmillan, at a Cabinet meeting on 20 June that year another of his ministers provoked more distress. Duncan Sandys, minister of defence and the son-in-law of Winston Churchill, confessed he was rumoured to be the person in the Polaroids. He offered to resign, but Macmillan talked him out of it – the war minister and then the minister of defence both going wouldn't do – promising that Lord Denning, who had been commissioned to investigate the Profumo Affair, would also investigate the identity of the headless man.

To this task Denning, the Master of the Rolls, brought his great legal mind. In four shots of the man in different states of arousal were handwritten captions: 'before', 'thinking of you', 'during – oh', and 'finished'. If he could match the handwriting, he could find his man. He invited the prime suspects – Duncan Sandys, Douglas Fairbanks Jr, American businessman John Cohane, Peter Combe, a former press officer at the Savoy Hotel, and Sigismund von Braun, the diplomat brother of the Nazi scientist Wernher von Braun – to the Treasury and asked for their help in 'a very delicate matter'. As they arrived, each signed the visitors' register. Their handwriting was analysed by a graphologist, and the result (confidential for many years) proved conclusive: the headless man was Douglas Fairbanks Jr. Which was a tonic for Duncan Sandys. He got even more relief when a Harley Street doctor said Sandys's pubic hair did not correspond with that revealed in the masturbation photographs.

Into this fellatio fanfare, low goings-on in high places, or the other way around, very much depending on your viewpoint, arrived the sad story of Gwyneth Rees, 22, found naked and dead in a rubbish dump in Hammersmith, west London, on 8 November 1963. Some teeth were missing, she'd been strangled in the same manner as Elizabeth Figg had been four years earlier and her body was discovered near the Thames. The killings became 'the Hammersmith Nudes Murders' by the time the morning papers reached the capital's news-stands.

With the assassination of JFK exactly two weeks later, the demise of young Gwyneth from Cardiff lost its headline potential. But not for long. The time of the moon for the killer came around swiftly – and repeatedly. It was on the towpath along from Hammersmith Bridge that the body of Hannah Tailford, 30, was found on 2 February 1964. She'd been killed almost identically to Gwyneth Rees. Tailford had been a 'party girl' at clubs and embassies in London. She'd been drowned in a bath and thrown into the Thames from the same towpath where Betty Figg had been found dead. Hannah's stockings were at her ankles, her knickers were in her mouth and the rest of her clothes had been taken away by her killer. There was speculation that she'd died during the making of a snuff movie (the money shot being death on screen) after film equipment was found in the apartment she'd worked from in London's Victoria. With the Profumo Affair and the Argyll divorce still topics of titillation, the dead girl was linked to society orgies. Hannah Tailford was said to have attended swinging parties and told friends of being forced to have sex with 'a toff dressed in a gorilla suit'.

The rumours, and the fear on the streets, heightened when Irene Lockwood, 26, was found strangled to death on the shores of the Thames in Hammersmith only a few weeks later, on 8 April 1964. The concerns did not stop prostitutes in the area working. These women got £1 10s for full intercourse; it was £3 in Curzon Street in the West End.

Death hurried tragically on. Twelve days later, the body of Helen Barthelemy, who'd moved to London from the outskirts of Edinburgh, was found in an alleyway in Brentford, near Hammersmith. She was a devotee of West Indian clubs in Notting Hill. Her teeth were gone and the only difference from the other victims was that she had paint particles on her body – some evidence for the police to follow. There were more paint flecks on the body of Mary Flemming, 30, which was found set against a private garage in Chiswick on 14 July 1964.

Margaret McGowan, also known as Frances Brown, 22, from Edinburgh, was found strangled and naked in an alley above Kensington's Civil Defence underground control centre on 25 November 1964. She'd been reported missing a month earlier by prostitute Kim Taylor, who said her friend had been picked up by a man driving a Ford Zephyr or Zodiac. McGowan was a good-looking woman, carried a knife for protection, and had a 'Mum and Dad' tattoo on her forearm. Shortly before her death, the society painter Victor 'Vasco' Lazzolo, Stephen Ward's friend and a devotee of young and available girls, had pestered her to pose nude with another girl at his studio.

It was her murder that pulled the bizarre and horrible events of 1963–4 together in a web of headlines. Ward, who revelled in the company of peers and prostitutes, in any combination, had gone on trial at the Old Bailey on 22 July 1963, charged with living off the immoral earnings of girls including Christine Keeler and Mandy Rice-Davies. In what is generally accepted as an Establishment set-up, Ward, 50, was severely prosecuted and evidence presented from prostitutes Ronna Ricardo and Vickie Barrett. During the trial, Ricardo withdrew her evidence against Ward of procuring, and Barrett's similar allegations were shown to be unsafe.

Christine Keeler and Mandy Rice-Davies were called as witnesses, as was Maggie McGowan, who gave evidence for the defence. On the eve of the last day of the trial, after a hammering of his character by prosecuting counsel Mervyn Griffith-Jones, Ward took an overdose of sleeping pills at the flat of his loyal and admirable friend Noel Howard-Jones, who, aghast, found him in a coma the next morning. The trial went on without him in the dock. Ward was still in a coma on Wednesday, 31 July, when the jury reached their verdict of guilty of the charge of living on the immoral earnings of Christine Keeler and Mandy Rice-Davies. The charges of procuring were rejected. Ward died in hospital three days later after what can certainly be argued was a serious miscarriage of justice by appointment to the British Establishment.

With her death, the notoriety of the Ward trial again caught up with Maggie McGowan, and the Jack the Stripper murders were linked to the Profumo Affair. As the vain hunt went on for the killer, the theories became more bizarre. It was reported that Christine Keeler was questioned about the murders; she assures me she wasn't. Several other prominent names of the time were, however, among the more than 7,000 people quizzed about the killings.

Then, shortly after 1965 began, on 16 February, another body was discovered. Bridget 'Bridie' O'Hara, 28, was found dead, with those flecks of paint on her body, in a shed behind the Heron Trading Estate in Acton. The body appeared to have been cocooned before being discarded like a pile of laundry. Indeed, all the girls seemed to have been taken from the streets, suffocated and stripped, and their bodies kept for some days before being dumped.

Weeks went by and there were no more dead good-time girls found along the River Thames. Had Jack the Stripper stopped killing or was he now hiding his victims' bodies? The failure to catch the killer fanned the flames of speculation in a world where, even for the casual newspaper reader, all seemed decadence and drama.

The proposal that Freddie Mills was Jack the Stripper surfaced amid this overheated, boiling atmosphere in London, some time before he was killed. It was a story that had been circulated, villain to villain, before rather than after the nude murders stopped. There has never been an official conclusion to the Jack the Stripper case, but there are still those around in the underworld who maintain that Freddie was the man and killed himself to escape his demons.

The only reason this story existed, however, was because the police investigation had publicly mentioned that the culprit might be a boxer; the suspect they had in mind was in fact a totally different man.

Chrissie Mills, of course, never accepted any of it. She was correctly convinced that Freddie was murdered following a prearranged meeting at his nightclub. Without any knowledge of Benny Huntman's involvement, something that has remained hidden for decades, she analysed her husband's death and, only weeks after the murder, she gave her verdict in the press, talking to the *Sunday Mirror* and the *Sunday Express*. It was closer to the reality of events than any other given then or since:

I would never be able to swallow three aspects of Freddie's so-called suicide and there's a whole lot of people who also reckon this verdict was based on some downright dubious 'facts'. First the gun, this unreliable, awkward shooting-gallery toy which Freddie is supposed to have chosen on two separate occasions as the ideal means of making his exit.

Anybody who believed that didn't know Freddie. He might have been a tiger in the boxing ring but outside it he was like a pussycat when it came to comfort. A wife knows more about her husband than any policeman or coroner and, believe me, if Freddie ever got to the stage of contemplating suicide it would be a gas-oven and cushions or a cosy dose of sleeping pills. I'm sure of that. And there were plenty of these in our house. Anyone who knew Freddie will tell you that once he made up his mind it was straight in and no second thoughts. The idea that he borrowed this gun from a woman in a shooting gallery to kill himself, then changed his mind and took it back and then changed his mind again would be laughable under less tragic circumstances.

What I feel in my very bones is that this gun was just a prop to threaten some villain who was on his back. It was for protection.

Why should Freddie Mills have to lean on a gun when he had fists that had won him fame and fortune? He had an almost pathological fear, which went back to his boxing booth days, of hitting anyone with his bare hands. He just couldn't do it, not even in the ultimate situation of a showdown. I think it was psychological, down deep.

At the inquest the impression was that it was unusual for Freddie to say he was going for a sleep in his car in Goslett Yard, by the side of the club, where I found him shot. The implication was that this was a big, unusual thing he was doing only to be matched by some extreme decision such as suicide. Well, that's the second thing that sticks in my gullet, for everyone knew that Freddie was always sleeping in that same car in that same yard.

The truth was that Freddie was the Great Sleeper. There were nights when he just couldn't keep his eyes open after twelve o'clock. That's why they gave him the nickname Cinderella Man. He could sleep anywhere. Sometimes, at home, he used to kneel on the floor in the lounge, rest his arms in a chair and sleep like that. Other times he'd just rest his head on my lap and off he'd go.

The third thing is that it was left to me to find the body. I had been worried during the final twelve months when I was no longer helping behind the bar at the club but was only a Saturday night visitor. Some time during this period Freddie started selling his property, the houses we had bought in south London as an investment. The only intimation I had that he was selling was his complaint once that it was too much of a headache. Anyway, the property is sold and where the money is or where it went I just don't know. It certainly isn't in the bank.

The more I look back to Freddie's last week the more certain I am that his movements only make sense if this was the showdown week: the one when he was going to have a once-and-for-all reckoning with some racketeer.

It was all played out against a background of high temperatures and a recent bout of pneumonia. On the Monday night I made him look into a mirror and told him, 'You know what we do with the children when they look like that, don't you? We put them to bed – where you should be.' But he insisted, 'No, no, I must go to the club,' and so off he went. He didn't stay terribly late. In fact, he was back by one o'clock. When he came back, he said he felt ropey and went straight to bed.

I don't think he would ever have gone out that night unless he had some vitally urgent business keeping a rendezvous with someone. My feeling is that the fellow didn't turn up that night. Tuesday was the day he borrowed the gun. Perhaps, during the extra day he had thought it all over, he had realised there was no money left. Perhaps, as he had a threat hanging over him, he had gone for the gun to 'shift these so-and-sos off my back'. I can well imagine that thought in his mind. But maybe on the Tuesday night he had no occasion to produce the gun. He could have said, 'Look, mate, I've no money but give me till Saturday and I'll see what I can do.'

And being stuck with the gun then, as it were, he

would have taken the common sense point of view and said to himself, 'Now what the bloody hell am I doing with this? I might have an accident with it.' And so he returned it. For that would be Freddie all over – just the sort of thing he would do. On Friday, according to the evidence at the inquest, he borrowed the gun again. I used the car to fetch our daughter Mandy from school at about four o'clock and I certainly saw no sign of it then unless it was in the boot.

Saturday, his last day alive, looked so much like being a nice, comfortable routine Saturday. If anything put the stamp on this feeling, it was Freddie's insistence that there should be smoked haddock for tea. He loved smoked haddock and, though it was late in the afternoon, he rang up a fishmonger to make sure they had some in. So I took Mandy and her sister, Susan, in the car and we went in search of his haddock. He was in bed when we got back and I told Susan, 'Well, leave him alone – I'll cook ours and we'll leave Daddy's till later.'

Susan woke him at half past seven and when he came down at about eight o'clock he sat in the dining room watching the girls do a little dance routine. Then we all went into the kitchen and he had a poached egg on his haddock and later he watched television before leaving for the club.

I reckon he had a rendezvous in Goslett Yard at eleven o'clock. It was the ideal place, because you certainly couldn't have a private talk in the club. And so he drove his car into the yard and, leaning out of the window, told the doorman he was going to have a sleep for an hour. I didn't leave the house for the club until 12.45 a.m. on Sunday. By that time it was over an hour since the doorman had found Freddie in the car. Five minutes after I left home Andy Ho rang the house to say that Freddie couldn't be aroused. So, when I got to the club I didn't know my husband was dead.

When I arrived, Andy took my elbow and started propelling me to the yard. When we got to the car, I noticed that the back window was down and Freddie was in the back seat. I talked to him through the window and, getting no answer, I climbed inside, put my arm round him and began to pat his face. I talked to him for some time, thinking how foolish he was to go to sleep in the back of the car on a cold night with the window right down. When I tried to get nearer to him, I felt something in the way, something resting against the seat. He sat there with his head lowered and his hands on his knees, perfectly relaxed. Then, when I pulled his face to mine, I felt wet and I noticed stains on my white suit and I thought it must be blood.

'He's dozed off and hit his head on the starting handle,' I thought, so I picked up this object and realised for the first time that it was a gun. When at last the penny dropped, I screamed to my son Donny, who was standing outside, to get a doctor. The next thing I knew I was in the club office. It was ten past one and Andy was ringing the hospital.

One thing I couldn't get over. They had failed to wake Freddie some time earlier, yet nothing was done till I arrived. It doesn't matter what was happening down there – and I quite believe that the fear of God was around the place – someone at least could have called a doctor or an ambulance.

So Freddie kept his rendezvous that night, whatever happened the other nights. And when you know the layout of the club you can see how easily it could have happened.

The doorman has said that he doesn't remember anyone going up the alley into the yard that night, but this proves nothing because a side door to the club opens into the yard. Normally the door is locked during opening hours, but Freddie could have arranged to keep it open. His visitor could have had a meal in the club, gone out through the side entrance, completed his 'business', returned, finished a drink, perhaps, and finally left through the main entrance.

As for the racketeers, what was more convenient than a suicide verdict? There were certain people I was sure would telephone me with offers of help. But there hasn't been a single call. They're too frightened even to dial my number.

I know Freddie didn't kill himself. The rifle was lying

so neatly by Freddie's side when I entered the car, it was impossible to imagine he could have taken his own life. My family and I believe that the death was stage-managed, that the fatal shot came from outside the car. Freddie couldn't have killed himself with the rifle. It was in an impossible place for that to have happened. He was shot with the rifle from outside the open window.

There were other anomalies in the strange investigation that followed. Before the police arrived at Goslett Yard, an ambulance removed Freddie's body. A man had been found shot dead and ambulancemen removed the body before the police arrived? Commander Leonard 'Nipper' Read of Scotland Yard was equally mystified:

> I agree it was unfortunate the ambulancemen removed the body before the arrival of the police. This precluded the taking of photographs, which in the event would have been most helpful in determining precisely what happened. I cannot account for this.

The Mafia hit men, Laurel and Hardy, were long back in America by the day of Freddie Mills's funeral. Despite the truth and Chrissie Mills's conviction about the death of her husband, his body was released by the Westminster coroner's office and he was a suicide statistic.

Freddie, one of Britain's most famous sportsmen, who'd earned more than £100,000 and died with £387 in the bank, was buried privately at Honour Oak Cemetery in Camberwell, south London, on 30 July, the Friday after his death. Earlier, more than 1,000 people had attended the parish church for the funeral service; the same number had crowded nearby streets. Jack Solomons led the pall-bearers, and among those with him were British heavyweight champion Henry Cooper, the *Daily Mirror*'s Peter Wilson and entertainer Bruce Forsyth, who gave the address.

Benny Huntman couldn't face that day. His son stayed away with him. Benny was busy, too. He had to get on with the business that Freddie might have disrupted. The American Mafia, like many lively organisations, wanted their own gambling establishment in London, this government-endorsed ongoing jackpot, and at the centre of the action, in the West End or Mayfair. For the past half-dozen years, Benny had been commuting to New York and Miami, often taking the boys' winnings in cash from the big fights in the UK and Europe. All the time, he'd been indoctrinated by Lansky about the European gambling empire.

Although he was acutely aware of the continuing interest in Freddie Mills's death, he could not be distracted from his primary missions; in a sense, the more outrageous and lurid the stories about Freddie, the easier he was.

Roger Huntman says his father could focus on a target no matter what was swarming around him: 'I don't think he was worried about the Freddie thing at the time. A few months after it, I went with him to the Savoy Hotel in the Strand, where Scotland Yard's Flying Squad were holding their Christmas party. I wondered what the hell we were doing there. We were sat at a round table with about six other people when, halfway through the meal, two men came over to my father and introduced a third. A short conversation took place, we finished our meal and left.

'On the way out to Covent Garden, where our car was parked, this third man walked up to my father and, although it was dark and I was walking a few feet behind my father, I saw him give this man an envelope. And the copper walked on. The Freddie Mills business was over.

'It was a classic Mafia hit. They sent someone to him, to set him up, whom he trusted. Me.'

1 2

THE ROARING SIXTIES

'Keep on Running', The Spencer Davis Group, 1966

The strongest currency in the world of avarice, outbidding the dollar, the yen and even gold itself, is the rich and powerful man's whim. The profit is always in indulging it. The passion for possession trumps prudence every time. Meyer Lansky had a lifetime of learning that.

He understood the fundamental psychology of gambling from a professional point of view. He knew high rollers wanted to gamble big and always, always, he had provided the opportunity in an environment that would play to their sense of entitlement.

He envisaged the Dorchester on Park Lane in Mayfair, London, as the pivotal step, the bridgehead, of his global gambling dynasty. It would be a playground for kings and princes, fast-set hedonists and international society. But there would be many others. He'd tasked Dino Cellini and Benny Huntman with locating the perfect places to take the world's money, in any currency whatsoever. There was one sacrosanct Lansky law: however the money went around, by train, plane, automobile, where or how it was gambled, it must always conclude its journey in his pocket. He'd personally do the counting and the accounting to his associates. Nothing could violate that process without a brutal reprisal. For despite his dog-eared countenance, the nicotine-creased brows and jowls, Meyer Lansky was a killer with a degree in the pure maths of malevolence if his profit was endangered.

Dino Cellini, for all the charm and culture, was equally determined. He'd always lived by games of chance and it was chance that gave him a link to set up London's most colourful gambling establishment. Enrolled in his croupier school was one Joel Salkin, whose uncle Alfred was the poker-room manager at Crockford's. Joel Salkin arranged a meeting between the two gambling men. Alfred Salkin took Dino Cellini's idea of an American casino in central London to his bosses, who were enthusiastic.

Crockford's sent a team to the Bahamas to study the syndicate's Lucayan operations; then Crockford's opened negotiations with the Lyons catering group for an American-style casino at the Cumberland Hotel in Marble Arch. It didn't work out and Alfred Salkin moved to the Isle of Man to run Crockford's casino there. And chance, or someone, intervened once again. Thomas William Parker, owner of the Colony Club, was suddenly outed for £65,000 in income tax fraud and sentenced to three years' jail at the Old Bailey in November 1964; with the help of Benny Huntman, the smart West End nightspot was sold to Silvio and Giovanni Tolaini. Others favoured the Berkeley Square location, including Jack Cooper of Miami, investor and arms supplier to the Trujillo dictatorship. Cooper met the Tolaini brothers with a view to buying the Colony. His partner in this was New York gambling promoter Stephen Tolk, who in early Lansky times had run casinos in Saratoga, New York and Miami.

Yet after talking with Dino Cellini, Cooper decided against buying the Colony; it was 'too small'. Cellini and Alfred Salkin went to see the Tolainis. Benny Huntman chaired the meeting, poured the drinks. They set up the Colony Sporting Club Company with £100 nominal capital in September 1965. Salkin resigned from Crockford's and moved to Berkeley Square as managing director in October. Four months later, the Tolainis, who'd worked with Benny Huntman to take over the Colony location, moved on with a handsome payout.

Those funds and much more came from new investors including Gordon Marks and Cyril Shack, directors of Phonographic Equipment Company Ltd, distributors of amusement and fruit machines, including the products of Bally of Chicago, of which Lansky's old pal Morris Kleinman was a prime operator. Sam Klein, treasurer, a director and a large stockholder of Bally Manufacturing Company of Chicago, makers of gambling and amusement machines, introduced several Americans who bought shares. It was all about hitting that jackpot.

And it was all as incestuous as the Steubenville connections.

Lansky's teams were everywhere in Europe. The French Sûreté were monitoring Lansky himself and his associates in Nice, Paris and Marseilles. American drug detectives followed Lansky and Joe Nesline in London. The Federal Bureau of Narcotics was especially interested in Charlie 'The Blade' Tourine, who worked with Mafia bosses Ruggiero Boiardo of New Jersey, linked with the Genovese family in New York, and Anthony Salerno of East Harlem. Tourine saw himself as 'an opportunist', and he discovered criminal opportunity in killing, gambling and drug-trafficking.

Joe Nesline mirrored those activities, but his job in London was to do with gambling. He had several meetings with Billy Hill, the crime mastermind who also operated out of Tangier. The dapper, quietly spoken Hill, who conducted his meetings over pots of lukewarm tea, had schemes running in casinos throughout Britain. He'd controlled the nation's underworld for many, many years and advised that the Colony should have an English 'face'.

His lieutenant Bobby McKew remembers suggesting the band leader Paul Adam: 'I met them with Bill because you couldn't really do anything properly in London without his cooperation. They wanted someone to run their club, the Colony. I was talking to Bill and I said that the ideal person would be Paul Adam. He'd be a marvellous front because he was Princess Margaret's favourite band leader, played in the Milroy and was a housewife's choice. He was tall, handsome, a very good-looking man. He'd bring them in.

'The Americans, two men, Joe Nesline and a guy who never gave his name – dark suits, white shirts, very smart-looking men with beady eyes – were staying in a hotel off Conduit Street and came over to see us. Nesline had close-set eyes. He looked at you and he could freeze you just by doing that. I asked them, "Drink?" They both growled, "Club orange." Paul was there and had had a few; he was pissed and he kept pulling up a girl's skirt. The Yanks were annoyed and the next day when we met they said, "He drinks. He's not for us."

'Which was when Bill told them, "You need an Englishman. You've got to realise the Mafia here is the police. If you haven't got an Englishman who can deal with the police, sort them, it won't work."

'The Mafia guys were from the Midwest, tough guys, and

didn't quite believe all this, and they said, "We'll put our guy in, there's no question about that."'

Hill was not listened to, a rarity in his life.

The gambling men on duty must have no fallibilities. And such men, such familiar faces, were arriving in London. Dan 'Dusty' Peters rolled into town and Vincenzo Spertino, who'd left the croupier school and been over at the Lucayan Beach Hotel and Casino, arrived soon after. The Colony Sporting Club was in business before the star turn showed up.

George Raft was still in his monogrammed dressing gown when he took the London call just before breakfast at his friend's villa on the Florida coast. He was wanted as the host of the Colony Club; it was a personal invitation from Dino Cellini, whom Raft knew from Cuba and the Bahamas. The star, whom Hollywood had demoted to a cameo man, went for it – in style.

He flew to London for meetings with Dino Cellini and at the same time raised his profile with an appearance on television's *The Eamonn Andrews Show*. He danced the Charleston on *Sunday Night at the London Palladium* after sending up his gangster image, bringing the Roaring Twenties back for a moment with the host, Jimmy Tarbuck. In front of a celebrity audience at the Grosvenor House Hotel, he appeared on *This Is Your Life*.

What was George Raft's life was George Raft, the negotiable image. OK, he wore a corset underneath his tuxedo, but he was hugely popular. He sold the myth and it sold well, with a wave of his red breast-pocket handkerchief. The Colony became George Raft's Colony Club in Las Vegas-style neon over the entrance. It ignited a spark in genteel Berkeley Square.

George Raft, at 71, got quite a deal: five points in the Colony, $200 a week in his pocket, a rent-free two-bedroom apartment (Belton Towers, 55 Park Lane), a full-time maid, all meals and a wine-coloured Rolls-Royce, registration NM777, with an on-call liveried chauffeur. Another of his needs was for his clothes to be pressed every day, giving 'a feeling of class to me and the place'.

Class was important. Raft organised the club's restaurant, insisted on the best food, fine wine, conviviality. It was the Lansky philosophy: create an environment where high rollers feel entitled to lose as much money as possible. It was also as close to American gaming as you could get without being in Vegas. Craps was played to East Coast rules and layout. Punto banco, a South American version of chemmy, was introduced and roulette wheels spun displaying two zeros. There were only 11 tables and the chips were a maximum £25 – some casinos ran to £1,000 maximum chips – but the turnover was constant and 'some players threw them away like confetti'.

As part of his London life, George Raft had a girlfriend, Helen Elliott, then 25, a former Miss Rhodesia who added to the glamour of his image and the Colony. She told the *Sunday Mirror*:

> George was the most charming and debonair man but an awful lot of work went into that image. He took longer to get ready to go out than any woman. He wore a corset under his tuxedo; before he set off for the Colony, he had a guy from a wig firm come round to fit his hairpiece. That cost him about £40 a week. He still had that trenchcoat look with the hat pulled down over the eyes.
>
> He wanted me to look the part, too. He supervised my clothes. He wouldn't have me looking like a dolly bird. My clothes had to be long and ladylike and dignified, what he called classy. I always had to be decorative at all times.
>
> George always gave me £30 to £50 to play the tables at the Colony. There was never a cross word if I lost it. And if I won, I could keep the winnings.

George kept the winnings, too – but only for transport. On a trip to California, he had his non-American mistress carry a case for him: 'He didn't tell me what was in it, so I had a peek when he wasn't looking. I found rolls and rolls of notes. Thousands and thousands of dollars. It frightened the hell out of me.'

It delighted Benny Huntman and Dino Cellini. The money was going in the right direction: towards Meyer Lansky. Couriers were laundering the cash from Britain and around Europe. Bagmen and -women, on a basic salary of £12,000 a year, moved worldwide with cases of bank notes, the syndicate's profits from casinos everywhere. They always worked in pairs between Britain and the USA: a native of each country. An American was never asked what currency he was taking out of Britain, and a Briton was never asked what currency he was taking into the States. The American carried the cash out of London and handed it over to the Briton on the flight. It worked in all geographical variations.

It seemed ridiculously easy, but keeping it simple was the charm of it all. When Benny Huntman had reported the plans for legalised gambling in the UK, the team assembled by Lansky presumed the British government was working for them. The set-up was perfect.

In America, their biggest hurdle was the IRS, and getting around the taxman was part of the Mafia way of life. No one ever forgot that accounts, not a bullet, ended Al Capone. Illicit drugs and gambling gains couldn't go on the official accounts, as the IRS could demand to know where they came from. But if the money was invested in legalised gambling in the UK, it became 'gambling profit'. The 1960s Mafia invasion of Britain, with Angelo Bruno appointed as one of the generals, was intended as a permanent occupation.

The usual rules were employed by the usual suspects: once in the syndicate consolidated its position by corrupting police, public officials and politicians. They did it quietly and over time, working on those already prepared by Benny Huntman while the charismatic Dino Cellini worked his own magic. Deals were done with British casinos by making handshake agreements with businessmen approved by the gaming authorities and licensing justices. The men who ran some casinos were puppets.

The Mob cut was skimmed off in the cashiers' cages each night: the accounts revealed only 70 per cent of the real returns. The one necessity, an intractable demand, was that a trusted syndicate lieutenant, the equivalent of a George Sadlo, had to 'count the take'. For this reason, there were a good number – the most accurate count is 19 – of Mafia 'sleepers', quiet and younger businessmen, in place and standing apart from those with a higher profile from the past or present. They were an essential part of the occupation, the secret army of the future.

At the start of 1966, a landmark meeting in London was requested and so organised by Benny Huntman. Meyer

Lansky was to be in town, as were Angelo Bruno, Charlie the Blade and Dino Cellini, as well as representatives of the interests of gangsters in Germany, France, Holland and Belgium and Yugoslavia, the criminal Common Market.

That the meeting was being held and even the supposed location was leaked by inside men to officers in Scotland Yard; to make themselves look good, the high-ranking officers discreetly put it around with their friends in the press that they had infiltrated the Mob men and this summit conference had been scuppered. It went ahead instead at a private home in Wimbledon, south-west London. At the meeting, courier routes for casino profits were organised, as well as locations for gaming establishments throughout the Continent.

And all the time the America–London connection of cash-trafficking was enhanced by the gamblers, high rollers, imported from across America, which in itself became a profitable travel business. Every mile of the way, there was a profit to be made. With the deal to make the Dorchester the flagship of American gambling still furiously being worked on, the syndicate aimed to keep Sir Maxwell Joseph happy. The American junketeers were given suites of rooms paid for by the Mob at his hotel.

Eric Steiner ran the Pair of Shoes nightclub-casino in London. It was an amiable environment and the aristocratic Mark Sykes, who worked with him for a time, described the action: 'Eric organised what he called the junkets for high rollers from Las Vegas who were flown over to London and stayed for a week at the Dorchester, all expenses paid. The American gangsters in Las Vegas sent over planeloads of people who would gamble at the Pair of Shoes. It was staggering business. It was wonderful. All these people who would come over and they all took over the floor of our casino.

'These people would open big lines of credit each and the gangster guy at the other end would guarantee the money. We were paid everything in two weeks. No money changed hands. All markers went into the accounts and within two weeks we had the money. Tremendously efficient, the Americans.'

David Cornwell found that out as well, courtesy of Dino Cellini. 'I'd become homesick for my family and London. As gaming was starting to open up in the capital, I decided to return. Dino Cellini had been told by the authorities he couldn't work in Grand Bahama, so he'd again taken over the school that was constantly turning out trained dealers for the expanding Bahama business. He was helped by Freddie Ayoub.

'Dino Cellini had some big news for me. He told me that he intended to open a casino in Berkeley Square and he wanted me to work there. I jumped at the chance, but as the casino opening was six months away, and as he wanted to keep my commitment, he suggested that I go to work for a man who had a small casino in Mayfair. This was Eric Steiner and the club was the Pair of Shoes.

'What an experience this would be. Dino took me around to the Pair of Shoes. He sits me down with Eric, who was absolutely nuts. I'm looking at Eric and said to myself, "Where do I know you from? I know you from somewhere." I twigged. When I worked in the shoe shop in Old Bond Street, one day I was outside cleaning the window and a sky-blue 1959 Thunderbird comes up, the one that Sinatra drove. It was Eric Steiner, with two of the most beautiful women you have ever seen. He was a little man, Eric, although he wore elevator shoes. He got out with these two women, one on each arm, and he comes into the shop. I always remember looking at him, looking at his shoes. I never had seen anything like it. He had alligator, buckled shoes on, with heels as high as you like. It was an exotic animal for 1961. He bought each of the women a pair of shoes; it was part of his patter.

'Originally, Eric had borrowed the money to open the Pair of Shoes from Charlie Matthews, a well-known Irish gypsy bookmaker who also ran a second-hand car business; afterwards he wouldn't let Charlie Matthews in because he said he was too rough for the place, which was in Hertford Street, Mayfair, just behind the Hilton Hotel. Eric was a degenerate Swedish poker player, well known in Southern California, but his former life was shrouded in mystery. He lived in a small apartment on the top floor of the club. I started to work for Eric and soon understood what a complete lunatic he was. He was terrified of being kidnapped and had two ferocious-looking Alsatian dogs, Lucky and Gangster.

'Most of his staff were stealing from him and Eric knew it. He had a coloured butler called Robinson, who shuffled around and talked and looked like Louis Armstrong. When anybody is an out-and-out thief, they always think everybody else is thieving from them. Eric was so paranoid that he had a sophisticated eavesdropping system installed around the club to listen to what dealers were saying, and he would listen to this while lying in his bed upstairs. All the dealers were aware of the secreted microphones and would deliberately set Eric up by having fictitious conversations about cheating that would bring Eric running downstairs to discover that nothing was happening. Every dealer in the place knew where the mikes were. There was one behind the craps table on the floor by the skirting, so every time you leaned over the table, you gave it a kick, and about five minutes later Eric would come running down in his dressing gown, saying, "What's going on? What's going on?"

'Crazy as he was, he made it work. All the stars turned up, Sophia Loren, Ursula Andress, Charlotte Rampling. It was an elegant club. It was small, but it was very elegant. Eric was a son of a bitch, but he had terrific taste. He was a character. There was a celebrity service that you could subscribe to and they would send you a printout every day of the stars that were coming to London. Eric would go out and buy two dozen roses and have them delivered to a famous actress with an invitation to his club.

'Eric was kinder to me than to the other dealers because he knew I was close to Dino and he respected him. Also, I was a great dealer. One night, an oil magnate landed in the club and played craps alone. At the end of the night, he'd lost £12,000, which was a very much needed and big score for Eric. There were always outstanding unpaid bills at the club and also Eric was playing a lot of poker. Before going home, Eric gave me a $200 tip for helping win the money, and he gave out some others. When I rolled up for work on the following night, there was a brand-new Mercedes-Benz soft-top coupé in front of the casino. Rather than pay his debts, Eric had gone out and bought himself a new car.

'I worked for Eric until I got the call from Dino, who was the front man for Meyer Lansky and his group, who were breaking into the booming casino business in the UK. The club also had some English shareholders in the amusement-machine business, who had been recruited in Miami Beach. The main players in the UK were Jewish, and Dino put Alfred Salkin in as the front man, thinking he'd bring in these players. Salkin was a man of limited social graces and charm, who in reality knew very few players. The Colony opened in February 1966, and for the first three months was practically empty.

'Then a man appeared on the scene who changed everything. George Raft might have been a fading movie star, but he had charisma and charm unsurpassed. The club was renamed George Raft's Colony Club. Immediately, it transformed into a very busy casino. Every American film star, celebrity, sportsman who hit London came to the club to dine and play. The song played every night by the live casino band was "A Nightingale Sang in Berkeley Square". George brought in a load of American junkets, and very rich and very colourful people, all Mafia-connected people. They used to have wild parties at the Mayfair Hotel. All the guys that worked there all went out together, even the manager. We'd go to a club and we would usually end up gambling ourselves till nine, ten, eleven o'clock in the morning, then go home broke. We used to close up later about four, five o'clock. We worked long hours. I saw them and dealt with them. They played.

'I was promoted to the job of inspector, so I could mix socially with the players. We had the whole cast of the film *The Dirty Dozen* playing in the casino most nights, with Telly Savalas being the lead player. John Huston, Ursula Andress, Sophia Loren, Robert Ryan, Barbra Streisand, Elliot Gould, Lee Marvin; Cubby Broccoli and another James Bond movie producer, Mike Frankovich, they were both big players.

'Frank Sinatra came in the club to play when I was on the table. Frank was very drunk and in the company of some tough-looking individuals who came up to the craps table, took some credit and started to play for Frank. All very normal, except that the man with Frank shooting the dice was a well-known dice mechanic who was "scooting" the dice down the table, a technique not allowed in casinos, and he started to win big money. This was potentially explosive, as Frank had a dangerous temper when drunk, so George Raft was brought out of the casino restaurant to defuse the situation. In his charming way, George convinced Frank to stop playing, although some of his entourage became argumentative. However, George insisted and the play stopped, much to my relief.

212

'One night, I heard the Colony restaurant maître d'hôtel, Mario, say to George that he thought Frank was an animal. It had been reported in the papers that Frank had slugged a reporter – normal behaviour for Frank. George immediately leapt to Frank's defence, telling Mario, "Listen, remember, there are two sides to every story." Maybe George's opinion was influenced by the fact that Frank Sinatra had settled some tax problems George had back in the US.

'After the Frank dice-shoot incident subsided, George was leaning on the craps table talking to Lucille Ball, who was absent-mindedly swinging her handbag, which bounced off George's crotch area. He told her: "If you swing that bag any more, you're going to knock my dick off." She laughed like hell. That was George, forever the ladies' man.

'George was a hell of a dresser who had his handmade silk shirts ironed by a lady in Conduit Street for £1 each: you could get a maid for £6 per week. He never had a suit cleaned, just sponged and pressed. He said that cleaning killed the material, and he was right. George was also a professional dancer, which was how he made a living in his youth, and he often took to the small dance floor in the club with some young partner, usually Helen Elliot, who was his girlfriend in London and who often visited the club.

'Working at the Colony was hard. We never closed while there was action and I often left the club when it was broad daylight outside, but every night was an experience. Adnan Khashoggi was at his zenith – they called him the richest man in the world – and he played for big money, as did the princes he brought into the club.

'There was a mysterious guy squiring Khashoggi around: you have never seen such an elegant man in all your life. He was a shareholder in one of the casinos in Vegas; he was always in the casino and he was always with Khashoggi. There was another guy who used to hang around with them, a Lebanese guy who had a travel company in Knightsbridge.

'One night, I was watching Dino, who was talking to Khashoggi, and there was something going on. Dino didn't want Khashoggi to go near a table, and he blocked him and was talking to him. Khashoggi was trying to leave and Dino was putting his arm up so that he couldn't. Dino was very good. Khashoggi was playing with half a dozen people around him, girls and others. They were all helping themselves to Khashoggi's chips, and somebody had taken quite a bit of money, put it in his pocket, hadn't cashed out. Dino didn't want Khashoggi to see that. One of Khashoggi's princes ended up being the king of somewhere.

'As the Colony backed onto a girlie club, the Astor, there was a passageway through which girls could be brought into the club discreetly. A player could have a look at them, and if he liked what he saw he could send a girl back to his hotel, the Mayfair around the corner usually. Many of those girls became very respectable in later years. One married one of the world's most celebrated movie stars.

'Another character who played around the club was Ben Cooper, brother of the enormously wealthy Jack Cooper of Miami Beach. Ben was always broke and he often came to me and others for a "loan" for playing money. Ben always got money; he was looked after.

'There was a mixture of showbiz celebrities and gangsters, people who were involved in various activities. The boxer Billy Walker's brother George was down there all the time in the company of some very doubtful people. Underworld characters like Patsy Murphy and the tough Italian Bert "Battles" Rossi and Albert Dimes were around. There were some dangerous types, too. And not always the gangsters. I went in the toilet one night and there was Lee Marvin having a pee, and he's peeing all over his shoes. As he came away, an attendant handed him a towel and Marvin growled, "I don't think that's necessary." He just walked out with pee all over his shoes.

'Apart from all the stars and celebrities coming to the club, there was another element that frequented the Colony that was more infamous than famous: major names in American organised crime. Every big-name gangster that came to Europe came to the club to pay their respects. I was introduced to Meyer Lansky at the training school for dealers that Dino continued to run. When Lansky met me, he said to Dino, "A good-looking kid like this should be in Hollywood." He was a small and unimposing man, but a real sharp mind and casino expert.

'We had regular gambling junkets hosted by some very heavy people from Boston, Massachusetts, Providence, Rhode Island, and Miami Beach. The games were honest and nobody ever got cheated. The turnover of cash was astonishing, which was the point.

'There was plenty of competition, clubs everywhere: Victoria Club, Twenty Club, Meadows, the Curzon House Club, Crockford's, the Clermont, the White Elephant, Les Ambassadeurs. There were hundreds of smaller clubs all over London, like the Cromwellian and the Mint. We had most of the business because they were clever operators. Dino and these guys, they knew what they were doing. They were sleek, experienced in every possible situation. We had the first American baccarat game in Europe, one that had its origins in Cuba, in the casino. Whatever was new, whatever would attract, we had in the Colony.'

It wasn't all tea and biscuits for the American visitors. The Mob were also involved in a club around Lower Sloane Street and Bobby McKew went to a meeting there. He remembers: 'It was a small basement club and they found out, well, someone told them, that one of the French croupiers was skimming with whoever ran the club and they were doing the business there. The Americans weren't happy. There was a lot of trouble about that and when I tried to go in there a charming, old-school lady who fronted the place said to me with her immaculate voice, "Ah, don't go down there, you'll find you'll get a fucking needle in your eye."'

It was a time when many people vanished. Anthony, who had gone to visit Freddie Mills with Roger Huntman, always carried a knife for protection. He explained to Roger Huntman it was because Benny Huntman 'had many enemies'. Anthony may have had some himself. As the only one out of the inner circle who could link Benny Huntman to Freddie's demise, it was convenient for all that he went AWOL. His name was never mentioned to Roger Huntman again. Anthony vanished from the scene completely. He wasn't alone.

London was contaminated with the outlaw behaviour that's somewhat compulsory in such circumstances. In the protection game, the bad guys carried business-disrupting, home-made petrol bombs along with their demanding attitude. Flames and mayhem were 'an encouragement'.

The clock was turning to high noon more often than was natural, especially after the drinks told gamblers they were tougher than George Raft – or Humphrey Bogart or Edward

G. Robinson. The snag was that they kept facing up to aristos who thought they were James Bond. Stick that lot in with the real bad guys and it could get nasty. For the crime statistics, bodies could be pushed under the carpet. More often, they were wrapped in carpets and taken to the south coast of England, a favoured route in London gangland for bon-voyage assignments.

One element frequenting the carpet-joint clubs was more of an irritation to the bosses than anything else: the Kray twins, or, as they were known to the casino workers, 'the Brothers Grim'. The Krays were shaking down many clubs in the West End for protection money and could be intimidating – but it was sorted out in an agreeable manner.

That was done, to no one's knowledge, by Angelo Bruno and a much-liked and clever Irishman called Johnny Francis. He had worked with the Krays in London, but they and he had decided it was in his interests to vanish to America. There, through connections, he became the chauffeur in California for one of the Mob's favourite entertainers, Nat King Cole. He then moved east to Philadelphia, where he worked as a driver for Angelo Bruno. Johnny Francis became fluent in Italian and a huge asset to his boss. He became seriously involved in the family business. And when the Colony versus the Krays confrontation loomed, he brought the twins and Angelo Bruno together again. The Mafia boss had met them first in 1963, during a scouting trip to the UK when he wanted to set up America's illegal game of numbers in Britain. It consists of betting on a number correlated from the results of a series of horse races.

Bruno regarded Ron and Reg Kray as 'neighbourhood toughs', something to be dealt with and kept sweet. It avoided trouble with the authorities, as well as a threatened gun war, and they might be of some strong-arm service. The deal was they would get £1,700 a week to stay out of all the casinos. It was spelled out that it was a take-it-or-take-the-consequences deal. The twins took the easy money. Why not? It was what every operator in town was doing. London was gambling crazy. And it was legal – the Lansky dream. Of course, the money financed more crime, more profit.

Most of the London underworld ran a parochial business; they did not often even glance north of Watford or towards

France; for Angelo Bruno and his boardroom members, London was an essential arena, the paymaster of their global ambitions. Long before casinos were granted a gaming licence in the UK, the Mob moved in like good businessmen; they presented themselves in the guise of legitimate companies and offered sound and very accountable business propositions, and – the hook – opportunities. They could and did talk huge amounts of investment from the fortune in profits from the rackets, especially narcotics-trafficking, which were spun into international semi-legitimate enterprises. Dino Cellini and Benny Huntman on one hand, Angelo Bruno on the other, could set share prices in casinos at levels no legitimate investor could afford. The Mob officers alone knew the extent of cash from the skim and the other huge enterprises it would finance.

To them, Britain wasn't a nation, like France, Germany, Holland, Italy and beyond: it was a revenue source. And the authorities were unfamiliar with how it all worked. It was essentially the same business as armed robbery: evil, cruel and sometimes fatal. The only difference was the bad guys wore smiles and tuxedos as they stole – and they didn't run away afterwards. They stayed, laid foundations and carried on plundering.

Europe had the added attraction of supposedly being out of bounds to the American authorities. There were almost continuous Senate investigating committees and Grand Jury inquiries into the syndicate. This drive was not sidetracked by the assassination of Senator Robert Kennedy at the Ambassador Hotel in Los Angeles on 5 June 1968.

Kennedy, who as US Attorney General had been a 'pain in the ass' for organised crime, died from his wounds on 6 June. The Mob had been wiretapped saying they'd get the Kennedy 'head and tail', with Angelo Bruno offering, 'We swagged the big one and the little one.'

Now the Mafia was pursuing even more vigorously its invasion of Europe. The American authorities, the intelligence and narcotics officers, the FBI, the CIA spooks on red alert, were as fearful as the British government, represented by a distracted, chinless Home Office, of the amount of illegal money streaming through London like a twin Thames. The banks could break at any moment.

13

ROSEBUD

'Puppet on a String', Sandie Shaw, 1967

The hush came as quickly as the fight had begun, and the knife flashed, a second of brilliant clarity in the subdued lighting of the late evening at the Colony Club. It was a moment to murder.

'Vinnie, for Chrissake, that's a cop there!'

Dino Cellini had seen the trouble building, and before Vincent 'Fat Vinnie' Teresa could stab to death a moonlighting Scotland Yard detective, he'd sent in the troops. The society people, the underworld guys, were breathless as they watched Teresa, who was stricken, aghast. 'I was gonna stab a cop.'

The fat mobster from New England had not one concern about the well-being of his almost victim; it was the consequences for his own future that concerned him. A London policeman's death in the Colony Club would have grabbed too much headline and government attention for even all of Benny Huntman's contacts to smooth over.

Dino Cellini's instincts had avoided that upset. He'd met the real Al Capone; this time, he'd only had to deal with the Hollywood version. In 1960, the thickset actor Neville Brand had played Capone in *The Scarface Mob* and he was in London en route to Los Angeles. He'd enjoyed the lavish hospitality at the Colony and his diction was no longer RADA intact. Neither was his choreography: his hands and arms were roaming all over the ample breasts of a party girl called Dawn. Unhappily for the actor, Dawn was with a 22-stone hoodlum called Danny Mondavano, who in turn was with his partner Vinnie Teresa. They were running a gambling junket.

Teresa had left the couple with his friend Telly Savalas when Brand had wandered over. Danny Mondavano was a huge man and he loudly asked Savalas to tell Brand to leave

Dawn alone. Brand had booze blocking his hearing and ignored the request. Suddenly, Brand was as flat out as the club's uncorked sparkling wine. And Mondavano was about to seriously hurt him when three Colony men went into action.

Looking back on this time in court testimony and, later, with more bravado in his book *My Life in the Mafia*, Teresa remembered:

> It looked like they were going to tear Danny apart. I grabbed a steak knife and started running towards the one holding Danny. Just as I was about to cut this guy up, Freddie Ayoub grabs my arm and shouts that he's a cop. I was going to stab a plain-clothes cop from Scotland Yard. There was a stink, but Telly stepped in and told the cop that Brand had started trouble with the girl.

It was close; an amorous Hollywood Al Capone came within the blade of a big, sharp steak knife of ending the Mafia's gambling invasion just as it was going at full throttle – with Vinnie Teresa very much part of the charge. The Swinging London of the '60s had its degenerate depths, but it was the disassembling of authority that most changed the future. It was when money envy replaced the class variety and gambling became a way of life.

The Gaming and Betting Act that had so excited Meyer Lansky and company was explained to the British Parliament as helping housewives play cards for sixpences with their friends and vicars hold raffles to boost church funds. In return, the UK had a casino culture, with the Mafia running much of the action. The zero was banned from roulette, to establish equal odds between the punter and the house. The ban was mostly ignored and the punter didn't complain. Indeed, British gamblers appeared to enjoy the absolute certainty of losing long term over the mere possibility of winning in the short term. Maybe it's something to do with the stiff upper lip.

Harold Macmillan brought in Premium Bonds in 1956, which earned no interest and, like most government offerings, lost value. The chance, the small chance, was of winning a £5,000 prize. The Labour Party leader Harold Wilson raged that this was 'a squalid raffle'. It was a reasonable view. When Labour took power in 1964 and Wilson became Prime Minister, he increased the Premium Bond jackpot prize to £25,000.

Britain became a land of medium rollers but the natives were no match for the American gamblers being flown over to London. Britain's tourist industry loved the junkets; more and more central London hotels – the Hilton, Londonderry House, the Royal Lancaster, the Mayfair, Grosvenor House, the Park Lane and the Royal Garden – occupied their rooms with gamblers, and business was good in the shops. Junkets started in the early days of Las Vegas with free flights in long-haul piston-engined aircraft to the only American state with legalised casino gambling. As the casinos opened in the Caribbean, junkets followed naturally, and when gambling got going in London the American promoters were quick to join the party. Then there were trips to Monte Carlo, Lisbon, Seville, Kenya and beyond. London was the world's junket hub for gambling, and travel agents on both sides of the Atlantic cashed in – with a little help from the boys.

The Mafia, of course, was pulling the strings. Junkets to London offered good returns for their promoters: 15 per cent of the aggregate loss of the gamblers on the junket, or 10 per cent plus a fee of $50 a head. The organiser would also take money on discounts arranged with airlines.

Which introduced the 'flying fleece'. Every moment counts when you're stealing money. The high-altitude swindles began on the five- and six-hour flights into Vegas from the East Coast. There was little time for gaming elegance, so the card games played were 'Skin' or 'Banker and Broker'. They were not sophisticated: in Skin you bet that your opponent will not match the card dealt to you before you do; if you pull a king and the other player draws one of the three remaining kings before you do, you lose, and vice versa. In Banker and Broker, it's even easier. Whoever draws the highest card wins. With stacked decks, the impatient gambler could lose big; a player dropped $38,000 on one flight.

It always came around to the Lansky code of creating the environment, of giving the punter the entitlement to lose lots and lots of money. Vincent Teresa, who in 1967 updated casino junket arrangements with Papa Doc Duvalier in Haiti, established the Esquire Sportsman's Club at 10 Emerson Place, overlooking the Charles River in Boston. From there, the global gamblers went to London, Haiti, Antigua, the Dominican Republic, Puerto Rica, the Bahamas, the island of Madeira and the Portuguese mainland.

Esquire's operations were signed off by Lansky and Angelo Bruno, who had approved arrangements with the involved Mob bosses. In London, it had been agreed that chartering planes was too complicated and that airline package deals were best: the rule was one free ticket for every fifteen passengers. A group about the size of a classroom of kids was the preferred number. Deals were done between the Esquire Sportsman's Club and the Lucayan Beach in Grand Bahama. Max Courtney made the arrangements for Lansky with Antigua, where Charlie the Blade organised the percentages, and also the Lido Casino in Santo Domingo, which was controlled by Santo Trafficante Jr. It was a closed club.

Papa Doc in Haiti was the toughest boss that Vincent Teresa encountered. His people were begging in the street and Duvalier was begging Teresa to make him more money. Foreigners were welcome if they did that, but if not they were often shot. The snake-eyed dictator agreed the Mob could use their own gaming gear and croupiers but insisted the brutal Tonton Macoutes, his zombie guards, watched the money. Papa Doc would not be cheated.

Teresa insisted he would be. Bugger voodoo. This was the Mob. Fat Vinnie maintained they weren't going to be intimidated by machine-gun-armed, sharp-suited secret policemen posing in reflector glasses. The operators spiked the Tontons drinks, placed false bottoms in the cash boxes and used a tricky system to switch the cash so that Papa Doc's cut was only ever of half of the actual cash available. The Mob were skimming for themselves.

The gamblers travelling to Port-au-Prince spent their first two or three nights in Miami at the Hilton Plaza Hotel. They were 'warmed up' there by Fat Vinnie and his team. One evening, a craps game was going in a penthouse suite when a Baltimore insurance agent, over-served earlier in the cocktail lounge, said he was going to bet against himself. The game was switched to dice and the guy lost $12,000 in 18 minutes. Distraught, he attempted to jump out of the hotel window.

Teresa saved him: 'He didn't pay us yet. After, we'd let him jump.'

However the profit was made, the Caribbean trips were set up like those to Europe. Everything was on credit. The gambler is given a 'free' flight and hotel, meals and drinks at the casino, but after paying a deposit of $500 to $1,500. In return for his money, he gets an equivalent amount of non-negotiable chips; they can't be changed into money or negotiable chips, but can be used only for gambling. There's a proven psychological urge: junketeers are desperate to get rid of their non-negotiable chips and often lose them instantly. That way, they can get on with the real gambling.

It is a different world and mindset. Obsessed gamblers can play for 24 hours and appear as if they've enjoyed a good night's sleep. The focus, the concentration is such that it seems to overtake normal physiology. Holding on to the 'funny money' chips brands the player 'a stiff'. He's not a person of interest and is ignored, or fed 'a mickey' and put out of action. The big spender – that is, loser – is lavished with the caviar-and-champagne treatment.

The operation was based on the assumption that the gambler is going to lose. The potential value of any junket was upwards of half a million dollars. Credit was advanced on markers. Yes, some of the players settled these IOUs before leaving the UK. But most paid their debts back in America. And from there it could go anywhere, like, say, Switzerland.

This was the core of the global cash turnover; at times, Lansky and his associates were doing their own laundry with their profits. It was essential, for the IRS was all over the Las Vegas casinos and their books. The skim never ever went on the books, but it had to look 'reasonable' – which was not something the boys liked being. The huge profits were to be made abroad.

Vincent Teresa, colourful, clinically obese, with an imaginative fancy to match his size, enjoyed attention and that at times damaged his reputation for veracity. It's hard to expect perfect testimony from an acknowledged swindler, thief and active member of organised crime. Yet this Humpty Dumpty with spectacles was working intimately with the most successful gangsters of the twentieth century. He had references. And he learned quickly. He remembered:

The really big money was in the foreign junkets. There were no tax men to count up the loot in the casino's back room, there was no heat over points, politicians were bought off, there was just good, solid crooked casinos owned by the Mob to deal with.

One of the best places was Antigua in the British West Indies. You couldn't have found a more crooked place. The big casino was the Mamora Beach Hotel and the Mob had carte blanche there. The two guys running the show were Charlie the Blade and Angelo Chieppa. Charlie the Blade worked with Meyer Lansky in Havana when Cuba was a Mob playland. Everything in Antigua was in the bag, starting with the government.

Antigua taught me that there was money to be made running junkets if you handled them the right way. The world was a Mob oyster. The Mob had its finger in the pie everywhere and usually it was Meyer Lansky's finger. London was a good example. There were half a dozen moving casinos in that city. A number of them had rigged games and Angelo Bruno had a piece of a couple of them I know about.

Teresa insisted his Esquire Sportsmen's Club wanted more than that. The rule was you took a gambler subtly, not with a sledgehammer to the head; which was why he went to Jimmy Blue Eyes.

He would check out people for Lansky to see they had the OK from their Mob to do business with him. Jimmy Blue Eyes is the Mob's watchdog. When you wanted to run junkets into the Colony Club, the man you made arrangements through was either Lansky or his right arm, Dino Cellini. They'd give you the clearance and make sure you got a piece of the profits.

If you were a Mob representative running a junket to the club, they'd kick back 15 per cent of all the money lost by the people you brought. That could result in some very serious money being made, because this was a class operation, on a par with some of the best casinos in Las Vegas.

The Colony, according to Fat Vinnie, provided around $4 million a week in action.

It was fronted by George Raft for Cellini and Lansky. We first met at the Capri in Havana. Raft was the official host and greeter for the club, which was controlled by Charlie the Blade, a good friend of Raft's. I was there with a couple of guys from Boston to gamble and have some fun. In London, Raft was there as an attraction to bring the suckers in. He did his job and entertainers would flock to the place because they were his friends; it became the place to be. Raft would come down every night dressed in a tuxedo. He'd meet all the people, sign autographs, dance with the women. He told me Cellini put him in the place as a figurehead to draw in the people. His movie career was over and this was a nice way to keep living off the hog. He was a helluva drawing card. That was the best investment Lansky and Cellini made at the Colony Club.

Not only did we beat the American government on taxes, but they beat the British government on the other end as well. I almost never had a trip to London that made less than 50 to 80 grand for me – that means the Colony was knocking down 600 to 900 grand on just one of my junkets – and that doesn't include what we were knocking down from suckers in rigged card parties at the Mayfair Hotel. I made the really big money in the hotel. Top-name entertainers, politicians, judges used to be at the parties, which were wall-to-wall broads, booze and food. We'd use the broads, all good-looking hustlers, to lay the suckers we wanted to bust out.

We were having a party at the Mayfair, a big cocktail party with 20 or 30 people. A crap game started and out of a clear blue sky Joe Swartz walked in and asked if he could join the party. Joe was a building contractor from Baltimore. The game was rigged and we beat him $17,000 in half an hour.

That was not how the money was made at the Colony Club. It was legal gambling and the games were straight. They always did it the old-fashioned way: they cleaned it. There were no grand mechanics there; if needs must, Dino Cellini was the king. The Colony legitimately expected to get $17 for every $100, such were the odds; the twist of the cards was in the reporting of the turnover and the profit: a 50,000 night to the house would go down as 25 or 30, always much lower but *always* an acceptable number.

Teresa detailed how it worked for his trips:

> We put up a grand for every man going to the Colony. Out of that, he got $820 in English-pound non-negotiable chips. After he worked his way through that, he'd go on credit and sign receipts for more chips. When he got back to the States, I'd collect what he owed the casino.
>
> Cellini would come to see me or I'd fly to Florida to see him. Everything was on paper; a guy like me handled all the payoffs to Cellini or Lansky. The playing customer never played with cash if he was on a junket. It was through a credit system we could keep track of what the club took in and what was owed me. Cellini came to my office in Boston at least four times to collect money owed to the Colony and I flew to Florida twice to pay him. Both times Lansky was there.
>
> The first time, I had over 40 grand and I laid it on the table in front of them. The second time, Lansky sat behind the desk and I handed him over 50 grand. He put his right hand out, took the money, put it on the desk and fingered through it. That was the day he and Cellini offered to arrange for me to run junkets to Paradise Island in the Bahamas and the Lucayan Beach casino run by Max Courtney. I took a trip to Paradise Island but I didn't like the set-up, even though Eddie Cellini, Dino's brother, was in charge of the operation.

In 1967, Meyer Lansky filed his income tax returns to the IRS in America, giving his income as $71,411.27. In the next tax year, he declared $42,563.23. During this time, IRS investigators and the FBI, along with some division from almost all US law-enforcement agencies, estimated that Lansky had rolled over many millions of dollars. They couldn't prove it. But they tracked $6 million from the Monte Carlo Casino in Grand Bahama alone. Similar takes were brought in from around the world. Las Vegas was the most regular paymaster; one IRS count put it at a conservative $40 million over a three-year period. Every 24 hours, cash profits were skimmed off the hotels' winnings and transported by rail to Miami and Lansky. Every courier was hand-picked and times and trains changed.

Looking for a 'million-dollar heist', one team from Canada attempted to rob the courier. Neither they nor the courier knew that two of Jimmy Blue Eyes' enforcers were escorting the money, watching the mule's back. The three Montreal hoodlums remained in the Nevada desert while the cash went on to Florida.

When the payments got there, Lansky and company would meet in the card room of the Singapore Hotel and share it out: any Vegas excess would be sent off to the International Credit Bank in Geneva. Lansky was acutely aware of how much his financial paperwork was scrutinised. He was canny enough to get hard cash out of his environment quickly but also to have it within reach. Lansky and company were magicians at making money vanish and police and politicians look the other way. Cash was the ultimate power, the proven corrupter.

One underappreciated irony is that Lansky had all the money in the world but couldn't safely spend it. His riches, his real wealth, could never be displayed. A huge wealth hibernated. It's the dream of every mobster to be legitimate; in their confused morality, they want to handle crooked money honestly – but only after they've cheated for every penny or cent. In this world, you were never doing your job properly if you weren't chiselling someone. The wiretapped Mafia man's view was: 'Every fucking day's a scam to keep your power and position. Especially at the top.'

Fat Vinnie and others could shake Meyer Lansky's pedestal. But, in truth, this deity of global gambling was the architect of his own demise. He was too successful. The long-range planning, the aptitude, of connected operators like Benny Huntman, the skill and experience of Dino Cellini and the gambling crew, made Lansky's dream come true; but what Harold Macmillan liked to call 'events' put a nasty scar across his grand design.

14

FAREWELL, MY LOVELY

'Albatross', Fleetwood Mac, 1969

Money was a worry for James 'Sunny Jim' Callaghan, the rising power in Labour prime minister Harold Wilson's Cabinet. It was a necessity of his job as Britain's Chancellor of the Exchequer. The pound was getting a kicking, which meant he was, too.

The nation's balance of payments was lamentable. After a tumultuous time, Sunny Jim's bets weren't working. With Roy Jenkins' Home Office, the Chancellor focused on the gambling industry. Harold Wilson's supporters had encouraged him to find a distraction for the media.

Wilson was aware of the underworld infiltration into Britain. There had been discussion with MI5 officers and also liaison operatives from MI6, and in conversation and notes the Prime Minister called it 'a Mafia invasion'. He took it very seriously. Wilson prided himself on the image of the UK as bright, clean and fun, like the early Beatles or sharp Vidal Sassoon haircuts, a flowered-tie confection complementing the pageantry and pomp. Chicago-style gangsters weren't at all Trafalgar Square.

The Cole Porter element – anything goes – added to the casino culture's damaging public image. Wilson could blame the previous Tory administration for it all. It was Harold Macmillan's lot who had brought in the Gaming Act. And they were indeed naive. The original legislation had become a mockery. It was intended, in a fluttering vicar's-tea-party sort of way, to allow gambling for fund-raising at garden fetes; instead it had created the bonanza of the commercial gaming industry. And as they couldn't understand the consequences of the new laws they were making, the legislators had put nothing in place to control them. There were no legal requirements on the way the games should be played.

It wasn't just Meyer Lansky and company who took advantage, but they were there at the kick-off thanks to Benny Huntman and the network of contacts he'd established. These inside men had also helped keep the British government off the backs of the Mafia gamblers. Yet as Callaghan talked of new taxes on the gambling industry, Roy Jenkins was pushing for a more immediate crackdown on the Mob – with the Colony Club the example to be made.

The headlines were screaming of protection rackets, of strong-arm men collecting debts and of the growing influence of the European Mafia in Britain. And there were the pictures of rich gamblers puffing on torpedoes of Cuban tobacco. All they had to do was chuck champagne in their faces to totally get the public going. Newspaper editorials demanded gaming reform. In Westminster, they predicted the eventual devaluation of the pound. And the roulette wheels kept spinning with the illegal zero showing and giving the house the edge.

Benny Huntman and his underground lobby countered the arguments about criminal venality, saying they were simply a ruse 'to put through measures which stem from the traditional Socialist moral dislike of gambling itself'.

The British government jumped over the arguments. And George Raft, who used to get his in the last reel of black-and-white celluloid in his Warner Bros days, was first in the firing line. Raft was at home in California in January 1967 when he received a telephone call at his neat, always neat, Beverly Hills house. He was told Home Secretary Roy Jenkins had branded him an undesirable alien and he was banned from Britain. Raft told his informant he was mistaken. He wasn't. After a few days and many phone calls, the disillusioned Raft knew it, too.

He was confused: 'I regard London as my second home. I pay taxes there and here, too. I have no idea what it is all about.' Normally, the elderly actor would have been banned without any Home Office announcement. But a UK newspaper, *The Guardian*, revealed the decision – one that had been discussed at the top Cabinet level for fourteen days. He was told his continued presence in the United Kingdom would not be conducive to the public good. It was more public relations than anything else. Raft was a figurehead. Yes, he took the Mob coin – so did a lot of people – but that was it. He enjoyed the reflected glory of being surrounded by the Mob boys and it worked vice versa, especially with those of similar pedigree and longevity, which was always enough to comprise a dinner party. George Raft was good for business, but, as Billy Hill had predicted, he wasn't English and he wouldn't survive.

From the outset, the Colony was apple-pie American, despite the scattering of British shareholders and directors; Dino Cellini introduced a team of veteran American gambling operators including Freddie Ayoub, Cal Simon, the daytime gaming manager, Whitey Steir, famous for his manner at the craps tables, and Mitch Vuceta. Under them, the Colony was the nearest establishment in London to the authentic atmosphere of an American club. Their imitators in other London casinos never achieved the same effect. They were the men who gave the Colony its style. When they were working, the gambling was intense.

Although the Colony was run straight, David Cornwell always felt the club was under threat: 'I think it was doomed from the beginning. There was a lot of jealousy, too. I think the other operators, people like John Aspinall at the Clermont, were saying to the friendly coppers, "You know what's going on down there? You know what's going on? Gangsters are coming in, and this is happening and that is happening." The worst for it was a guy at a trademark club. What a piece of shit he was. Oh, yes. I've been in the club working and he's come round with a policeman, saying, "You see what they are doing here? They are doing wrong." Greed is what upsets most people. I've seen it so many times. Greed always upsets everybody. If you are sensible and intelligent and you let everybody get a bit to eat, there's not a problem. It's when people want to hog the lot that there's trouble.'

The heat became relentless. The apparently affable but deadly Angelo 'Gentle Don' Bruno was banned from Britain. Albert Dimes and Benny Huntman took over his hands-on responsibilities. Bruno took an apartment in Nice where another, younger associate visited him with the usual suitcases. Dino Cellini, with his great foresight and experience, thrown out of Cuba, banned from the Bahamas in 1964, too hot to handle in Chicago and Las Vegas, on Papa Doc's blacklist, had predicted the events; other arrangements had been made. Yet he went through the protests when his turn came to become *persona non grata* in the UK.

He was ordered to leave Britain by midnight on 20 March 1967, but said he would remain until a plea for a three-week extension of his permit was answered by the Home Office. He wanted to bring a libel case case against the BBC and two of its reporters from *24 Hours*. They'd said he was some sort of gangster, knew connected people.

He most certainly knew Meyer Lansky, who was number one on the Home Office's Top Ten Most Unwanted List. And other chart favourites, Charlie 'The Blade' Tourine (Home Office memos called him 'a hatchet man'), Anthony 'Tony Ducks' Carollo and resident but background enforcer John Joe Simocie. A series of other names were given to airports and ports to stop entry.

The surveillance became as intense as the gambling at the Colony. Alfred Salkin seemed at a loss following the departure of George Raft and Dino Cellini from day-to-day activities. Maybe he missed them. He made several trips to Miami for meetings with Dino Cellini, who had not pursued his libel action and had left Britain on 21 March 1967, by train from Victoria Station. When Salkin was asked about him, he replied, 'I have met Dino Cellini lots of times. He was one of the finest men you could wish to meet. I am proud to know him.'

They would have had business to discuss in Florida. After his Home Office expulsion, Dino Cellini went to Miami and worked with the travel agency, Travel and Resort Enterprises Inc., operated by his friend and associate George Berger from Suite 721 at the Dupont Plaza Centre. They sent over a steady flow of high-powered junkets to the Colony Club. The company also sent groups of gamblers to casinos in their ever-increasing network, in Estoril, Paris, Rome, Athens and South America. There were also trips to South Africa and Indonesia. Exceedingly lucrative were the junkets to the Bahamas, to Paradise Island, which Cellini and others now knew as 'Meyer's Island'.

Dino Cellini was a pragmatic man. George Raft made a noise about his ban; he contacted J. Edgar Hoover through their mutual friend, the newspaper columnist Walter Winchell. Hoover stuck to the official line: he had no jurisdiction in England. Winchell wrote a column saying a casino competitor had paid to have Raft thrown out. Cellini got on with business. Benny Huntman flew out to see him and they talked of staging transatlantic fights, but not just in the UK, also throughout Europe. The plan was to have the boxing in Mob casino cities. It would also help clean cash.

The Mob were getting more and more into entertainment enterprises and communications. Cellini told a rather startled Benny Huntman that he was going into the rock 'n' roll business. The Beatles and all these other guys were making a fortune: they wanted to dip their beaks.

'I know nothing about music and you'll have to do it.' That's how Benny Huntman broke the news to his son Roger that he was about to become a rock-music manager. With a talented band. The Drag Set were originally formed as the Apaches in 1965. They made a comfortable living throughout 1966, working in London on the blues circuit with acts like Wilson Pickett and John Lee Hooker. In 1967, they worked with the eccentric Joe 'Telstar' Meek, but a week after making their recordings the weird Mr Meek, who thought his cat was Satan, inexplicably shot his landlady to death and killed himself. Those violent events in north London stopped the commercial release of the Drag Set's music, and their hopes. They reformed as the Open Mind and appeared with Pink Floyd, Jimi Hendrix, the Soft Machine, Joe Cocker, Arthur Brown and Jon Anderson.

In an effort to help his father, whose health was failing, Roger Huntman became the group's manager and quickly learned the music game. 'We were going to make them a major act in America. My father's friends had entertainment connections in television and music in New York and with films, too. But the main business was in New York, where the big corporations were based. I found it really easy to get music contracts because of my father and Dino. They never sat still. The gambling was going and they wanted to move on to other profits. When my father died, the deal all fell apart.'

And so did Roger Huntman's life for a long time: 'I believe a large reason Benny died of a heart attack wasn't because he could see everything falling apart because of police investigations into gambling in this country and the enactment of the Gaming Board under the Wilson government, but because he was himself directly involved in the contract he put on his good friend Freddie Mills.

'Deep down in his heart, he never came to terms with it. He kept thinking he could have handled it differently, but, of course, with the people he was working with that wasn't possible.

'Way back, that fight in front of Frankie Carbo, the rumble with Darby Sabini, that was the first sign of my father's true nature and the violent world he chose to live in. There was no turning back. He laid the final foundation of his destiny in those moments.

'People found out how far he was prepared to go. I believe that to the day he died he never regretted that decision. It later afforded him beautiful homes, money, travelling the world, respect and a certain fame. Wonderful, yet there was a terrible price attached.'

That summer before he died, Benny Huntman had worked with Jack Solomons on their 23rd world championship contest, with the popular Welsh featherweight champion Howard Winstone defending his title against José Legrá. After Benny Huntman's heart gave out at home in London on 25 October 1968, Jack Solomons paid tribute to his long-time partner and friend: 'Benny was one of England's top managers, who obtained more money for his boxers than any other manager of his time. He knew everybody.'

And then some. Mae Huntman received a huge postbag of condolence messages. One was a telegram which was handed to her by her son Roger. It offered sympathy and was signed 'Meyer'.

Benny Huntman's death and the end of his personal connections arrived at a time when the British government introduced their new, stricter Gaming Act. For the Colony Club, the deck was stacked.

David Cornwell was still working at the club. 'When this happened, the atmosphere deteriorated. Alf Salkin was completely lost without the support of Dino and George. George blamed Salkin for his barring, stating that Salkin had informed on him to the authorities. The two did not take to each other.'

232

With the new legislation and the expulsion of the prime front men, the deal with Sir Maxwell Joseph was in disarray. Benny Huntman, with Dino Cellini's help from Miami and often Amsterdam, had tried to keep the deal going, but his death severed the syndicate's closest contact with Sir Maxwell. Other arrangements were looked into. It was time to perform elsewhere.

Just before Christmas in 1968, police had raided the Colony and taken away gaming equipment. A woman screamed: 'I'm on a streak, a winning streak! Do you have to take away the wheel now . . . do you have to?'

It was an appropriate moment of metaphor. Salkin called the Colony Club staff together on 31 January 1969 to announce the sudden, and instant, closure of the operation. It was going into voluntary liquidation and the 140 staff were being paid off:

> Due to the difficulty of operating this type of business profitably without conflicting with the law as it stands at present, the board has decided that it would be in the best interests of the shareholders and of the club as a whole to cease trading voluntarily forthwith.

On 4 February 1969, the Colony Sporting Club Ltd, Salkin and his American gaming manager, Freddie Ayoub, were fined a total of £1,000 at Bow Street Magistrates' Court for illegal gaming as a result of the police raid on 22 December 1968, when officers caught croupiers attempting to cover the zeros on the roulette wheels and tables.

That 1969 night, Ayoub flew out of London to Portugal to meet his brother Bobby, who supervised the dice tables at the Estoril Casino outside Lisbon, and the next day he flew on to Miami. That day in London, Salkin, at exactly 10.30 a.m., left his home in Eyre Court, St John's Wood, climbed into what had been George Raft's Rolls-Royce, NM777, and was driven to Heathrow Airport. He caught the noon BOAC Flight 531 to New York. He took several pieces of luggage.

Some months after her husband's death, Mae Huntman also went to America. She went to live in California with her niece, the actress Jennifer O'Neill. She took with her the telegrams of commiseration about Benny Huntman's death including the one signed 'Meyer'. Mae Huntman believed it was a telegraphic error and that the kind message had come from Israel's Prime Minister Golda Meir.

THE FAT LADY SINGS

'Götterdämmerung', Richard Wagner, 1876

Vincent Teresa didn't want to be Fat Vinnie any more. The only thing he wanted to be overweight was his wallet. Come to that, he didn't want to be Vincent Teresa. He wanted to be Mr Anonymous. Which was why the Federal Marshals kept telling him if he kept bolting down the fried chicken with extra spicy sausage and sauce it would probably get him killed.

It wasn't just the cholesterol threat. If he could lose weight, it would be the best disguise of all; he'd be a less obvious target for the assassins who were intent on silencing him. In this opera, the intention was that Meyer Lansky's freedom would be over when this fat mobster sang.

The effervescent Teresa had turned government informer for the reason that it paid well, supported his family and new life, and kept him out of a long, long jail term. His testimony had convicted nearly two dozen mobsters, but the big number was his claim he could bring down Meyer Lansky. He told the authorities that he personally had taken bags of cash to Lansky and Cellini, had handed it to them himself.

This was gold to the prosecutors. The US Justice Department had 17 strike forces aimed at disrupting organised-crime business in the same number of cities. Strike Force 18, set up in February 1971, had one purpose: the downfall of Meyer Lansky. They knew of the skimming in Las Vegas, of the revenues from and in the Bahamas run through the Bank of World Commerce in Nassau, from where it was dispatched to any destination in the world. They knew of the money going to Switzerland. They knew there was so much money coming out of the islands that it was sometimes sent parcel post in quarter-of-a-million-dollar air-drops. They knew cash was being brought back into America by laundering it through fake companies. They knew much, but they could prove nothing.

But now they had cash being hand-delivered, which was why the US Marshals Service was nervously guarding the slightly less fat Vincent Teresa 60 miles from Miami in the Florida Everglades in preparation for his evidence against Meyer Lansky in the city.

Which was where the Meyer Lansky crowd were gathered. They looked the part, leathered skin with deep-heat tans, neat and geriatric gangsters strolling around Miami. They'd meet at the card room on the mezzanine of the Singapore Hotel and play some poker but mostly talk and make plans and organise their ongoing enterprises. Jimmy Blue Eyes was living in Hallandale, where they'd 'had a lot of laughs' with the Colonial Inn; Dino Cellini was in Miami Beach; and Meyer Lansky was under constant surveillance in a comfortable but modest house in the north of the city. He'd breakfast at Wolfie's deli on Collins Avenue. He played golf at a public course, booking his tee time as 'Mr Jones'. If the movies had wanted to cast him as an innocent little rich man retired to the sun, which he enjoyed while out walking his shih-tzu, Bruiser, there would be no protests about accuracy.

The FBI and the US prosecutors had been willing to try anything to convict the mobster who'd become a mythical, ghostly figure, a deity of shadowland; their frustration often revealed itself. In 1970, returning to Miami from Acapulco, Meyer Lansky was found with prescription pills for which he had no prescription. They jumped on him with drug charges, which were, after legal kerfuffles, thrown out. The incident cracked Lansky's patience with America. His wife, Teddy, was furious.

Her version of events, as reported in New York and Miami newspapers: 'We were in Acapulco, I got ill, stomach problem, and thought I died. Got pills, over-the-counter, Donnatal, which Meyer also took for his bad ulcer conditions.

'Finally, I was able to travel to the US after being detained by being ill, when, much to our surprise, as we were reaching the door at the airport in Miami, someone approached Meyer and asked that he come to a private room. After an hour or so, I became alarmed and opened several doors and found Meyer with inspectors who had opened our bags and found the Donnatal, a legal drug. When finally released, two men came to the apartment the following day and arrested Meyer for drugs. The newspaper headlines were that Meyer Lansky was in jail on $250,000 bail for drugs. It appeared that it was drugs – cocaine and the like – when all it was was one Donnatal. All the while, it was evident they were trying to frame him.'

The real frame came when one of the FBI tipped Meyer off that he was definitely going to be framed. Connections – a wonderful thing. It's the edge the advance warning allows.

The US Justice Department issued a subpoena for Lansky to appear before a Grand Jury, saying that from Las Vegas wiretaps the FBI was able to charge him and three others with skimming $36 million from the Flamingo Hotel between 1960 and 1967. Immediately before he was indicted for tax evasion, Lansky went to Israel, on 27 July 1970, and applied for a permanent visa under Israel's Law of Return, granting citizenship to any Jew who was not mentally ill nor had a major criminal record. In turn, the US Embassy in Tel Aviv was told to tell Lansky to return his passport to them and himself to the United States. The headlines in the Tel Aviv newspapers ruined his Israeli citizenship application and it was denied; he was a threat to public safety, as was his bitter appeal.

Teddy was distraught: 'Meyer and I flew to Europe to seek out refuge in Israel. Only a man like Meyer with his connections could have accomplished this, but when his case came up, Israel forgot, although M. knew the score and realised they didn't have a choice.'

The US cancelled Lansky's passport and the Israeli government issued him a travel document for any country willing to admit him. For $50,000 cash, Lansky received a visa allowing him to enter Paraguay as an agricultural worker. It was not good. He had flown there with a lawyer while his wife stayed on in Israel.

Teddy Lansky: 'After a tumultuous trip home, after 37 hours of being denied entry into Paraguay, he arrived in the US and was taken directly to the hospital. When the news came over the air, I flew back at the break of dawn, through friends, to avoid publicity. I arrived in New York, was met by air officials, saying that the press and television people were there, so they

VIP'd me discreetly and put me on a plane, but I had to put Bruiser in baggage. It broke me up, as he never travelled without me, always on the plane with me. But I had no alternative. My son and daughter-in-law were waiting for me in Florida, but had I not had my dog in baggage, I would have left the plane in Fort Lauderdale and taken a cab to Miami. But Bruiser was not with me so I stayed on the plane, and when I arrived in Miami it was bedlam.

'My son rushed to the plane to tell me there were reporters and photographers by the score. I felt defeated after a long trip. A reporter from television, Bernice Norton, attacked me verbally, called me "Godmother". I spat in her face.'

It's questionable whether her husband would have had the energy to do that. He'd all but been around the world, stopping in Switzerland, Argentina, Bolivia, Peru and Panama; everywhere he went, they said he made an offer of $1 million for sanctuary. It was one every nation could refuse.

On his arrival in Miami on 7 November 1972, FBI agents bounded into the first-class cabin and arrested the wandering Lansky. His lawyer David Rosen got him out on a quarter of a million dollars' bail and into Mount Sinai Hospital. His client was suffering from cardiac insufficiency. When Teddy joined her husband, she was told he'd suffered a heart attack on the plane from South America.

Vincent Teresa was also suffering chest pains – and giving the evidence we heard earlier. 'Everything was on paper; a guy like me handled all the payoffs to Cellini or Lansky. The playing customer never played with cash if he was on a junket. It was through a credit system we could keep track of what the club took in and what was owed me. Cellini came to my office in Boston at least four times to collect money owed to the Colony and I flew to Florida twice to pay him. Both times Lansky was there.'

The chief witness against Lansky might have been suffering more than chest pains – fear, terror, being the biggest ailment. But his heart *was* dodgy, and doctors said he too had suffered a heart attack. The stress of having to do what he'd never expected, testify against Lansky, could have squeezed his arteries a little too tight.

After postponements on both sides, Teresa finally got to the witness stand: he tried to look like a court-room regular in a suit and tie; he carried a briefcase and wore a wig, a false moustache and goatee. It wasn't just the accessories that didn't fit.

The FBI's case against Lansky included the Las Vegas Flamingo Hotel skimming charges, the contempt of court for failing to answer the subpoena issued when he was in Israel and hiding money from the IRS as part of a skim from the Colony Club in London. If found guilty on all counts, the money maestro of the Mafia faced the rest of his life in jail. He was found guilty of contempt of court in a ruling that was later overturned through a technicality. The Flamingo skimming charges were eventually dropped after protracted legal wrangling and delays because of the ageing gangster's quite obviously deteriorating health.

And the Colony connection? Vincent Teresa testified to his Grand Jury evidence that he had taken the cash from the Colony Club junkets to Lansky in Miami and given it to him at the Dupont Plaza Hotel around 17 May 1968. David Rosen was precise in his dissection of the veracity of it. It was like filleting fish; he picked the flesh from the bones of Teresa's version of events. This chief government witness could not describe or detail the rooms where he'd met Lansky. He was rubbish on times and places. Then he was told Lansky wasn't even in Miami when Teresa had supposedly given him the money. As the jury listened, Rosen explained that his client was at the time in Boston, recovering from a double-hernia operation. He produced Mrs Lansky to elaborate. She said later: 'It showed the lack of skill and ethics that the Government presented anything to frame my husband, and the judge ruled in our favour. Truth will come out.

'Meyer later told me that had he gone to jail for this low-down filthy liar, he didn't think he would have survived, so thank God for keeping the records and proving the Government was using very bad procedures. Maybe they should all be in jail instead. This fat man Teresa was used and abused. I'm sure he was a sorry liar.'

The jury also heard medical evidence of Lansky's 10 May hernia operation and his inability to travel following it. There were Boston hotel records. What with Rosen's colourful characterisation of Vincent Teresa's penchant for abandonment of the straight and narrow, it was no surprise

Lansky got off. Teresa's only rebuttal was that Lansky must have had a double.

It was a strange business and has never been fully explained. Why did Vincent Teresa flounder with his evidence? Had he made it all up to get attention, expecting it to come to nothing? Was he fearful for his family if he went ahead? There had been constant talk that they were to be kidnapped. Teresa was an old and long-time mafioso, and he understood the true consequences of providing convincing minutiae in his evidence. By waffling, he may have kept his family alive.

Whatever the core truth of it, when this fat man sang he joined a US government chorus determined to put Meyer Lansky out of business. They were assisted more by time, the enemy of all, in getting what they wanted.

16

THE PAINT JOB

'Voodoo Chile', Jimmi Hendrix, 1970

Dino Cellini slipped the net of tax evasion charges from the Colony Club skim by doing what he did best, travelling fast and light. He reckoned by the time he left London he'd worked in most gambling emporiums of note across the world. In Miami, he'd organised global gambling junkets involving jets packed with punters sent off in style to be comfortably deprived of their money. Still, he was never content with paperwork profit.

The Bahamas were booming. The operation with Mary Carter Paints, the Delaware outfit headquartered in Tampa, Florida, following the deal with Huntington Hartford had paid off many times over. Mary Carter paint stores were all over America and the British West Indies. A subsidiary, Bahamas Developers, owned 3,500-acres of land in Wallace Groves territory on Grand Bahama. Mary Carter was no Caribbean virgin.

Without Huntington Hartford, the company was able to get a casino licence for Paradise Island; using the good graces of Sir Stafford Sands, they paid $750,000 for a certificate of exemption for the Bahamian Club, a gaming establishment in Nassau owned by Wallace Groves.

The agreement stipulated that the Bahamian Club permit was to be transferred to the Paradise Island casino on condition that Mary Carter relinquished four-ninths of the casino's profits as well as management of the casino to Wallace Groves's Bahamas Amusements Ltd.

Meyer Lansky, through his associates, was managing the Bahamian Club for Wallace Groves, as well as the Monte Carlo Casino on Grand Bahama. They took over the Paradise Island casino for a flat 15 per cent of the gross gaming profits.

241

Mary Carter's Paradise Island was linked with Nassau on New Providence Island by a $2-million toll bridge, which Huntington Hartford, five years earlier, had been refused permission to build. The $15-million Paradise Island Hotel and Casino opened in January 1968. The casino was managed by Eddie Cellini. Two-thirds of the profits were created by junkets of gamblers sent to the Bahamas by the banned Dino Cellini.

It was a very tropical and potent mix. And into it arrived Lynden O. Pindling, the new young political leader of the Bahamas, whose opponents claimed he'd received payments from the Lansky syndicate. Yet Pindling had campaigned against his homeland becoming 'a lucrative centre of international crime' and that had resulted in a British Royal Commission looking into gaming in the Bahamas. That investigation was led by Sir Ranulph 'Rasher' Bacon, a towering figure from Scotland Yard.

It would be some years later that Rasher Bacon revealed a little more of his thoughts about gaming in the Bahamas. Leonard 'Nipper' Read, the detective who had built a strong enough case to convict Ron and Reg Kray at the Old Bailey on 4 March 1969, was looking forward to an executive job on Grand Bahama when he retired from Scotland Yard. He went to the Bahamas to be interviewed for work and residency permits. He was introduced to all who mattered, including Lynden Pindling, who said he looked forward to Mr Read arriving to stay. The detective was taken for a game of golf and to lunches and dinners by the islands' development establishment. He was assured it was all formality, but it was later whispered to him there were 'problems'. He was told nothing officially.

One of his referees had been Sir Ranulph Bacon, whom he caught up with at a chief constable's dinner.

'You never got that job in the Bahamas, did you, old son?'

'As a matter of fact, I didn't. But how did you know?'

'Come on, you didn't expect to get in with your background and reputation, did you? They couldn't afford to let a man like you in there with all the corruption going on.'

George Raft never understood why he was banned from Britain. I met him several times in Los Angeles and interviewed him there, too. He always admitted knowing Benny Siegel and Meyer Lansky, Dino Cellini and the rest. But, he said, other than his host duties in Havana, Las Vegas and London, he had no business dealings with them. Yet when I saw him, he was very much back in the gambling business.

Every morning at 10 a.m., he turned up at the offices of the Riviera hotel-casino on Wilshire Boulevard in Beverly Hills. His job was to promote the casino and help lure gamblers to Las Vegas. He'd stare out from beneath his silver toupee and wave to passers-by who peered in the windows at him. He was the $500-a-week 'ambassador of goodwill'.

He'd never talked in detail about the Colony Club, the Kray twins, or his lifetime ban from Britain. 'What did I do? I'm still very hurt, very bitter. What was my crime? I'm not a member of the Mob, never was. Rocky Marciano had organised the whole thing. He picked me up at my hotel in London one Sunday afternoon and said we were going to meet some poor kids in the East End of London. So I met the Kray twins. I had my picture taken with them, but I didn't know who they were.

'No, no, they didn't look like poor kids. No, sure they didn't. I admit I was wrong, but I couldn't get any work after the London business. I liked to gamble; I once had 20 racchorses and I still go to the races, to Hollywood Park and Santa Anita. I lost a fortune. But it was that club in London that finished me off. They just wouldn't let me do that job. I'd hardly got to London and they kicked me out.'

It was a couple of years later, on 24 November 1980, that one of the original movie gangsters bought it in real life. He died from leukaemia at his home, the neat, always neat, place in Beverly Hills.

Bobby McKew simply nodded at the story: 'We never fell out with the Mafia over the Colony. In fact, they paid more attention to us over other matters. They understood we knew what we were talking about. We had even more clout.

'The next ones who did come in were the Playboy Club. I went up there once and in the lounge there were half a dozen people all drinking and they were policemen, plain-clothes. Must have been having a night out. '

By then, Dino Cellini was once again pushing the company line in Europe. He also had a job description: he was the European representative of the Bally Amusement Machine

Company of Chicago. His contacts were impeccable, especially from the croupier schools in Havana and Hanover Street in London that he'd operated for Bahamas Amusements Ltd, the Wallace Groves/Lou Chesler set-up. These trainees were now working throughout the world and fed back the gossip; every piece of intelligence was an edge.

The American Mafia, through the Lansky syndicate, worked alongside their brotherhood members in Italy and across the Continent. Dino Cellini was particularly close to Dutch organised crime, an often overlooked worldwide criminal power, and with Freddie Ayoub he set up syndicate stakes in Amsterdam's greatest interest other than tulips: sex. Sex clubs were a perfect game because they could be played alongside heavy drug-trafficking and gambling. There was an underground trade in weapons and pornography. The syndicate also provided escorts for cash shipments, itself a tribute to hope over experience.

Joe Nesline, using a string of aliases and passports created in a fourth-four apartment in Hammersmith, west London, was as busy as Dino Cellini. With Charlie the Blade, he had moved into the Hotel Lav casino operation in Split, Yugoslavia. Dino Cellini had an office there and, his bones wearying at times, took sessions in the hot springs. David Cornwell worked there as a croupier and saw many familiar faces.

Nesline had kept close contacts with Benny Huntman and others with influence in the boxing world. One of them was a former boxing manager who had found more profit and, surprisingly, fewer tantrums in the sex business. His headquarters were the rosy-red-tinted districts of Hamburg. From there, working with suppliers of girls and drugs from Beirut to Manchester, England, he'd built a lucrative empire across the Alps.

They had connections in Milan and West Berlin. In Amsterdam, Nesline was in business with Goffredo Cellini, operating the Club Caballa casino. With another partner, they had the Casa Rosso Club, which was at one stage the umbrella organisation for European sex shops and brothels.

While Meyer Lansky fought with the cancerous cells in his lungs, his close partners Dino Cellini and Jimmy Blue Eyes pursued his interests: profit and power. They joined up with that swashbuckler of a swindler Robert Vesco, who, with neat irony, after stealing $240 million from investors, found refuge in 1982 in Cuba. In 1970, Vesco had made a hostile takeover of Investors Overseas Service Ltd (IOS), a mutual-fund enterprise operated by the Turkish-born, charming and amorous crook Bernie Cornfeld.

The affable, bearded and ebullient Cornfeld – catchphrase: 'Do you sincerely want to be rich? – had built up IOS holdings to more than $1.5 billion but attracted the attention of the Securities Exchange Commission (SEC). Vesco took the chance to grab control of IOS. It got messy, with Cornfeld rushed into jail in Switzerland while the wily Vesco looted IOS for many, many millions of dollars. A huge amount of the IOS loot was placed in a corporate enterprise set up in Amsterdam with the help of Dino Cellini. When it got too messy, Vesco went on the run and popped up all over the Caribbean, including the Bahamas, where Cellini had the appropriate contacts. What surprised many was Vesco's bail-out to Cuba, where his death, something that has never been confirmed, was announced in 2007. The Vesco-IOS affair was only one of the Cellini-axis endeavours, as they also laid the foundations of schemes and enterprises around the world. At much the same time, the main players of their turbulent times left the scene by chance or cruel intention.

Handsome Johnny Roselli got a Mafia farewell in the hot July of 1975 when he was still in charge of the Chicago Mob's gambling interests in Las Vegas. He was living quietly with his sister, Mrs Joseph Daigle, in Plantation, Florida, a little to the west of Fort Lauderdale. He was, his neighbours said, a nice, silver-haired gentleman who liked to walk his poodle and talk about such local environmental concerns as the caterpillars munching the foliage. Although he had arthritis of the spine, he played golf regularly. Another local wiseguy – we're talking Meyer Lansky County, where corpses happened to turn up every now and then – had been assassinated on the golf course earlier in the year, and Roselli never played the same course twice in a row. Still, he rejected his lawyer's advice to hire a bodyguard.

He was choked to death and then his body was sealed in an empty 55-gallon oil drum. Heavy chains were coiled around this casket and holes punched in the sides to make it stay underwater when it was dumped in the ocean off the Florida Golden Coast. Roselli rose from the depth: the gases from his decomposing body floated the oil drum to the surface. Three fishermen found it in Dumfoundling Bay near North Miami Beach. Police ran the victim's fingerprints with the FBI and up came the ID: John Roselli, 71, emphysema sufferer and a Mafia executive who'd been involved in landmark capers and made the error of telling about them.

In June 1975, Roselli had testified before a special Senate Intelligence Committee (SIC) investigating the excesses of the CIA. This is where he should have counted up to five and pleaded the Amendment. Roselli not only talked, he provided the details of how he and Sam Giancana had been recruited by the CIA to assassinate Fidel Castro. He also told about his partner from the Sans Souci casino days in Havana, Santo Trafficante Jr, who had worked with them.

Five days before Roselli sang, his Chicago boss Sam Giancana took seven .22 bullets at immediate range in the face and neck in his house at Oak Park in Illinois. Giancana, who knew more secrets than most, was scheduled to testify, like Roselli, before the SIC.

Santo Trafficante Jr did the Caribbean hop – Costa Rica, the Dominican Republic – to stay ahead of his notoriety. And this clever, evil man was able to escape the horrors he'd conjured; he never spent a night in jail and died from natural causes in 1987 at home in Houston, Texas. It was news, with errors, that was quickly sent around America and the world. Yet even in death his demise was carefully couched; he was a reputed mobster. Of course, Santo Trafficante Jr knew the voodoo folk and you never can tell.

The Associated Press reported his death as follows:

> TAMPA, Fla. – Santo Trafficante Jr., one of the last of the old-time reputed Mafia dons, has died at the age of 72.
>
> Henry Gonzalez of Tampa, Mr. Trafficante's long-time friend and attorney, said Mr. Trafficante died late Tuesday at the Texas Heart Institute in Houston, where he had gone for heart surgery.
>
> Mr. Trafficante's Sicilian-born father allegedly presided over what federal authorities call Tampa's "era of blood," when rival crime families fought for control of lucrative

Florida gambling from 1937 to 1945. When his father died in 1954, Mr. Trafficante took over the family business, according to testimony before a US Senate committee in 1963.

Over the years, the younger Mr. Trafficante was linked to at least four gangland slayings and testified about a plot to assassinate Cuban President Fidel Castro. But Mr. Trafficante escaped lengthy jail terms.

A federal judge last July dismissed racketeering and conspiracy charges against Mr. Trafficante in a case that grew out of a $2 million FBI sting undercover gambling investigation. Mr. Trafficante was accused of giving permission to underworld organizations in Florida to run gambling operations, in return for a share of the profits.

But the judge declared a mistrial after refusing to admit the key prosecution evidence: tape-recorded conversations between Mr. Trafficante and a mob figure who had been found dead with his hands cut off.

Still pending against Mr. Trafficante was a 1981 Miami indictment charging him with participating in a kickback scheme to milk millions of dollars from a health and welfare fund set up for Laborers International Union of North America.

Mr. Trafficante lived modestly, with homes in Tampa and North Miami Beach, and suffered from many health problems in his later years. Attorneys cited his heart, kidney and memory problems in gaining delays of his trial.

His attorneys said government allegations that Mr. Trafficante was Florida's "boss of bosses" and a leader of La Cosa Nostra were sensational exaggerations.

Mr. Trafficante was among 57 alleged mobsters arrested when authorities broke up an apparent underworld convention in Apalachin, N.Y., in 1957. Those charges were later dropped.

Also that year, Mr. Trafficante was questioned about the death of Albert Anastasia, a maverick who headed a group dubbed "Murder, Inc." Anastasia's throat was slashed while he sat in a hotel barber chair. Mr. Trafficante was never charged in relation to that crime.

Throughout rounds of gangland wars, Mr. Trafficante suffered only an arm wound from a 1953 shotgun blast fired into his car. Cuban police in the 1950s said they intercepted four would-be mob assassins.

In 1978, appearing before a House panel looking into assassinations of political figures, Mr. Trafficante said he participated in an alleged CIA assassination plot against Castro because "I thought I was helping the United States government."

Mr. Trafficante denied there was any mob plot to kill President John F. Kennedy.

There has been testimony that Mr. Trafficante once promised that Kennedy would not be re-elected.

Mr. Trafficante leaves his wife, Josephine, two daughters and four grandchildren.

The Gentle Don, Angelo Bruno, went violently in 1980, with a shotgun blast in the back of the head. The killing had not been sanctioned by the syndicate, and the killer and Philadelphia wannabe, Antonio Capronigro, Bruno's consigliere, was himself assassinated. His body was found in the trunk of a car in New York with $300 in $20 bills pushed into his mouth and up his backside. It was a message not to be greedy.

Harold Christie, who had played such a prominent role in the life and death of Sir Harry Oakes and the Bahamas, was a winner financially. He speculated on marshy land to the west of Nassau and sold it for redevelopment as the luxury gated community Lyford Cay Club, one of the world's wealthiest and most exclusive neighbourhoods. In 1962, President John Kennedy hosted talks there with Britain's Prime Minister Harold Macmillan. The membership was international, from England, France, Switzerland, Cuba, America, Italy, Canada and Greece. The Bahamas had always attracted money. Harold Christie died there in 1973.

Meyer Lansky was gone ten years later of lung cancer in Mount Sinai Hospital in New York, at the age of eighty-one. The funeral was family only – small, sedate, with none of the fanfare of old, or the style of the always overdressed Frankie Yale and his $25,000 silver casket.

The debate followed as to how much money he had and

where it was. You could pick almost any place – a city, a street, a skyscraper in New York, a resort in Miami, a development in London, a shopping centre in Belgrade, a couple of corners of Monte Carlo – and chances are Lansky had part of it. Throughout his life, he never left his fingerprints on anything. He was unlikely to leave them on his legacy.

Benny Huntman's sister-in-law Renee had married an American bomber pilot, Oscar O'Neill, after the Second World War and had gone to live in New York. They had a son, Michael, who became a successful lawyer, and a daughter, Jennifer, who became a successful model and actress in films like *The Summer of '42*. After Benny died, Mae Huntman stayed with her niece in California for eight years. She returned to Britain and lived with her son Roger in west London before she died in 1987. She spent her time reading and going over her memorabilia, including the telegraph from Golda Meir.

Dino Cellini also enjoyed reading and was a lifetime devotee of F. Scott Fitzgerald. He was especially fond of *Tender Is the Night*, set in the south of France, where the Fitzgeralds, Scott the novelist, Zelda the novelty, had danced their personal Charleston over many lives. He spent more and more time there as his health weakened. He was still a wanted man in America, but arrangements were made with the US government for him to return on compassionate grounds. The skill of the magic mechanic remained. His sleight of hand was intact. He appeared before dozens of US government committees investigating organised crime and was asked 565 questions. He gave nothing away. No one saw all the moves of Dino Cellini. They never had. Much to the distress of his immediate family – his wife, Helena, son and three daughters – he died aged 63 from cancer in Miami in 1979.

In 2011, his brother Bobby Cellini was aged 70 and operating a casino in Malindi in Kenya. His brother Eddie, 89, was still beating the odds and working, running a casino in Honduras.

The others had all gone on to entertain elsewhere.

ROGER HUNTMAN'S
SIGNED STATEMENT

'Que Sera Sera (Whatever Will Be, Will Be)', Doris
Day, 1956

The facts, details, names and circumstances laid out in
Shadowland leave me, after many years' deliberating, with
only one conclusion: that on the night of 24 July 1965, Freddie
Mills was shot dead on the orders of Meyer Lansky because
he tried to blackmail my father. Thereby Mills posed a threat
to the Mafia operations in London and Europe, by saying he
would go to Fleet Street with his story about the gambling
structures they were setting up in England and Europe.

You do not threaten people such as these – if you do, you
will pay the ultimate price. Freddie Mills paid that ultimate
price, his life, which I now realise.

By going to see Mills at his Club to tell him my father would
lend him the £2,500, and for Mills to be there on the night of
24 July to meet my father, I unwittingly set Mills up, and it was
also their way of what my father described as 'bringing me in'
eventually.

The readers must of course make up their own minds – just
as I have had to. Fortunately, they can draw their own
conclusions quicker with this book – for me, it has taken
much longer because I could not believe I was used in such a
way by people I loved and trusted. I was young and naive, and
earning big money, and I was told by my father never to ask
questions and always to do their bidding.

I can only hope that what has been disclosed in this book
can bring closure to Freddie Mills's family, but sadly it cannot
bring him back.

I fully understand the police may wish to talk to me re this
book, but I must tell them now, I will only be able to reiterate
what has been written – nothing more, nothing less.

The reason I have come forward now with what I know is

because I have diabetes and could die at any time and am the only person still alive who knows what happened to Mills, and his family and the public can now know what I believe is the end of the Freddie Mills mystery and until-now unsolved death.

Signed: Roger Huntman, 15 May 2011

In June 2011, Roger Huntman added to this statement:

I have revealed this story for myself and for my mother and father, Benny and Mae Huntman, who I have such fond and loving memories of. I wanted to take this opportunity to thank them for everything they did for me. Difficult as it will be for many people to understand, I feel enormous gratitude towards Gaetano 'Tommy' Lucchese, Frankie Carbo, Jimmy Blue Eyes, Dino Cellini and Meyer Lansky for what they did for my father. They looked after him in America and for the rest of his life. They admired his loyalty and in turn I am thankful that they acted the same way to my father.

Postscript

Legacy

'You Don't Mess Around With Jim', Jim Croce, 1972

There are many players in the story of organised crime, the entertainment business and politics in the twentieth century, and almost as many conspiracy theories. I've spent a professional lifetime encountering and reading about them, investigating them, disregarding, forgetting and being convinced by one or other. Some of the conclusions reached in *Shadowland* are arrived at with access to new material and archives and also by circumstantial evidence. They are influenced by primary testimony of those who were involved or around the participants. Freedom of Information in America provides exotic access to National Archives and FBI files from Al Capone's first bootleg murder to Edward Kennedy's life and times and death in 2010. The UK archives at Kew were truly pertinent. The Hans Tasiemka Archive in London was a rich source for the minute detail missing from official files, with reports that not only provided facts but also a vivid snapshot of the moments when what is now history happened. All provided evidence and indications of how those involved would react in given situations. All the fragments came together for me in *Shadowland*. There are thousands of 'for your eyes only' documents involving the FBI and the 'dirty tricks' CIA, which, if they've not been shredded, may enlighten us more one day with perhaps fascinating details of the Duke of Windsor, spies and Nazi gold in the Bahamas, and the Kennedy family and the Mob. In our age of electronic information and leaks, it surely can't take too long. New American official files on the JFK assassination will be made available in 2017.

I have no caveat for the story of Benny Huntman and the many ramifications from it. Roger Huntman held back nothing of the brutal truth about his father and his father's life. To him, there were two men, Benny Huntman, whom he obeyed, and his father, whom he loved. In our three years of talks, picking over times, dates, birth, marriage and death certificates, the turned-up corners of lives past, he always instinctively separated the two in conversation. He's lived with the story for many years and for his own health reasons wanted to reveal it at a time when he's the only one left the past could possibly punish. He was a young man doing his father's duty; at that time, he didn't know the extent to which Benny Huntman served two families.

I believe *Shadowland* ends the decades-long puzzle of how Freddie Mills met his death and provides a fresh prism through which to view many landmark events, not least some pivotal sporting occasions.

Of course, we are insatiable. We hunger for more. What we don't know will always intrigue. That goes for the past and the present, too. There are many rumours today around Vladivostok, Russia's largest port city on the Pacific Ocean. It's situated close to the Russo-Chinese border and North Korea and is a place of sharp wind, intrigue and seriously threatening people, including drug-cartel soldiers. Hey, everybody has to unwind, and there are said to be a couple of gambling dens, including a more upmarket place, what we could call a carpet joint. It's run by some guy out of Miami . . .

Some puzzles, not least the secret of longevity for so many in a tricky trade, go on.

Sonny Liston was found dead at his home in Las Vegas and the police called it a heroin overdose. His friends pointed out that Liston abhorred needles. His death certificate is dated 30 December 1970, the day he was found. His body had decomposed. The truth remains elusive about the end of the man who always ragged at the lead the Mob put on him. Frankie Carbo, Mr Gray, who ran Liston, was 72 when he died from heart disease in 1976. He'd been released from jail on health grounds. He spent his last days in Miami Beach. He knew a lot of old guys there.

Jimmy Blue Eyes was last seen playing golf in Las Vegas. They say he looked pretty good for 90 years old but complained about getting a desert chill. He'd gone to Nevada to visit relatives, but, lest we think of him as a nice old guy, a geriatric gangster, there is a story told that reflects how he and his associates operated: he was approached by an acquaintance in Miami Beach who suggested to him the idea of opening an informal café that would import the northern newspapers for the huge number of Florida visitors who missed the news from home. Jimmy Blue Eyes agreed to finance the operation, but with one permanent proviso: there would be one table set aside for him in a corner that no one else would ever be allowed to sit at. The café became an instant success. Almost everyone visiting Miami Beach from the north ate breakfast or lunch there and read the news from New York, Philadelphia, or Boston. Queues formed to get in. One day, Jimmy Blue Eyes passed a queue of waiting diners and stopped dead in his tracks: 'What the fuck!'

There were customers at his table. His partner explained he was so overwhelmed with business that he'd sat a group at the table but swore they would be leaving soon. Jimmy Blue Eyes left and returned later, when that meal's rush was over. He ate and drank while his partner continued to apologise, swearing this gaffe would never be committed again.

'I'm sure it won't,' said Jimmy Blue Eyes. A little later, his restaurateur partner collapsed and died from a cup of coffee laced with arsenic. Jimmy Blue Eyes, a silent partner, paid out more cash when he bought the café from the dead man's wife for a new partner of record to run.

The American House Select Committee on Assassinations (HSCA) ruled that JFK was the victim of a conspiracy based on the recording of the gunshots fired in Dealey Plaza, captured over the police radio. A total of seven impulses were recorded on tape, but only four of them were analysed. This concluded that all four were gunshots, two of them occurring within half a second of each other, too close to be fired by one man. Comparisons of the echoes with test shots fired in Dealey Plaza confirmed that at least one of the recorded shots was fired from the grassy knoll. Five, rather than three, shots rules out Oswald as the solo assassin. Research in 2009 confirmed both the location and time of the recording as being in Dealey Plaza at the time of the assassination, that there were at least four gunshots in Dealey Plaza, two of them within a half-second of each other, and at least one of them was fired from the grassy knoll.

The National Archives and Records Administration in Washington DC has a section on the Kennedys versus organised crime and balances it against the events in Dallas. The following is the most pointed section, as it appears in the Archives:

War on organized crime

The Kennedy administration made an unprecedented effort to fight the insidious menace of organized crime. The President had first encountered the problem when he became a member of the Senate Select Committee on Labor Racketeering. Robert Kennedy was chief counsel of the committee, and later, as Attorney General, he became the President's surrogate in a campaign against the underworld.

Dramatic developments in the war on organized crime had occurred just before Kennedy came to the White House. A roundup of hoodlums in Apalachin, N.Y., in 1957, followed by an abortive prosecution of many of the leaders, demonstrated the impotence of Federal enforcement. The Senate testimony of Mafia member Joseph Valachi in 1963 became the catalyst for a renewed effort to strengthen Federal criminal laws that could be used to control the threat of organized crime.

The zeal of the Kennedy brothers signified the roughest period for organized crime in Department of Justice history. Historian Arthur Schlesinger, Jr. wrote in "Robert Kennedy and His Times" that, as a result of the Attorney General's pressure, "the national Government took on organized crime as it had never done before."

Schlesinger observed: "In New York, Robert Morgenthau, the Federal attorney, successfully prosecuted one syndicate leader after another. The Patriarca gang in Rhode Island and the De Cavalcante gang in New Jersey were smashed. Convictions of racketeers by the Organized Crime Section and the Tax Division steadily increased – 96 in 1961, 101 in 1960, 373 in 1963. So long as John Kennedy sat in the White House, giving his Attorney General absolute backing, the underworld knew that the heat was on."

The Attorney General focused on targets he had become acquainted with as counsel for the Rackets Committee. He was particularly concerned about the alliance of the top labor leaders and racketeers as personified by Teamster President James R. Hoffa. Schlesinger wrote that "the pursuit of Hoffa was an aspect of the war against organized crime."

He added: "The relations between the Teamsters and the syndicates continued to grow. The FBI electronic microphone, planted from 1961 to 1964 in the office of Anthony Giacalone, a Detroit hood, revealed Hoffa's deep if wary involvement with the local mob. For national purposes a meeting place was the Rancho La Costa Country Club near San Clemente, Calif., built with $27 million in loans from the Teamsters pension fund; its proprietor, Morris B. Dalitz, had emerged from the Detroit [sic. Cleveland] underworld to become a Las Vegas and Havana gambling figure. Here the Teamsters and the mob golfed and drank together. Here they no doubt reflected that, as long as John Kennedy was President, Robert Kennedy would be unassailable."

As with the Civil Rights Division, Robert Kennedy expanded the Organized Crime Division at Justice. As a result of information collected by the FBI syndicate operations were seriously disrupted in some cases, and leading organized crime figures were concerned about the future.

As the policies of the Kennedy administration broke new ground, political extremists in the United States seemed increasingly willing to resort to violence to achieve their goals. In an address at the University of Washington in Seattle on 16 November 1961, President Kennedy discussed the age of extremism: two groups of frustrated citizens, one urging surrender and the other urging war.

He said: "It is a curious fact that each of these extreme opposites resembles the other. Each believes that we have only two choices: appeasement or war, suicide or surrender, humiliation or holocaust, to be either Red or dead."

The radical right condemned Kennedy for his "big Government" policies, as well as his concern with social welfare and civil rights progress. The ultraconservative John Birch Society, Christian Anti-Communist Crusade led by Fred C. Schwarz, and the Christian Crusade led by Rev. Billy James Hargis attracted an anti-Kennedy following. The right wing was incensed by Kennedy's transfer of Gen. Edwin A. Walker from his command in West Germany to Hawaii for distributing right-wing literature to his troops. The paramilitary Minutemen condemned the administration as "soft on Communist" and adopted guerrilla warfare tactics to prepare for the fight against the Communist foe. At the other extreme, the left labeled Kennedy a reactionary disappointment, a tool of the "power elite".

President Kennedy saw the danger of a politically polarized

society and spoke against extremist solutions, urging reason in an ordered society. In the text of the speech he had planned to deliver in Dallas on November 22, 1963, he wrote: "Today . . . voices are heard in the land – voices preaching doctrines wholly unrelated to reality, wholly unsuited to the '60s, doctrines which apparently assume that words will suffice without weapons, that vituperation is as good as victory and that peace is a sign of weakness."

At the beginning, John F. Kennedy had been an extremely popular President. His ratings, ironically, were highest in the aftermath of the April 1961 Bay of Pigs invasion, when he received a remarkable 83 percent approval rating in the Gallup Poll. But by the fall of 1963, he had slipped to 59 percent, and he became concerned about the political implications. In October, Newsweek magazine reported that the civil rights issue alone had cost Kennedy 3.5 million votes, adding that no Democrat in the White House had ever been so disliked in the South. In Georgia, the marquee of a movie theater showing PT 109 read, "See how the Japs almost got Kennedy."

An inveterate traveler, Kennedy interspersed his diplomatic missions abroad with trips around the country. He made 83 trips in 1963. In June he visited Germany, Ireland and Italy; later in the summer he toured the western United States – North Dakota, Wyoming, Montana, Washington, Utah, Oregon, Nevada and California – to gain support for his legislative program.

Not only did Kennedy enjoy traveling, but he almost recklessly resisted the protective measures the Secret Service urged him to adopt. He would not allow blaring sirens, and only once – in Chicago in November 1963 – did he permit his limousine to be flanked by motor-cycle police officers. He told the special agent in charge of the White House detail that he did not want agents to ride on the rear of his car.

Kennedy was philosophical about danger. According to Arthur M. Schlesinger, "A Thousand Days," Kennedy believed assassination was a risk inherent in a democratic society. In 1953, Schlesinger recounted, then-Senator Kennedy read his favorite poem to his new bride, Jacqueline Bouvier Kennedy. It was "I Have a Rendezvous with Death," by Alan Seeger.

> It may be he shall take my hand
> And lead me into his dark land
> And close my eyes and quench my breath . . .

But I've a rendezvous with Death
At midnight in some flaming town,
When Spring trips north again this year,
And I to my pledged word am true,
I shall not fail that rendezvous.

During the November 1963 Texas trip he told a special White House assistant: ". . . if anybody really wanted to shoot the President . . . it was not a very difficult job – all one had to do was get on a high building someday with a telescopic rifle, and there was nothing anybody could do to defend against such an attempt."

Kennedy had decided to visit the South to bolster his image in that region. He chose to visit Florida because it had voted Republican in 1960, and Texas because it only had been saved by Lyndon Johnson by an extremely slim margin. According to Texas Governor John B. Connally, Kennedy first mentioned a political trip to Texas in the summer of 1962 when Connally, a former Secretary of the Navy, was running for Governor. Kennedy broached the idea to Connally again the following summer.

Despite some obvious political reasons for a Texas visit, some members of Kennedy's staff opposed it because the State was not favorably disposed to the President. From 1961 to 1960, the Secret Service had received 34 threats on the President's life from Texas. Political embarrassment seemed a certainty. The decision to travel to Dallas was even more puzzling. Many perceived Dallas as a violent, hysterical centre of right-wing fanaticism. There, in 1960, then-Texas Senator Lyndon B. Johnson had been heckled and spat upon. In October 1963, just a month before the President's scheduled visit, Ambassador to the United Nations Adlai Stevenson was jeered, hit with a placard and spat upon. Byron Skelton, the National Democratic Committee-man from Texas, wrote Attorney General Robert Kennedy about his concern for President Kennedy's safety and urged him to dissuade his brother from going to Texas.

There are several probable explanations for the decision to visit Dallas. Kennedy was to visit four other cities – San Antonio, Houston, Austin and Fort Worth – and it was feared that ignoring Dallas would harm his image in Texas. Kennedy also was anxious to win over business, and Dallas was the place to address business leaders in Texas. As a result of his economic policies, particularly the rollback of steel prices, Kennedy believed he was perceived as hostile to business. Before the November Texas trip, he shared his

258

concern with Governor Connally: "If these people are silly enough to think that I am going to dismantle this free enterprise system, they are crazy."

All the other trips that summer and fall, including the visit to Florida, had been successful. In his testimony before this committee, Governor Connally explained that he believed that Texas was a State crucial to a Kennedy victory in 1964, and contended that Kennedy came to Texas for two reasons: to raise money and to enhance his own political prospects in Texas.

Word of the trip to Texas first appeared in the Dallas papers on September 13, and Kennedy's itinerary for Texas was announced by Governor Connally on November 1. The President was scheduled to address a luncheon of business leaders at the Trade Mart in Dallas on November 22. He decided to travel into the city in a motorcade that was to follow the normal Dallas parade route. Kennedy liked motorcades, for they afforded an opportunity to get close to the people, and he made a special point of arranging one in Dallas because he believed it would be his one chance that day to greet workers and minorities. The final motorcade route through Dealey Plaza in downtown Dallas was selected on November 15.

In 1963, the Secret Service had identified six categories of persons who posed a threat to the President: right-wing extremists, left-wing extremists, Cubans, Puerto Ricans, Black militants, and a miscellaneous category that included mental patients. It identified two cities as particularly threatening – Miami and Chicago. Dallas was considered a potential source of political embarrassment. Prior to the trip to Dallas, the Secret Service had not uncovered any serious threats there, and no extensive investigation was conducted in the city. Beginning a week before the trip, defamatory posters and leaflets excoriating the President appeared throughout Dallas. Some carried Kennedy's picture with the caption, "Wanted for Treason: This Man Is Wanted for Treasonous Activities Against the United States." It was suggested the President's Dallas parade route should not be published, but at the urging of Kennedy's staff, it appeared in the Dallas newspapers on November 18 and 19.

The President and Mrs. Kennedy traveled to Texas on November 21. That day, Kennedy visited San Antonio and Houston, where he was warmly greeted by enthusiastic crowds. He flew to Fort Worth that evening.

One of the President's first acts on the morning of November 22 was to call the woman who had arranged the accommodations that he and the First Lady occupied at Fort Worth's Texas Hotel. She had hung the walls with original paintings by modern masters such as Vincent Van Gogh and Claude Monet, and the special effort of the citizens of Fort Worth greatly impressed the Kennedys. That rainy morning, the President addressed the Fort Worth Chamber of Commerce. The speech was well received and, as Governor Connally recounted, it was laced with fun. Later in the morning, after a query from Dallas, the President said that if the weather was clear, he did not want the protective bubble used on the Presidential limousine.

The President and his entourage took off for Dallas at approximately 11:20 a.m. While the Presidential plane, Air Force One, was airborne, the President looked out the window and remarked to the Governor with a smile, "Our luck is holding. It looks as if we'll get sunshine." A clear sky, brilliant sunshine, 68-degree temperature – a marvelous autumn day – provided the backdrop for the President and Mrs. Kennedy as they arrived at Love Field in Dallas. The First Lady was presented with a bouquet of roses, and the couple attended a reception held in their honor at the airport by the community leaders of Dallas. After greeting them, the President moved to shake hands with the enthusiastic crowd which according to some estimates may have numbered 4,000 persons. For a few minutes, the President and the First Lady walked along the security barrier, greeting people. Then they joined Governor and Mrs. Connally in the Presidential limousine. Two Secret Service agents, one the driver, sat in front. The President and his wife sat in the rear seat, with the President on the right, in keeping with military protocol, as Commander in Chief of the Armed Forces. Governor Connally sat on a jump seat directly in front of the President, with his back to Kennedy, and Mrs. Connally occupied the left jump seat. Two cars with members of the Dallas Police Department, including Chief Jesse Curry, and Secret Service agents, preceded the Presidential limousine. Behind a follow-up car carried Secret Service agents and members of the White House staff. To the rear of that car, the Vice President and Mrs. Johnson and Senator Ralph Yarborough rode in another limousine. Next came the Vice President's follow-up car, and then a long line of limousines, trucks and various vehicles containing Members of Congress and other dignitaries, photographers, the President's physician, and members of the White House staff and the press.

The motorcade left Love Field at about 11:50 a.m. Governor Connally recalled he was worried not about violence but about the possibility that some incident might occur that would embarrass the President and disrupt the atmosphere of confidence that had been building throughout the trip. That morning a hostile full-page advertisement, sponsored by the "America-thinking Citizens of Dallas," had appeared in the pages of the *Dallas Morning News*. It charged, among other things, that Kennedy had ignored the Constitution, scrapped the Monroe Doctrine in favor of the "Spirit of Moscow," and had been "soft on Communists, fellow-travelers, and ultra-leftists in America." The Governor was apprehensive that there might be unfriendly demonstrations during the motorcade or that the crowd's mood would be indifferent or even sullen.

The Governor's concern subsided as the motorcade passed through the outskirts of Dallas and neared the center of the city. The crowds grew larger and they were unmistakably friendly, with people smiling, waving, and calling the President's name. In Connally's words: "The further we got towards town, the denser became the crowds, and when we got down on Main Street, the crowds were extremely thick. They were pushed off of curbs; they were out in the street, and they were backed all the way up against the walls of the buildings. They were just as thick as they could be. I don't know how many. But there were at least a quarter of a million people on the parade route that day and everywhere the reception was good."

Governor Connally noticed that Mrs. Kennedy, who had appeared apprehensive the previous day, was more relaxed and enjoyed the Dallas crowd. The only hostile act he remembered was a heckler with a placard that read "Kennedy Go Home." The President noticed the sign, and asked Governor and Mrs. Connally if they had seen it. Connally said, "Yes, but we were hoping you didn't."

"Well, I saw it. Don't you imagine he's a nice fellow?" Kennedy asked.

The Governor said, "Yes, I imagine he's a nice fellow."

Connally's fear of an embarrassing incident seemed to be unfounded.

He recalled: "The crowds were larger than I had anticipated. They were more enthusiastic than I could ever have hoped for."

This enthusiasm was apparent in a number of incidents. A little girl held up a sign with the request, "President Kennedy, will you shake hands with me?" The President noticed the sign, had the car stopped and shook hands with the little girl. The car was mobbed by an admiring crowd that was only separated from the Presidential limousine by Secret Service agents. At another stop, as the motorcade approached downtown Dallas, the President caught sight of a Roman Catholic nun with a group of schoolchildren. He stopped and spoke with the group. Several times enthusiastic onlookers broke away from the curbside throng and attempted to reach the limousine. Secret Service agents cleared the admirers from the street.

The crowds grew thicker as the Presidential parade approached downtown. The motorcade followed the traditional Dallas parade route into the downtown business district, turning onto Main Street, which brought it through the centre of the Dallas commercial district. It moved westward along Main toward Dealey Plaza. People crowded the sidewalks, surged into the street and waved from office building windows. The motorcade tunneled through the throng. The Governor later remarked that the business community, the group Kennedy sought to impress, would have to be affected by this remarkable reception. Connally said, ". . . the trip had been absolutely wonderful, and we were heaving a sigh of relief because once we got through the motorcade at Dallas and through the Dallas luncheon, then everything else was pretty much routine."

President Kennedy was clearly delighted by his Dallas welcome. At the corner of Main and Houston, the motorcade made a sharp 90-degree turn to the right and headed north for one block, toward the Texas School Book Depository. As the limousine approached Houston and Elm, Mrs. Connally, elated by the reception, said, "Mr. President, you can't say Dallas doesn't love you." "That's obvious," the President replied.

At Elm Street, the limousine made a hairpin turn to the left and headed west, passing the book depository.

At about 12:30 p.m., as the President waved to the crowds, shots rang out. Mrs. Connally heard a noise, turned to her right, and saw the President clutch his neck with both hands, then slump down in the seat. Governor Connally immediately thought the noise was a rifle shot. He turned from his straight-backed jump seat in an attempt to catch sight of the President because he feared an assassination attempt.

The Governor described the scene: "I never looked, I never made the full turn. About the time I turned back where I was facing more or less straight ahead, the way the car was moving, I was hit. I was knocked over, just doubled over by the force of the bullet. It went in

262

my back and came out my chest about 2 inches below and to the left of my right nipple. The force of the bullet drove my body over almost double, and when I looked, immediately I could see I was drenched with blood. So, I knew I had been badly hit and I more or less straightened up. At about this time, Nellie [Mrs. Connally] reached over and pulled me down into her lap.

"I was in her lap facing forward when another shot was fired . . . I did not hear the shot that hit me. I wasn't conscious of it. I am sure I heard it, but I was not conscious of it at all. I heard another shot. I heard it hit. It hit with a very pronounced impact . . . it made a very, very strong sound.

"Immediately, I could see blood and brain tissue all over the interior of the car and all over our clothes. We were both covered with brain tissue, and there were pieces of brain tissue as big as your little finger . . .

"When I was hit, or shortly before I was hit – no, I guess it was after I was hit – I said first, just almost in despair, I said, 'no no, no,' just thinking how tragic it was that we had gone through this 24 hours, it had all been so wonderful and so beautifully executed.

"The President had been so marvelously received and then here, at the last moment, this great tragedy. I just said, 'no, no, no, no,' Then I said right after I was hit, I said, 'My God, they are going to kill us all.'"

Mrs. Connally initially thought the Governor was dead as he fell into her lap. She did not look back after her husband was hit, but heard Mrs. Kennedy say, "They have shot my husband." After one shot, Mrs. Connally recalled, the President's wife said, "They have killed my husband. I have his brains in my hand."

Roy Kellerman, the Secret Service agent in the right front seat, said, "Let's get out of here fast." Bill Greer, the driver, accelerated tremendously. "So we pulled out of the motorcade," Mrs. Connally recalled, "and we must have been a horrible sight flying down the freeway with those dying men in our arms."

She added, "There was no screaming in that horrible car. It was just a silent, terrible drive."

The wounded President and Governor were rushed to Parkland Hospital.

At 1 p.m., the 35th President of the United States was pronounced dead, 1,037 days after his term had begun.

Consider this along with a 2,352-page FBI dossier on the life and chicanery of Senator Edward Kennedy, the surviving brother of America's First Family, which was released in 2010 when he'd also moved on. It highlights the Kennedy family's ability to anger both the Mob and the FBI by their behaviour. Edward Kennedy died, aged 77, in August 2009, from a brain tumour. It was reported that his widow, Victoria, did not want the FBI files released, but the Freedom of Information law allows us to see what was reported over the years to the powerful J. Edgar Hoover. The files reveal that, throughout his public life, the agency received many warnings that the Mafia were going to kill the youngest Kennedy brother. They were not alone: enemies included embittered Vietnam War veterans angered by his 'Communist' views; many infuriated by his support for the IRA; the Ku Klux Klan; and the crazies who wanted him dead because he was a Kennedy.

Many Americans were outraged by the married Kennedy's serial womanising and his cowardly behaviour after the death of Mary Jo Kopechne, 28; he fled the scene when his car plunged off a bridge following a drunken party at Chappaquiddick.

J. Edgar Hoover, the enigmatic and obsessive FBI chief, was mesmerised by the sex lives of others and every scrap of information was filed away for use one day. Others' sins gave him power.

Hoover must have been contented in his job in July 1965, when so much pertinent to *Shadowland* was happening. The until recently secret dossier reported that clean-cut Senator Edward Kennedy, 33, had attended rather louche parties at the Carlyle Hotel in Manhattan during the first half of the '60s. It detailed:

Mrs Jacqueline Hammond, age 40, has considerable information concerning sex parties in which a number of persons participated at different times. Among those mentioned were the following individuals: Robert F. Kennedy, John F. Kennedy, Teddy Kennedy, Sammy Davis Jr, Mr and Mrs Peter Lawford, Frank Sinatra, Marilyn Monroe.

The party hostess Mrs Hammond was divorced from the former US ambassador to Spain, and kept rooms at the

Carlyle. Actor Peter Lawford was married to the Kennedys' sister, Pamela. When Hoover got his information, Marilyn Monroe and JFK were both dead but their names remained in the report, which swelled the FBI Teddy Kennedy files. It also contained the story of how Frank Sinatra was being used by the Mafia to discredit Robert and Teddy Kennedy and their British brother-in-law Peter Lawford. The plan was to put them in a 'compromising situation', which, given the cast, wouldn't cause much difficulty.

Even more intriguing and buried in this colourful chapter of the FBI vault is the paperwork recounting the story of a man whose name is censored but who says he has been a Mafia member since 1948, based in the UK. He says he was brought into the assassination of President Kennedy when JFK's killer was sent to him in 1965 for rest and recuperation in west London. The assassin was sent to the city to escape the stress of his Mafia assignment to kill a president.

In two typed letters postmarked Wimbledon, logged by the FBI in April 1970 and personally vetted and read by J. Edgar Hoover (see pp. 281–90), he says that Senator Edward Kennedy is another target for the Mob, as is new US President Richard Nixon:

> In 1961 I attended a general meeting of the Mafia, during which time the main discussion was the Killing of John F. Kennedy and Martin Luther King. Although you may have closed your files on the killing of the President, you are wrong, the man who actually killed him, also the man who paid the killer is alive and at this moment preparing to kill Senator E. Kennedy and Mr. Nixon.

The letter writer offers to help catch the killer but insists in one letter, 'if any of this leaks out I am a dead man'.

Hoover, who'd witnessed more than most and instigated many of his own far-fetched conspiracies, ordered his London-based agents to meet the informer and fully investigate his story. If it was a puzzle and we were looking for the link to Wimbledon Man, could JFK assassination + Mafia + Corsican connection + London = Benny Huntman and his associates? Frustratingly, few further clues are revealed in the files that cover 1961 to 1985.

History gets more retouched than rewritten as time goes on. We learn more and it might not only be the knowledge that is new to us but the understanding of it. Which is why, like evening primrose, we always seek new light, especially when men like Benny Huntman emerge from the shadows, where we should not doubt our world continues to turn.

LAST CALL

'The Gambler', Kenny Rogers, 1979

Dino Ricardo Cellini was born in Havana in 1953, when his father, in partnership with Meyer Lansky, was running the Mafia's most profitable gambling interests in Cuba. He was given the name Ricardo because of his parents' favourite television show, *I Love Lucy*. In the second series, Lucille Ball and her Cuban husband, Dezi Arnaz, were having a baby, as they were in real life, and the TV couple called their son Ricardo. The 'Lucy Goes to Hospital' episode, shown for the first time on 19 January 1953, was the most-watched television programme of the era, and America watched 'Little Ricky' grow up.

Dino Cellini and his wife, Helena (who was 86 and living in Miami in 2011), adored the show; it reminded them of their own close-knit family life. Dino Jr, who is known to his friends as 'Ricky', recalled in 2011, a couple of days before what would have been his father's 95th birthday, 'I was Mom and Pop's "Little Ricky".'

At the age of three, Ricky Cellini was the ring-bearer at the wedding of the oldest daughter of Santo Trafficante Jr, one of the most powerful Mafia chieftains of the twentieth century. Trafficante was godfather to his sister Donna. In March 1987, he flew to America from London to act as a pall-bearer at Santo Trafficante Jr's funeral.

His father moved his family around his gambling world, so Ricky Cellini and his three sisters were present for a great part of the events described in this book, and Dino Cellini's son believes this book has got 'close to the true story as never before'. For this reason, he broke decades of silence and

267

spoke to me several times in July 2011, while staying at his new beach home in Miami, where he is recovering from treatment for cancer.

'First, you must understand that Pop and Meyer Lansky were partners. Dad looked after the casino business, Jimmy Blue made sure no one bothered him and Meyer looked after other business.

'Jimmy Blue was the boss. He was the boss after Charlie Lucky left. After Charlie Luciano got deported, it was Jimmy that became the boss. Meyer was a brilliant mathematician. That's my uncle. We called him "Uncle Meyer". The only one that really knew these guys like Sadlo and Meyer, Charlie Lucky and Jimmy Blue was my father.

'My uncles never knew them like that. My dad was ten years, eleven years older than Uncle Eddie, and these men were his age. You understand? My uncle Eddie is a brilliant man, so is my uncle Bob and so was my uncle Goff. They were all intelligent men, so Dad didn't have far to go to pick people to work with him, but Dad was the one. You see, Dad had started to get the reputation in gaming of being the master mechanic. He had worked for Meyer earlier in New York and they were a brilliant combination.

'I remember being in the office at Resorts International and they didn't have emails in those days or fax machines. We had telex machines. I put the tape through the thing and I'm reading it and I'm going, "Jesus, Dad, I don't understand this thing . . . It says Sweden." As soon as I said "Sweden", he yelled across the office, "Bring that to me right away." It was a calculation, a mathematical calculation. He'd joined a mathematical college in Sweden that would send like twenty people a problem and they would calculate the problem and the first one telexed back the answer. They wouldn't win any money or anything like that; it was a game. But Dad took it serious.

'Meyer Lansky was a great judge of character and that's why he chose Dad to take their gambling empire around the world. From the early days, they had this plan – and they did it. Cuba, Haiti, the Bahamas and London – Dad loved London – and from there into Europe, Africa. They were everywhere and we went with them. They fed off each other. When Meyer talked, my dad listened. When Dad talked, Meyer listened.

268

They had every move planned in advance, every obstacle taken care of, fixed.

'Meyer was like that, and they understood each other, but the most important thing they understood about each other was that their word was beyond reproach. They could shake each other's hands, and time proved that. My father in front of a Senate Committee – I mean 500, 600 questions and every threat in the world, not a fucking word came out of his mouth. They knew that that was the make-up of the person, and that was why he was the man he was.

'Hey, one day Meyer and my dad were sitting out back of our house in Keystone Point out in north Miami. Mom was out back making hamburgers and my dad and Meyer are sitting close to each other, they were whispering into each other's ears and you'd think they were making out. Dad's in a bathrobe and Meyer's relaxed and they're getting out pencils and paper and making all sorts of calculations. Dad called to me and told me to buy 10,000 shares in Resorts International. I did it without question and the shares did nothing but grow in value big-time. These guys were running the world.

'Dad took working with Meyer as an opportunity to clear all of the tough stuff away from him. No more. Be the straight guy. He was Meyer's partner. My father would have thought you to be an idiot to sit there with a piece of burning paper in your hand or go through some blood ritual. My father would have thought you were out of your mind if you even asked him to do something like that. These were just men that were real men. What I mean is, their handshake was better than a signed paper, you know? Truly. You can't find them any more. They walked into fire for each other. They were brilliant people.

'I was six years old and we were in Havana when Fidel moved in and it was the only time my dad went mad at us kids. He'd got us back to the Riviera Hotel and we were up in our suite. My sister and I were looking out the window at Fidel and his guys coming in. They were firing guns in the street, there were tracers going everywhere, bullets were hitting the walls of the hotel, and Dad came in and saw us at the window and he raced over and pulled us away. He was mad as hell. We might have been hurt.

'The fix had been in with Cuba through Meyer all the way

back to when they were bringing liquor through the country. It was Dad and Meyer who gave Santo permission to have a place in Havana. They gave him a joint called the Sans Souci, which was outside the city of Havana. There was nobody that would go out there. Of course, they complained. Santo said this wasn't fair because it was an organised system – all for one, one for all – at this time. It was the time of the Apalachin Meeting [the American Mafia summit on 14 November 1957, when around 100 mafiosi met at Joe Barbara's house in Apalachin, New York] and all that. The guy who took Charlie Lucky's place when he left was Jimmy Blue Eyes. This is who the boss was, OK? No question about that.

'So Meyer asked my dad, "Listen, go do me a favour. Go to the San Souci and see what you can put together, because we want to be fair to everybody. We don't want any bad feeling." Dad went out there and put in a bingo parlour. They gave away a convertible Cadillac. Well, from not being able to get a car into the parking lot, they went to having to have close to 20 off-duty policemen to park the cars at the San Souci, and it became a success. That was what Dad did. He knew what to do to get the people to go there.

'He was a genius at gambling, at calculating the odds, the pure math of it all. And he knew people. He wasn't bothered by competitors. He said they, the gamblers, would always find their way to our tables because we offered a better deal and environment. But if somebody bothered us, tried to get in on our business, then Jimmy Blue would look after that.

'Jimmy Blue had a guy who was his right arm, a guy who would, you know, take care of things. He was a guy called Dan Stromberg who was known as 'Nigger Dan' – he'd go into Harlem and take care of situations, anything – and if Dan knocked on your door you might as well shoot yourself, you know what I mean? You weren't leaving.

'But Dad was the casino man, the master of the gaming. The guy who explained that best was Martin Fox, who owned the Tropicana in Havana. He had wanted my dad to come down in 1949 and run the Tropicana, but they had the joint in Cincinnati and they were doing real good, so my dad sent my uncle Eddie. My uncle Eddie is a very educated guy in gaming. He's a great. If there is a hall of fame, he's in there.

'My uncle Eddie was down in Cuba and he tried to do what

my dad did. My uncle Ed didn't like it there. They changed
places. My uncle Ed came to Cincinnati and my dad went
down to Cuba. Martin Fox said, "Before, we had the student.
Now, the professor has arrived." It was always like that.

'My mom is Scots-Irish. She was 20 when she met my dad.
She was the second runner-up in the Miss America contest,
Miss Boston, back then. She was very, very beautiful. She still
is. In 1949, Dad had a whack-out [illegal] joint in Cincinnati,
Ohio. Dad had already gotten the reputation that he was a
master mechanic. Mom was telling me a story about those
times the other day. It was hysterical.

'They were getting a new sheriff, and Dad had to close
because his guy was running. So he closed the joint up for
two weeks while the election was going on. Mom and Dad are
both sitting in the coffee shop at the hotel where they have
the joint. My mother is just young, barely 22. This guy comes
in and my father looks up and he goes, "Oh God, no."

'A guy comes walking up and he goes, "Oh, Dino, how are
you?" He's tapping my father up and he's obviously drunk.

'My father looks up and says, "Sam, how are you?"

'He was a rich son of a gun and Dad had been whacking
this guy out for months. He's a big player and Dad didn't
want to lose him – you want to keep the players who come
into your joint – so he can't tell him to go away. So he's talking
to him, and he says, "Sam, listen, we can't stay. This is my wife,
Helena. We're just getting ready to leave." The guy is drunk
and he doesn't want any drunks around my mother.

'The guy goes, "Well, where you goin'?"

'Dad says they're leaving town, going out of town. They had
no plans whatsoever.

'"No kiddin'. Where you goin'?"

'My father says, "New Orleans." My mother is just sitting
there across the table wondering what on earth he's talking
about.

'The guy says, "That's no problem. I'll take you to the
airport."

'Dad still didn't want to make the guy feel like he was
unwelcome. My mother said he walked them to the ticket
counter! She said, "Your father buys two tickets to New
Orleans." They got on the plane. The guy walked them there.
In those days, you could walk right to the aircraft. He thought

he was doing my father a favour. She said the first time she went to New Orleans, she had to buy a new wardrobe. They didn't even have a toothbrush.

'When my mother met my father, she was part of a dance group and they were very high end. They played New York and all this, they were very, very good, and what happened is that there was a lady who played their music and she knew my mother well. They just thought my mother was adorable. I have an Aunt Joneen and she's also beautiful, but she's blonde. She'd work with my dad. She'd sit at the table with her purse open and Dad was so good that when he switched dice he'd spin the discards into the purse, which she'd close. It's a natural move if you know what to do.

'This woman who'd played the piano for my mother saw my father coming in the casino with this blonde. She does not know that this is my mother's sister. She was thinking, "That son of a bitch, coming in with that blonde every fucking night. He's a got a beautiful wife at home and a child."

'She says something and my father gets spooked: "Helena, you'd better speak to Mary, for crying out loud. She's going to get me nailed. She thinks I'm bringing Joneen as a date. She doesn't know Joneen has got the purse with the dice."

'My mother came in the next day with Joneen, and my father said to Mary, "Hi, Mary. How are you?"

She's grabbing my mother: "You poor child."

'Mom says, "Mary, I'd like to introduce you to my sister."

'My mom and dad were never away from each other for more than a month. If my father was away for three months, my mother would be away from him for a month and then go and be with him for two months . . . They were solid and Meyer had seen that early. Dad was a man who saw the vision and would not to be distracted by any piece of skirt that passed his way, or by anything else.

'We would go to eat dinner, and Dad would see somebody working, a busboy that would be working hard and really doing his job, and he would make a point of going over and saying, "Listen, I've got a school where they're learning how to be croupiers," and he would give the kid a card and he would come down to the school and see if he was interested in being a dealer to go to the Bahamas.

'When I first went to Freeport, there was a whorehouse

and a place where you could land private planes. They were just making the airport and the Lucayan Beach Hotel and Casino was nothing but a bunch of stakes in the ground with little red flags. That had to be 1962, when they were just making the plans. There was never any question that it would all go ahead. All the arrangements had been made.

'With Dad, everything went as smooth as it ever could. The casino guys wanted my dad to be everywhere, but clearly he couldn't do that. We always had our home base, which we always returned to. We lived in Keystone Point in north Miami when we had the Colony in London. I was a young kid. Dad always took me everywhere with him. I was his only son.

'I remember meeting with Al Salkin and his lawyer in the Rhône Hotel, Geneva, right there by the lake. We met there and we had a suite and Dad gave me a hundred dollars. I was downstairs in a cafe and I was trying to pick up a hooker. I think I was like eleven or twelve! It was a hundred dollars – fuck my age! I was figuring that she might not notice that I was so young. Alf and Dad were making the deal to make the Colony. We flew back to London, and by then they had given us the licence.

'Before the Colony, we would go and stay at the Hilton, and we stayed there a couple of years while they were making the Lucayan Beach. Then Dad got a residency where he got a place for George Raft there, too, at 55 Park Lane, right next door to the Dorchester, which was convenient.

'George Raft was a guest and he had all the broads in London. He was a friend of Meyer's all the way through. He knew the guys. My mother used to say the women were always all over him. He was a great dancer. He would be in the Colony and Dad had him all set up. He lived across the hall from us at 55 Park Lane. The picture that you see of him in front of the Colony, the one of them on the Rolls – I remember sitting with my father standing right there. We've got the park behind us and they're taking a picture in front of the Colony.

'And right after they took that picture, George looked over at my father and he said, "Dino, come here and take one for me. You're the one who owns this joint." Exactly what he said to him.

'Dad goes, "I don't like the lights, George."

'George nagged, "Just one, for me." My father struck the

same pose as George and they took a picture. There were two copies of that picture made. One was given to George, one was given to my mother, who gave it to me.

'John was the driver. He used to come and pick us up in the Rolls to go riding in Hyde Park all the time. We'd go about three times a week. Not Dad, just me and my sisters. It was a very enjoyable time. A great time. When the Colony opened, Dad left Park Lane and went over because he wanted to be able to walk to the joint, and we lived at 40 Berkeley Square, up there in that first apartment. Nice apartment, bigger than Park Lane.

'Out of all of his places, I want to tell you, the one he loved most, where he put himself into it more than any place that we've ever had – and we've had many, many places – was the Colony. Dad loved that place and when they made him not welcome and he had to leave England he was truly hurt, because he truly enjoyed getting dressed up with the hat and going to Ascot. He loved London and the scene at that time.

'There was not much trouble at the Colony. Dad never liked Frank Sinatra, so if he saw him there he'd leave and avoid any confrontation. We had a lot of fun with Telly Savalas, who was a good guy. He and some of the other guys filming *The Dirty Dozen* in London often had to haul Lee Marvin's ass out of there. It wasn't a difficulty.

'There was a guy called Bill Davies, who's retired now, and my dad called him "the original Jesse James", so you can imagine what this guy was like. A cooler guy you could never meet. He's the one who took me to No. 1 Savile Row, to Gieves & Hawkes, to get a suit for the first time.

'There was some serious stuff, but we had Jimmy Blue. There were some English guys called the Krays, two brothers, one was a fag, I think. What happened was Bill Davies came to my dad and said, "Hey, listen, these guys, they want you to pay 'em. We opened the Colony and this is London, this is their town."

'And Dad said, "Well, we don't need any more partners."

'"Dino, if you don't pay 'em, they're going to blow the place up."

'"Well, let 'em blow it up. We'll just make another one. Let 'em blow it up."

'"No, Dino, they're going to wait until you're in the building and then they're going to blow it up."

'My father just said, "OK," and he called Jimmy, and Jimmy talked to those guys. You understand? My dad didn't know how to talk to those guys.

'When Jimmy Blue got done with you, you knew. Let's put it this way: this man could kill me, have me killed, in a minute, and I wouldn't be number 250, you know what I mean?

'The Krays were a nuisance. After Jimmy talked to them, we never heard from them again. If there was any problem, Jimmy made it go away. That was Dad's partner. He just didn't work in the casino. He was the one made sure that nobody bothered Dad. Everyone wanted Dad to be allowed to do the business.

'Dad circumvented the law in Holland to get us a gaming licence there. Once they figured out what we did, they made another law so no one could do that again, but they couldn't take away our licence. We were the only ones that were legal. That was Dad. He would go and do things like that. He opened up Atlantic City to where its revenue is huge. The volume – that was always the difference. He believed in slot machines and they paid off for him big-time through his association with the Bally Manufacturing Company, which again was contacts. He knew everybody.

'I remember being in Angelo's in Rome getting suits made. Angelo was fitting me. He had a bust of Dad. Every time he got new material, he would make this jacket or this suit and he would send it to Pop. But I had to get fitted there and, as we lived in Rome, it was just right down the street. Anyway, all of a sudden Dad came in. He took me into the place next door, where there were bodyguards there and everything like that. "Rick, I want you to meet Constantine." It was the King of Greece.

'He knew many wealthy men. When Adnan Khashoggi's father got sick in the United States, he didn't know where to go. He called my father up and asked him. My father is the one who sent the doctor over to him. I think they were in Nevada. They all loved Dad. They all knew Dad from London, Havana, Amsterdam, Portugal – all over the world.

'Once, at home, I opened the door and suddenly there's James Caan and some other actor there to see Meyer, Jimmy,

Dad and some others. These guys were shaking. They're excited to meet these guys. I'm a young kid and going, "Wow, man! James Caan!" I wanted to talk to him. What the heck.

'Dad really didn't talk about stuff that much. It was always very QT. You knew he was the boss not because he told you but because when he walked in that aura would come from him. This guy was the boss; there were no two ways about it. Dad always liked to stay under the radar.

'My grandfather Marcello owned a restaurant in Steubenville called the Lindbergh, and the only reason he called it the Lindbergh was because Charles Lindbergh had crossed the Atlantic on his solo flight three days before he opened. He was trying to bring people inside. Then they later changed the name only because they got caught selling whiskey too many times. They took the licence away from the Lindbergh, so it became the Roma.

'My grandfather was low-key too. People don't know he was the one gave Dino Crocetti, who you know as Dean Martin, the 25 dollars to take the bus from Steubenville to New York to go meet an up-and-coming comedian; he also put him in a hotel for a week or so until they got going. They were in a poor town in Ohio. We were actually one of the ones that were coming from a little bit of bucks. Some of those bucks started Jerry Lewis and Dean Martin's double act. Dean Martin did work with my dad, but that was at the Imperial, which was in a different class to Rex's Cigar Store. There's been a lot of myth, but that's how it was.

'I've seen so many books, so much stuff written, that's just not correct. I know because my father or my mother told me – or I was there myself.

'Santo. Christ. There was an agent that was in charge of investigating Dad. His name was Special Agent Harrison. We were at the office in Rome and I was about 17 years old, so this has to be about 1970. I'm at the office with Pop and he's in there doing some work and all that. Meanwhile, we've got to get home for dinner. They had dinner ready at a certain time. We had a butler and a maid, and they would make the dinner. My mother was over, too. It's six, seven o'clock, time for us to leave, and the front doorbell rings.

'Dad goes, "Go get that door." I go over to the reception area and everybody has gone home. I open the door and there's Santo. He puts his finger to his mouth and says, "Don't say nothing. Go tell him Special Agent Harrison is here."

'It was my Uncle Santo. I have known him my entire life. I had to do what he said. I walked into the office and I look at my dad and he says, "Who is it?"'

'I said, "Some man. His name is Special Agent Harrison. He said you would know who he is."'

'My dad. His eyes look up to the sky and he grabs his pencil and he throws it up in the air, just in the air, and looks at me and says, "Look, son, go on home and tell your mother I'll be there in a bit."

'In the meantime, Santo is turning the corner and coming through the door. Now my dad one second is, "Oh God. This bastard . . ." The next, he looks up and there's Santo and it's, "Oh my God . . ." Then they start laughing.

'He said, "We're all going out for dinner. Call your mother." I mean, shit like that would happen all the time. The characters were amazing.

'When Meyer started laughing, it was infectious. Lansky was a great one. After my father died, he came to our house to see my mother and told her, "Don't worry about anything. You are one of us." That was a rare thing.

'As nice as Meyer was, he knew how to focus a person's attention. I used to drive Meyer after my father passed away. Meyer would call up and he wants somebody to come and get him and he has some places to go. I would be assigned to go get him and drive him where he wanted to go. I'm sitting there driving the car and I say, "Meyer, if you want to tell somebody something and you really want them to hear what you have got to say, what do you do? How do you do it?"

'He said, "Well, if you really want to get your point across and you really want someone to hear what you say, you stare at them and you whisper. Then he can't do anything but listen to you."

'Straight from the horse's mouth. With these guys, at least you knew what was going on. It was their way, unless you negotiated some way to make it different than was how it was. I think the people in the world have looked at their own governments and found out that these guys are far more corrupt.

'John Kennedy got elected because of the help of the

Teamsters union in Chicago during the convention that they had there, the Democratic Convention. That's what got him elected. They turned it around. Who got that one for them was Joe Kennedy, because he went way back and he dealt with those guys, Jimmy and Meyer. They knew him well. He was a bootlegger, for Christ's sake.

'The upset after John Kennedy's election! To tell the truth, I think Bobby's attitude to the whole thing would have been a lot different if Joe Kennedy hadn't had a stroke right after John got elected president. He was not able to tell them so proficiently, "These are the guys that did this favour for me, fellas. This is why you're here." I think he got popped too, but that's another story. Everyone had their connections. Meyer got Franklin Delano Roosevelt his White House seat. People don't realise so many things. It's a strange world, but it's a small one.

'Bobby Kennedy was a fucking prick, but the guy Nixon was the one, he was just . . . he was out of line, and he was the one that wanted my dad in jail. He got on to Edgar J. and put the FBI on us. The FBI agents, they would break my brake light on the back of my car. Then when I went out on a date and I drove down the street, I would press on my brake and they would have the police pull me over, and then the federal car would pull up in front of me. Then this guy would write me a ticket for a broken brake light and the feds would be asking me, "Is your father home?"

'The creep Nixon kept that up until he waved goodbye to the White House. Dad and I watched it on TV and Dad said, "They'll pardon him. He'll get off. These pricks always do."'

Dino Cellini returned to America after charges against him, instigated by the testimony of 'Fat Vinnie' Teresa, were dropped by federal prosecutors. His wife, Helena, was with him when he died after a long struggle with cancer, aged 63, at Mount Sinai Hospital in Miami.

Their son remembers: 'My sister Donna was singing an Italian folk song in his ear and he looked over at my mother, who was standing right next to him, and he went, "Helena, Helena, Helena." He threw her three kisses and then he passed away. That's exactly how he died.

'For days afterwards, it was madness. When there was the wake, people couldn't understand why so many Mafia families were there being represented. People who don't communicate with each other were there. Everyone in the world seemed to come to pay respects.

'The croupiers in the Bahamas chartered planes to be present. They flew in between shifts, some for the services, some for the burial. The casinos never close. That's business, how Dad ran gambling around the world, and it's still the way it works.

'Wayne Ferris on the ABC news said, "The genius of international gambling passed away today." He got that right.'

Appendix

THE SHADOWLAND DOSSIER

'Behind Closed Doors', Charlie Rich, 1973

Legat, London   4/15/70

Director, FBI 62-112941

                                                    1 - Mr. Rappach
                                                    1 - Foreign Liaison
ASSASSINATION OF PRESIDENT   (Cleared telephonically)
JOHN FITZGERALD KENNEDY,
DALLAS, TEXAS, 11/22/63
MISCELLANEOUS - INFORMATION CONCERNING
OO: DALLAS

              ReBulet to Legat, London, 4/7/70 captioned.
"Mr. [   ]
London, England, Research Matter (Correspondence and Tours)."

              Enclosed for Legat, London, are two copies of Dallas   b6
airtel 4/7/70 and two true copies of a letter written by   b7C
[   ] which was mailed to the Dallas Office. This
second communication from [   ] is similar in content to
his letter furnished to you by referenced communication.

              Leads set forth by referenced Bureau letter should
be handled promptly so that information concerning [   ]
can be disseminated by the Bureau.

              Enclosures (4)

              KMR:dvj
              (5)
                                                                      b6
                                                                      b7C
NOTE: [   ], who lives in London, England, directed
individual letters to our New York Office and also to our Dallas
Office. [   ] was not identified in Bureau Files and the
first communication received from New York was handled by the
Crime Records Division. The second communication is being furnished
for the information of Legat London. Legat London was instructed
in Bulet 4/7/70 to determine appropriate background of the subject
and his creditability through established sources and submit results
of inquiries in a form suitable for dissemination. U. S. Secret Service has been advised and the Office of Senator Kennedy has been
advised due to an alleged threat against him.

MAILED 20
APR 16 1970

April 9, 1970

GENERAL INVESTIGATIVE DIVISION

Attached concerns letter received by our Dallas Office from [   ] of Wimbledon, England. [   ] indicates he is going to get assassination of President Kennedy case reopened if it takes 20 years. He claims assassin of President Kennedy still at large as well as individual who planned it, and he knows this individual.

[   ] also claims another assassination is to take place (last of Kennedys) apparently referring to Senator Edward M. Kennedy. [   ] concluded if we wish to find out more from him, contact with him should be discreet or he will be a dead man.

There is no record for [   ] in Bureau or Dallas files. By separate communication, Legal Attache, London, will be furnished full background and requested through sources to have [   ] located and interviewed thoroughly and develop full background. Secret Service and Senator Kennedy's office being advised of this information.

KMR:jny

Mr. [illegible]
Mr. [illegible]
Mr. Mohr.
Mr. Bishop
Mr. Casper.
Mr. Callahan
Mr. Conrad.
Mr. Felt
Mr. Gale
Mr. Rosen
Mr. Sullivan
Mr. Tavel.
Mr. Soyars.
Tele. Room.
Miss Holmes.
Miss Gandy

F B I

Date: **4/7/70**

Transmit the following in _____
(Type in plaintext or code)

Via _____ **A I R T E L** _____
(Priority)

TO: DIRECTOR, FBI (62-109060)

FROM: SAC, DALLAS (89-43) (P*)

SUBJECT: ASSASSINATION OF PRESIDENT
JOHN FITZGERALD KENNEDY,
DALLAS, TEXAS, 11/22/63
MISCELLANEOUS - INFORMATION CONCERNING
Threats Against Senator M. Kennedy
OO-DALLAS

    Enclosed for the Bureau is the original and one
Xerox copy of a letter and the envelope in which it was
mailed, postmarked 4/2/70 at Wimbledon, England, from an
individual identifying himself as [ ].

b6
b7C

    In this letter addressed to the FBI at Dallas,
Texas, [ ] indicates he is going to get the assassination
case re-opened if it takes him the next 20 years. He indicates that he joined the Mafia organization in 1948. He
also states that the man who really pulled the trigger in the
assassination is still at large as well as the individual
who planned it and that he knows such individual. He
describes the individual as a maniac who wants power and
wants to be President.

    The writer of this letter states that another
assassination is to take place, which is the last of the
Kennedys, and apparently is referring to Senator EDWARD M.
KENNEDY.

    He closes by saying that should we wish to find
out more from him we should be discreet in contacting him
or he will be a dead man.

(4)-Bureau (Encl. 2) (R.M.)
1-Dallas
RPG:jls
(5)

2 ENCLOSURE

62 - 112941

NOT RECORDED
133 APR 27 1970

ORIGINAL FILED IN 62-109060 - 6929

ENCLOSURE
Approved: _____   Sent _____ M   Per _____
Special Agent in Charge

DL-89-43

      The general indices and the special assassination
indices of the Dallas office are negative concerning [   ]

b6
b7C

      It is suggested that the Bureau have Legat, London,
fully identify [   ] and submit a letterhead memo-
randum containing contents of the enclosed letter with the
background information for appropriate dissemination,
especially in view of the statement that another assassination
is to take place.

-2-

London
England

Dear Sir,

I am writing in the hope you will do something, for I promise you that if you don't, if it
takes over the next 20 years I am going to get the
case of President John F. Kennedy re-opened.

In the past your department have been
ridecouled in the handling of the case.

Let me make it clear that I am quite
prepared to give myself up to you and give you
everything you want.

In 1948 I joined the Mafia organization
and was inoguarated by the Supreme Boss who is a
Governor of one of your states in America. From
1948-1960 I did a lot of gun smuggling, and held
many secret documents relating to the security of
America. In 1962 I attended a meeting during which
the main discussion was the killing of President
John F. Kennedy. Now, although you did tap a
conversation on Nov the 9th relating to the killing
this was deliberately done for you to hear. But
although you caught one man and he was shot by
another, up to now the man who really pulled the
trigger is at large still, and the man who planned
it all, for we knew we could not miss. In 1965
the killer was sent to me for a rest, but last
October I sent him back upon instructions, for
another assanin is to take place which is the
last of the Kennedy's.

As I said before this is entirely up to
you, but I can assure you that there is going to be
quite a lot of killings.

TRUE COPY

This man is a maniac, he wants power, he wants to be president, and will stop at nothing to get it. Is a man's life only worth $20,000 dollars.

All the disturbances that is going on in America, is being back by him.

Should you wish to find out more from me, please be discreet as possible, for if any of this leaks out, I am a dead man.

Your's truly,

- 2 -

4/7/70

Airtel

To: Legat, London   62-112941-

From: Director, FBI

MR.

LONDON, ENGLAND
RESEARCH MATTER (CORRESPONDENCE AND TOURS)

b6
b7C

     Enclosed are two copies of a self-explanatory letter
which is not being acknowledged. Through established sources and
contact with appropriate [   ] you should determine
the background and credibility of Mr. [   ] and, based on the
information developed, you should determine the advisability of having
him interviewed. Upon completion you should advise the Bureau of
the results of your inquiries in a form suitable for dissemination, if
appropriate, together with your recommendations as to the handling
of correspondence which might be received from Mr. [   ] in the
future.

b7D

Enclosures (2)

ALL INFORMATION CONTAINED
HEREIN IS UNCLASSIFIED
DATE 7/27/93 BY [   ]

1 - New York
Reurs 3/30/70.
1 - Foreign Liaison Unit

MAILED 20
APR 8 1970
COMM-FBI

NOTE: Bufiles contain no record of correspondent. Contents of this letter
were telephonically furnished to [   ] Protective Intelligence
Division, U. S. Secret Service, at 3:45 p.m., on 4/2/70, who requested that
a copy be furnished his agency by courier. A copy of Mr. [   ] letter
was furnished the Liaison Section of the Domestic Intelligence Division on
4/2/70 for appropriate delivery.

b6
b7C

Tolson
DeLoach
Walters
Mohr
Bishop
Casper
Callahan
Conrad
Felt
Gale
Rosen
Sullivan
Tavel
Soyars
Tele. Room
Holmes
Gandy

DMW:cfj (7)

TELETYPE UNIT

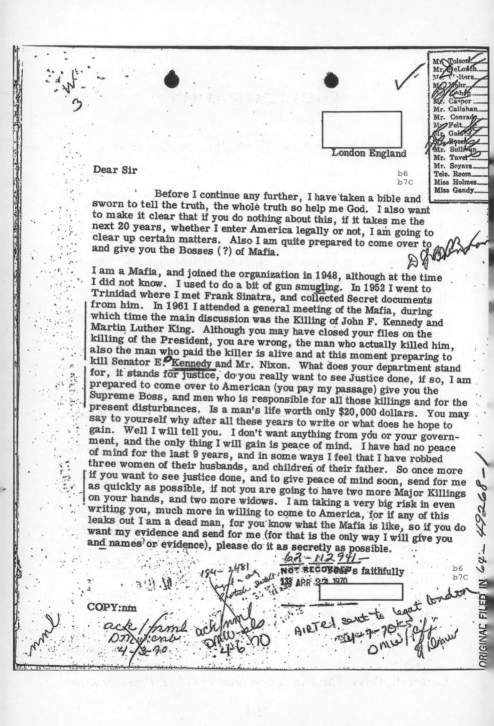

Mr. Tolson
Mr. DeLoach
Mr. ___lters
Mr. Mohr
Mr. ___hop
Mr. Casper
Mr. Callahan
Mr. Conrad
Mr. Felt
Mr. Gale
Mr. Rosen
Mr. Sullivan
Mr. Tavel
Mr. Soyars
Tele. Room
Miss Holmes
Miss Gandy

London England

Dear Sir

b6
b7C

      Before I continue any further, I have taken a bible and sworn to tell the truth, the whole truth so help me God. I also want to make it clear that if you do nothing about this, if it takes me the next 20 years, whether I enter America legally or not, I am going to clear up certain matters. Also I am quite prepared to come over to and give you the Bosses (?) of Mafia.

I am a Mafia, and joined the organization in 1948, although at the time I did not know. I used to do a bit of gun smugling. In 1952 I went to Trinidad where I met Frank Sinatra, and collected Secret documents from him. In 1961 I attended a general meeting of the Mafia, during which time the main discussion was the Killing of John F. Kennedy and Martin Luther King. Although you may have closed your files on the killing of the President, you are wrong, the man who actually killed him, also the man who paid the killer is alive and at this moment preparing to kill Senator E. Kennedy and Mr. Nixon. What does your department stand for, it stands for justice, do you really want to see Justice done, if so, I am prepared to come over to American (you pay my passage) give you the Supreme Boss, and men who is responsible for all those killings and for the present disturbances. Is a man's life worth only $20,000 dollars. You may say to yourself why after all these years to write or what does he hope to gain. Well I will tell you. I don't want anything from you or your government, and the only thing I will gain is peace of mind. I have had no peace of mind for the last 9 years, and in some ways I feel that I have robbed three women of their husbands, and children of their father. So once more if you want to see justice done, and to give peace of mind soon, send for me as quickly as possible, if not you are going to have two more Major Killings on your hands, and two more widows. I am taking a very big risk in even writing you, much more in willing to come to America, for if any of this leaks out I am a dead man, for you know what the Mafia is like, so if you do want my evidence and send for me (for that is the only way I will give you and names or evidence), please do it as secretly as possible.

62-112941

NOT RECORDED   Yours faithfully
133 APR 22 1970

b6
b7C

COPY:nm

ack/fnml   ack/nml
D.M./cnb   DMW-nls
4/3-70   4-6-70

AIRTEL sent to Legat London

BIBLIOGRAPHY

'It's All Over Now', The Rolling Stones, 1964

Allsop, Kenneth, *The Angry Decade* (John Goodchild Publishers, 1958)

Andrew, Christopher, *The Defence of the Realm: The Authorised History of MI5* (Allen Lane, 2009)

Atherton, Mike, *Gambling: A Story of Triumph and Disaster* (Hodder and Stoughton, 2006)

Baker, Carlos, *Ernest Hemingway* (Scribner, 1969)

Bartlett, Donald, and Steele, James B., *Empire: The Life, Legend and Madness of Howard Hughes* (Norton, 1979)

Birtley, Jack, *Freddie Mills* (New English Library, 1977)

Bloch, Michael, *The Duke of Windsor's War* (Weidenfeld and Nicolson, 1982)

Block, Alan A., *Masters of Paradise: Organised Crime and the Internal Revenue Service in the Bahamas* (Transaction, 1991)

Blond, Anthony, *Jew Made in England* (Timewell Press, 2004)

Brenner, Teddy, and Nagler, Barney, *Only The Ring Was Square* (Prentice-Hall, 1981)

Breslin, Jimmy, Damon Runyon, (Ticknor and Fields, 1991)

Breslin, Jimmy, *The Good Rat* (Mainstream Publishing, 2008)

Burke, Carolyn, *No Regrets: The Life of Edith Piaf* (Bloomsbury, 2011)

Cable Street Group, *The Battle of Cable Street, 1936* (Cable Street, Whitechapel, 1995)

Cantor, Bert, *The Bernie Cornfeld Story* (Lyle Stuart, 1970)

Catterall, Peter, *The Macmillan Diaries 1950–1957* (Macmillan, 2003)

Catterall, Peter, *The Macmillan Diaries Vol. II: Prime Minister and After: 1957–1966* (Macmillan, 2011)

Chepesiuk, Ron, *The Trafficantes* (Strategic Media Books, 2010)

Cirules, Enrique, *The Mafia in Havana* (Ocean Press, 2004)

Cockburn, Alexander, and St Clair, Jeffrey, *Whiteout: The CIA, Drugs and the Press* (Verso, 1998)

Conrad, Harold, *Dear Muffo: Thirty-Five Years in the Fast Lane* (Stein and Day, 1982)

Dale Scott, Peter, *Deep Politics and the Death of JFK* (University of California Press, 1996)

Dale Scott, Peter, *Crime and Cover-Up: The CIA, the Mafia, and the Dallas-Watergate Connection* (Open Archive Press, 1977)

Dallek, Robert, *Nixon and Kissinger* (Harper Collins, 2007)

Davis, John H., *The Kennedy Clan: Dynasty and Disaster, 1848–1984* (Sidgwick and Jackson, 1995).

Deitche, Scott M., *The Silent Don: The Criminal Underworld of Santo Trafficante Jr* (Barricade Books, 2007)

Denker, Henry, *The Kingmaker* (Mayflower, 1974)

Dorril, Stephen, *Black Shirt: Sir Oswald Mosley and British Fascism* (Penguin, 2007)

Eisenberg, Dennis, Uri, Dan, and Landau, Eli, *Meyer Lansky: Mogul of the Mob* (Paddington Press, 1979)

English, T.J., *The Havana Mob* (Mainstream Publishing, 2007).

Evans, Sir Harold, *Downing Street Diary: The Macmillan Years, 1957–1963* (Hodder and Stoughton, 1981)

Exner, Judith Campbell, with Demaris, Ovid, *My Story* (Grove, 1977)

Fabian, Robert, *Fabian of the Yard* (The Naldrett Press Ltd, 1950)

Fabian, Robert, *London After Dark* (The Naldrett Press Ltd, 1954)

Fallon, Ivan, *Billionaire: The Life and Times of Sir James Goldsmith* (Hutchinson, 1991).

Farr, Tommy, *Thus Farr* (Optomen Press, 1989)

Farrell, Nicholas, *Mussolini* (Weidenfeld and Nicolson, 2003)

Fitzgerald, F. Scott, *The Great Gatsby* (Charles Scriber's Sons, 1925)

Fleming, Ian, *Casino Royale* (Jonathan Cape, 1953)

Foreman, Freddie, with Lisners, John, *Respect: The Autobiography of Freddie Foreman* (Century Books, 1996)

Fraser-Cavassoni, Natasha, *Sam Spiegel: The Biography of a Hollywood Legend* (Little, Brown, 2003)

Goldsmith, Lady Annabel, *Annabel: An Unconventional Life* (Weidenfeld and Nicolson, 2004)

Gibson, Ian, *The Shameful Life of Salvador Dalí* (Faber and Faber, 1997)

Heller, Peter, *Bad Intentions: The Mike Tyson Story* (Da Capo Press, 1995)

Henessy, Peter, *Having It So Good: Britain in the Fifties* (Penguin/Allen Lane, 2006)

Hersh, Seymour, *The Price of Power* (Summit Books, 1983)

Hill, Billy, *Boss of Britain's Underworld* (The Naldrett Press, 1955)

Houts, Marshall, *Who Killed Sir Harry Oakes?* (Robert Hale and Company, 1972)

Kahn, Roger, *A Flame of Pure Fire: Jack Dempsey and the Roaring '20s* (Harcourt, 1999)

Keeler, Christine, with Thompson, Douglas, *The Truth at Last* (Sidgwick and Jackson, 2001)

Kelley, Kitty, *His Way: The Unauthorised Biography of Frank Sinatra* (Bantam Books, 1986)

Kessler, Ronald, *The Richest Man in the World: The Story of Adnan Khashoggi* (Warner Books, 1986)

Kynaston, David, *Austerity Britain, 1945–1951* (Bloomsbury, 2007)

Lacey, Robert, *Little Man* (Little, Brown, 1991)

Lamb, Richard, *The Macmillan Years, 1957–1963* (John Murray, 1995)

Leasor, James, *Who Killed Sir Harry Oakes?* (Heinemann, 1983)

Leigh-Lyle, Terry, *Personalities of Boxing* (Scion Ltd, 1952)

Leigh-Lyle, Terry, *From the Ringside* (Corgi, 1958)

Lewis, Norman, *The Honoured Society* (Eland Books, 1984)

Mailer, Norman, *Oswald's Tale: An American Mystery* (Random House, 1995)

Manchester, William, *The Death of a President* (Michael Joseph, 1967)

Mass, Peter, *The Valachi Papers* (Putnam's, 1968)

McDougal, Dennis, *The Last Mogul: Lew Wasserman, MCA,*

and the Hidden History of Hollywood (Crown, 1998)

Messick, Hank, *Lansky* (Putnam's, 1971)

Mills, Freddie, *Twenty Years: An Autobiography* (Nicholson and Watson, 1950)

Moldea, Dan E.W., *The Hoffa Wars: Teamsters, Rebels, Politicians and the Mob* (Paddington Press, 1978)

Moldea, Dan E., *Dark Victory: Ronald Reagan, MCA, and the Mob* (Viking Penguin, 1986)

Morton, James and Parker, Gerry, *Gangland Bosses: The Lives of Jack Spot and Billy Hill* (Time Warner Books, 2004)

Morton, James, *Fighters* (Time Warner Books, 2005).

Morton, James, *Gangland Soho* (Piaktus, 2008)

Noguchi, Thomas T., *Coroner* (Simon and Schuster, 1983)

Norwich, John Julius, *The Duff Cooper Diaries* (Weidenfeld and Nicholson, 2005)

O'Sullivan, Ronnie, *Ronnie: The Autobiography of Ronnie O'Sullivan* (Orion, 2003)

Oglesby, Carl, *The JFK Assassination* (Signet Books, 1992)

Owen, Frank, *The Eddie Chapman Story* (Allan Wingate Ltd, 1953)

Owen, James, *A Serpent in Eden* (Abacus, 2005)

Pereiglio, Milo, *The Marilyn Conspiracy* (Pocket Books, 1986)

Piaf, Edith, and Cerdan, Marcel, *Moi pour toi: Lettres d'amour* (Ud-Union Distribution, 2004)

Pileggi, Nicholas, *Wiseguy* (Pocket Books, 1985)

Plimpton, George, *Shadow Box* (Lyons Press, 2010)

Raab, Selwyn, *Five Families: America's Most Powerful Mafia Empires* (Thomas Dunne Books, St Martin's Press, 2005)

Ragano, Frank, and Raab, Selwyn, *Mob Lawyer* (Charles Scriber's Sons, 1994)

Read, Leonard, with Morton, James, *Nipper Read: The Man Who Nicked the Krays* (Futura Paperbacks, 1992)

Reid, Ed, and Demaris, Ovid, *The Green Felt Jungle* (Trident Press, 1963)

Reynolds, Bruce, *The Autobiography of a Thief* (Bantam Press, 1995).

Richardson, Charlie, with Long, Bob, *My Manor* (Sidgwick and Jackson, 1991)

Robert, Randy, *Jack Dempsey: The Manassa Mauler* (University of Illinois Press, 2003)

Runyon, Damon, *Guys and Dolls* (Penguin Books, 1992)

Sandbrook, Dominic, *Never Had It So Good: A History of Britain from Suez to the Beatles* (Little, Brown, 2005)

Sandbrook, Dominic, *White Heat: A History of Britain in the Swinging Sixties, 1964–1970* (Little, Brown, 2006)

Schulberg, Budd, *The Harder They Fall* (Random House, 1947)

Schulberg, Budd, *Ringside* (Mainstream Publishing, 2008)

Schulberg, Budd, *Sparring with Hemingway and Other Legends of the Fight Game* (Robson Books, 1995)

Sheehan, Jack, *Players: The Men Who Made Las Vegas* (University of Nevada Press, 1997)

Sinkow, Barry, *The Count in Monte Carlo* (Authorhouse, 2008)

Solomons, Jack, *Jack Solomons Tells All* (Rich and Cowan, 1951)

Summers, Anthony, *The Kennedy Conspiracy* (Warner Books, 1992)

Summers, Anthony, *The Arrogance of Power: The Secret World of Richard Nixon* (Phoenix Press, 2001)

Summers, Anthony, Swan, Robyn, *Sinatra: The Life* (Corgi, 2006)

Tate, Barbara, *West End Girls* (Orion Books, 2010)

Teresa, Vincent, with Renner, Thomas C., *My Life in the Mafia* (Doubleday, 1973)

Thomas, Donald, *Villains' Paradise: Britain's Underworld from the Spivs to the Krays* (John Murray, 2005)

Thompson, Douglas, *The Hustlers* (Sidgwick and Jackson, 2007)

Tosches, Nick, *The Devil and Sonny Liston* (Little, Brown, 2000)

Tosches, Nick, *Dino: Living High in the Dirty Business of Dreams* (Doubleday, 1992)

Turkus, Burton B., and Feder, Sid, *Murder, Inc.* (Da Capo Press, 1992; reproduction of 1951 edition)

United States Treasury Department, *Mafia: The Government's Secret File on Organised Crime* (2007)

Unsworth, Cathi, *Bad Penny Blues* (Serpent's Tail, 2009)

Vaill, Amanda, *Everybody Was So Young* (Little, Brown, 1998)

Van Dern Bergh, Tony, *Who Killed Freddie Mills?* (Penguin, 1991)

Von Tunzelmann, Alex, *Red Heat: Conspiracy, Murder and the Cold War in the Caribbean* (Simon and Schuster, 2011)

Waldron, Lamar, with Thom Hartmann, *Legacy and Secrecy: The Long Shadow of the JFK Assassination* (Counterpoint, 2008)

Waldron, Lamar, with Thom Hartmann, *Ultimate Sacrifice: John and Robert Kennedy, the Plan for a Coup in Cuba and the Murder of JFK* (Constable, 2005)

Wilkerson, Tichi, Borie, Marcia, *The Hollywood Reporter: The Golden Years* (Coward-McCann, 1984)

Wilson, Harold, *The Labour Government 1964–1970: A Personal Record* (Weidenfeld, Michael Joseph, 1971)

Yablonsky, Lewis, *George Raft* (Mercury House, 1989)

Ziegler, Philip, *King Edward VIII* (Collins, 1990)

INDEX

The following abbreviations have been used: BH – Benny Huntman; DC – Dino Cellini; FM – Freddie Mills; JFK – John F. Kennedy; ML – Meyer Lansky